Helion & Company Limited
Unit 8 Amherst Business Centre
Budbrooke Road
Warwick
CV34 5WE
England
Tel. 01926 499 619
Email: info@helion.co.uk
Website: www.helion.co.uk
Twitter: @helionbooks
Visit our blog http://blog.helion.co.uk/

Designed and typeset by Farr out Publications, Wokingham, Berkshire
Cover design by Paul Hewitt, Battlefield Design (www.battlefield-design.co.uk)

ISBN 978-1-804514-63-4

British Library Cataloguing-in-Publication Data
A catalogue record for this book is available from the British Library

CONTENTS

Note: In order to simplify the use of this book, all names, locations and geographic designations are as provided in *The Times World Atlas*, or other traditionally accepted major sources of reference, as of the time of described events.

ABBREVIATIONS AND ACRONYMS

AABn	Air Assault Battalion
ABn	Airborne Battalion
AFV	Armoured Fighting Vehicle
APC	Armoured Personnel Carrier
ASCC	Air Standardization Coordinating Committee, which at the time was responsible for generating NATO reporting names
BMD	Russian: *Boyevaya Mashina Desanta*, airborne infantry fighting vehicle
BMP	Russian: *Boyevaya Mashina Pekhoty*, infantry fighting vehicle
BRDM	Russian: *Bronirovannaya Razvedyvatelno-Dozornaya Mashina*, literally 'armoured reconnaissance patrol vehicle,' an amphibious armoured scout car armed with a 14.5mm heavy machine gun
BTR	Russian: *BroneTRansporter*, armoured personnel carrier, one of a number of eight-wheeled vehicle designs, usually armed with a 14.5mm heavy machine gun when in the troop transport role
BTR-D	Russian: *BroneTRansporter Desantny*, airborne armoured personnel carrier derived from the BMD-1
GAD	Guards Airborne Division
GAR	Guards Airborne Regiment
GRU	Russian: *Glavnoye Razvedyvatelnoye Upravleniye*, officially Main Intelligence Directorate of the General Staff of the Armed Forces of the USSR, Soviet military intelligence
IFV	Infantry Fighting Vehicle
ISI	Inter-Services Intelligence, intelligence agency of Pakistan
KGB	Russian: *Komitet Gosudarstvennoy Bezopasnosti*, officially Committee of State Security of the USSR, Soviet secret police
KhAD	*Khadamat-e Aetla'at-e Dawlati*, literally 'State Intelligence Agency,' the main security agency and intelligence agency of the Democratic Republic of Afghanistan, the Afghan secret police
MANPADS	Man-Portable Air Defence System
MRBn	Motor Rifle Battalion
MRBr	Motor Rifle Brigade
MR Coy	Motor Rifle Company
MRD	Motor Rifle Division
MRR	Motor Rifle Regiment
MT-LB	Russian: *Mnogotselevoy Tyagach Lyogky Bronirovanny*, literally 'multi-purpose towing vehicle light armoured,' multi-purpose amphibious auxiliary armoured tracked vehicle
NATO	North Atlantic Treaty Organization
PTS	Russian: *Plavayushchy Transporter Sredny*, literally 'amphibious personnel carrier medium,' amphibious transport vehicle often used as a ferry
Spetsnaz	Russian: *SPETSialnogo NAZnacheniya*, literally 'of special purpose,' used here to refer specifically to Soviet Special Forces
SSR	Soviet Socialist Republic
USA	United States of America
USSR	Union of Soviet Socialist Republics
V-VS	*Voenno-Vozdushnye Sily Soyuza Sovetskih Sotsialisticheskih Respublik*, the Soviet Air Force

EDITORIAL NOTE

This is a very unusual book – and for many reasons – so much so that when the author submitted his project proposal for the first time, the @War team at Helion was not entirely sure whether or not we should publish it the way it was written. The text was extremely detailed but did not offer the usual fluid narrative. Instead, it was entirely focused on facts and figures: listing events, units, operations, crucial military figures, and losses, on a day-by-day basis. However, eventually, we concluded that this is also the primary reason why it *should* be published: it is one of the most detailed operational histories of any war we have ever prepared, and an unprecedentedly detailed chronology of the Soviet military intervention in Afghanistan of 1979–1989, containing an extraordinary mass of information for the interested reader. Indeed, this is a book of cold facts: one not whitewashing the reasons or the deeds, and not attempting to emphasise the heroism of those who excelled or waving away or covering-up systematic massacres of civilians, nor to damn the participants – but one prepared with the sole intention of informing the reader about what exactly was going on during the conflict in question. Eventually, this also became the primary reason why we did decide to publish it: because it excellently performs the task of informing in such a magnificent fashion.

As such, this book is certainly anything other than easy to read and to follow as a flowing text. However, the task its author, Ilya Milyukov, has taken upon himself was not to write a work comparable to Tolstoy's *War and Peace*, but one of painstaking and merciless reconstruction of every military operation, and every action undertaken by the Soviet Armed Forces in Afghanistan over a period of almost 10 years. After publishing over 200 titles in the five @War book series, we are not only certain that Ilya has accomplished precisely this mission, but also confident that our readers are going to appreciate the sheer volume of the information presented.

It is our usual editorial policy to reduce the use of abbreviations and acronyms to a minimum and to use them only where they may be useful to the reader and avoid the tedious repetition of long names or terms written out in full. In this particular volume there is much repetition of common unit titles, there are also however very many unit titles that the reader will likely be less familiar with, particularly for Soviet support units. We have therefore adopted something of a 'halfway house' solution with this volume; for Motor Rifle Division, Brigade, Regiment, Battalion and Company we have used MRD, MRBr, MRR, MRBn and MR Coy respectively. The names of airborne units (the VDV) are inevitably prefixed with the 'Guards' honorific and are thus rendered herein GAD for Guards Airborne Division and GAR for Guards Airborne Regiment. For other units the Guards honorific is written out in full prefixing other abbreviations (e.g. 'Guards MRR' rather than 'GMRR'). Air Assault formations played a significant role in Afghanistan whereas anti-aircraft units, while present, did not play a major role; the use of AA therefore signifies Air Assault in this work and anti-aircraft will be written out in full. The remaining units, those that appear less frequently, have their names written in full *in situ* in order to avoid requiring the reader to constantly check the list of abbreviations and acronyms.

Finally, as the reader may expect, it has often been difficult to place a precise figure upon casualty numbers as sources and estimates often vary wildly. This work offers the range of reported casualties where precise numbers are not available.

INTRODUCTION

This book is a detailed chronology of the main events of the war conducted in Afghanistan by the USSR and the Democratic Republic of Afghanistan (the official title 1979–1987: subsequently, the Republic of Afghanistan), which began in December 1979 and lasted for more than nine years, ending in February 1989.

Afghanistan is a medium-sized landlocked country in Central and South Asia. It is bordered by Iran to the west, Turkmenistan and Uzbekistan to the north, Tajikistan and China to the northeast, and Pakistan to the east and south. At over 652,864 square kilometres (252,072 square miles), Afghanistan is, according to various sources, the world's 40th or 41st largest country and about the size of the Arkhangelsk Oblast in Russia or Texas in the United States of America.

The geography of Afghanistan is mostly mountainous and rugged, with some unusual mountain ridges accompanied by plateaus and river basins. It is dominated by the Hindu Kush range, the western extension of the Himalayas that stretches to eastern Tibet via the Pamir Mountains and Karakoram Mountains in Afghanistan's far north-east. Most of the highest points are in the east consisting of fertile mountain valleys. The Hindu Kush ends at the west-central highlands, creating plains in the north and south-west, namely the Turkestan Plains and the Sistan Basin. These two regions consist of rolling grasslands and semi-deserts, and hot windy deserts, respectively. Forests exist in the corridor between Nuristan and Paktika Provinces in the east, and tundra in the northeast. The country's highest point is Noshaq Mountain in Badakhshan Province in north-eastern Afghanistan, at 7,492 metres above sea level. The lowest point lies in Jowzjan Province in the north-west of country along the banks of the Amu River, at 258 metres above sea level. Despite having numerous rivers and reservoirs, large parts of the country are dry. The endorheic Sistan Basin is one of the driest regions in the world.

A view of Kabul and the Kabul River in 1975. (Mark Lepko Collection)

Afghanistan has a continental climate with harsh winters in the central highlands, the glaciated north-east (around Nuristan), and the Wakhan Corridor, where the average temperature in January is below -15°C and can reach -26°C, and hot summers in the low-lying areas of the Sistan Basin of the southwest, the Jalalabad basin in the east, and the Turkestan plains along the Amu River in the north, where temperatures in July average over 35°C and can go over 43°C. The country is generally arid in the summers, with most rainfall falling between December and April. The lower areas of northern and western Afghanistan are the driest, with precipitation more common in the east. Although proximate to India, Afghanistan is mostly outside the monsoon zone, except for Nuristan Province which occasionally receives summer monsoon rain.

Several types of mammals exist throughout Afghanistan. Snow leopards, Siberian tigers and brown bears live in the high-elevation alpine tundra regions. Marco Polo sheep exclusively live in the Wakhan Corridor region of north-east Afghanistan. Foxes, wolves, otters, deer, wild sheep, lynx and other big cats populate the mountain forest region of the east. In the semi-desert northern plains, wildlife includes a variety of birds, hedgehogs, gophers, and large carnivores such as jackals and hyenas. Gazelles, wild pigs and jackals populate the steppe plains of the south and west, while mongoose and cheetahs exist in the semi-desert south. Marmots and ibex also live in the high mountains of Afghanistan, and pheasants exist in some parts of the country. The Afghan Hound is a native breed of dog known for its fast speed and its long hair; it is relatively

A street scene from Kunduz in the 1980s. (ArtOfWar – Vladimir Shchennikov)

Afghanistan was an underdeveloped agricultural state almost without any industry. People were poor, uneducated, lived mainly in rural areas and were engaged in farming and cattle breeding. The illiteracy rate in the country was high.

Throughout millennia several cities within the modern day Afghanistan served as capitals of various empires. The country has been home to various peoples through the ages, among them the ancient Iranian peoples who established the dominant role of Indo-Iranian languages in the region. At multiple points, the land has been incorporated within vast regional empires, among them the Achaemenid Empire, the Macedonian Empire, the Maurya Empire, and the Islamic Empire. For its success in resisting foreign occupation during the nineteenth and twentieth centuries, Afghanistan has been called the 'graveyard of empires.'[1]

well-known in the West. Endemic fauna of Afghanistan includes the Afghan flying squirrel, Afghan snowfinch, Afghanodon (or the 'Paghman mountain salamander'), Afghan leopard gecko, Stigmella kasyi, Vulcaniella kabulensis, Wheeleria parviflorellus, and others. Endemic flora includes Iris Afghanica. Afghanistan has a wide variety of birds despite its relatively arid climate – an estimated 460 species of which 235 breed within.

The forest region of Afghanistan has vegetation such as pine trees, spruce trees, fir trees and larches, whereas the steppe grassland regions consist of broadleaf trees, short grass, perennial plants and shrublands. The colder high elevation regions are composed of hardy grasses and small flowering plants.

Due to Afghanistan's geography, transport between various parts of the country has historically been difficult. The backbone of Afghanistan's road network is Highway 1, often called 'the Ring Road', which extends for 2,210km and connects five major cities: Kabul, Ghazni, Kandahar, Herat and Mazar-e Sharif, with spurs to Kunduz and Jalalabad and various border crossings, while skirting around the mountains of the Hindu Kush. The Ring Road is crucially important for domestic and international trade and the economy. A key portion of the Ring Road is the Salang Tunnel, completed in 1964, which facilitates travel through the Hindu Kush mountain range and connects northern and southern Afghanistan. It is the only land route that connects Central Asia to the Indian subcontinent. Several mountain passes allow travel between the Hindu Kush in other areas. Serious traffic accidents are common on Afghan roads and highways, particularly on the Kabul – Kandahar and the Kabul – Jalalabad road.

The population of Afghanistan by the end of 1979 was between 15 and 18 million people and made up of many ethnic groups, mostly Pashtuns, Tajiks, Hazaras and Uzbeks. There are two official languages in the country – Pashto and Dari. Almost all Afghan people are Muslim. Most Afghans are tribal; Pashtun tribes form the world's largest tribal society.

Afghanistan was a monarchy for almost 50 years, but in 1973 the country became a republic and in 1979 it was divided into 28 provinces. The capital of the country is the city of Kabul, and the largest cities are Herat, Kandahar, Mazar-e Sharif and Jalalabad.

The modern state of Afghanistan began with the Hotak and Durrani dynasties in the eighteenth century. In the late nineteenth century, Afghanistan became a buffer state in the 'Great Game' between British India and the Russian Empire. There were three Anglo-Afghan Wars: in 1839–1842, in 1878–1880 and in 1919. Following the Third Anglo-Afghan War, the country became free of foreign dominance, eventually becoming the Kingdom of Afghanistan in June 1926 under King Amanullah. There was a civil war in Afghanistan in 1928–1929. In 1933 19-year-old Mohammed Zahir Shah became the King of Afghanistan.

From its earliest days, Soviet Russia enjoyed close relations with Afghanistan and diplomatic relations were established in 1919, and in 1921 a friendship treaty was signed. In 1929 and 1930 Soviet troops, then named The Red Army, fought in Afghanistan at the official request of the Afghan government. After that the two countries maintained friendly relations for decades – Soviet engineers and constructors built roads, bridges, tunnels, schools and hospitals in Afghanistan, Soviet doctors helped their Afghan colleagues to treat people, Soviet officers were involved in creating the new army, and the Afghan citizens, in their turn, studied in Soviet universities.

In 1973 Mohammed Zahir Shah was overthrown in a relatively bloodless coup, and the country became a republic. The Prime Minister of the Kingdom of Afghanistan, Mohammed Daoud Khan became the President of the Republic of Afghanistan and established the National Revolutionary Party in 1974. In April 1978 Mohammad Daoud Khan along with 17 members of his family were killed as a result of the so-called 'Saur Revolution.' Power passed to the group of people who called themselves the People's Democratic Party of Afghanistan. There were two factions in this party – the radical Khalq ('Masses' in Pashto) faction and the supposedly moderate Parcham ('Flag' in Pashto) faction. One of the two Khalq faction leaders, Nur Mohammad Taraki, became the prime minister of the

A typical village in the Kelagay Valley in Baghlan Province. (ArtOfWar – Vladimir Shchennikov)

Tents of Afghan nomads. (ArtOfWar – Vladimir Shchennikov)

country now named the Democratic Republic of Afghanistan. These people launched a reign of terror, with mass killings, purges within their own party, persecution of religion, expropriations and exiling of opponents.

There are two main versions about the nature of the Saur Revolution. A Finnish scholar Raimo Vayrynen states: 'There is a multitude of speculations on the real nature of this coup. The reality appears to be that it was inspired first of all by domestic economic and political concerns and that the Soviet Union did not play any role in the Saur Revolution.'[2] Russian author Igor Bunich wrote: 'On 27 April 1978 the communist coup, which Andropov's people were planning for a few years, took place in Afghanistan. The democratic Government of Mohammad Daoud was toppled by one of the communist factions called the 'People's Democratic Party of Afghanistan', and a direct agent of Moscow Taraki became President.'[3]

In mid-1978 a rebellion started in eastern Afghanistan and soon after that the civil war began in the country. In December 1978 the USSR and Afghanistan signed another friendship treaty, allowing Afghanistan to call upon the Soviet Union for military support. In March 1979 the Herat uprising took place, up to 20,000 people were killed and thousands of other people were wounded.

In September 1979 the Deputy Prime Minister of the Democratic Republic of Afghanistan, Hafizullah Amin, seized power and declared himself the leader of the country. Nur Mohammad Taraki was arrested and then killed. By that time, Afghanistan had a red flag and a coat of arms closely resembling those of the USSR. The People's Democratic Party (i.e. communist party) was ruling the country and there were many advisers from the Soviet Army and Committee of State Security of the USSR (the KGB) in Afghan towns. Some researchers say that Afghanistan became a Soviet colony.

1

AFGHAN AND SOVIET ARMED FORCES

The Armed Forces of the Democratic Republic of Afghanistan consisted of the Afghan Army, Afghan Air Force and paramilitary formations. The army's chain of command began with the Supreme Commander, who also held the posts of People's Democratic Party of Afghanistan General Secretary and Head of State. The order of precedence continued with the Minister of National Defence of the Democratic Republic of Afghanistan, the Deputy Minister of National Defence of the Democratic Republic of Afghanistan, Chief of the General Staff, Chief of Army Operations, Air and Air Defence Commander and ended with the Chief of Intelligence.

The officer corps numbered 8,000 people. An estimated 40 to 45 percent of these officers were educated in the Soviet Union, and of them, between five and 10 percent were members of the People's Democratic Party of Afghanistan or communists. By the time of the Soviet intervention, the officer corps had decreased to 1,100 members. This decrease can be explained by the number of purges centred on the armed forces. The purge of the military began immediately after the People's Democratic Party of Afghanistan took power. Most of the officer corps during the Soviet-Afghan War were new recruits.

The strength of the army was greatly weakened during the early stages of the rule of the People's Democratic Party of Afghanistan. One of the main reasons for the small size was that the Soviet military were afraid that Afghan Army servicemen would defect to the enemy if total personnel increased. There were several sympathisers of the Mujahideen within the military. Even so, there were several elite units under the command of the Afghan Army, for instance, the 26th Airborne Battalion, 37th, 38th and 444th Commando Brigades (according to another source, there was the 444th Commando Regiment in the Afghan Army). The 26th Airborne Battalion proved politically unreliable, and in 1980 they initiated a rebellion against the People's Democratic Party of Afghanistan Government. The Commando Brigades were, in contrast, considered reliable and were used as mobile strike forces until they sustained excessive casualties, after which the Commando Brigades were reduced to battalions.

The Afghan Army

The army consisted of 14 divisions, of these 11 were infantry and another three were armoured (according to the other sources, there were three tank or armoured brigades in the Afghan Army), all of which were part of three Army Corps. While an infantry division was supposed to be composed of 4,000 to 8,000 men, between 1980 and 1983 a division normally mustered only between 2,000 and 2,500. The strength of armoured divisions in contrast was maintained and stood at 4,000. During the Soviet-Afghan War, the Afghan Army used light weapons, and a lot of old equipment. During the counter-insurgency, heavy equipment, tanks and artillery were most of the time, but not always, operated by Soviet soldiers. A problem faced the Afghan government and the Soviet military, in the form of the

Table 1: Democratic Republic of Afghanistan Army Order of Battle (ORBAT), 1979

Formation	Base	Notes
I Army Corps	Kabul	
444th Commando Regiment	Kabul, then Anawa	Later reorganised as the 2nd Infantry Division
7th Infantry Division	Kunduz	
8th Infantry Division	Kabul	
9th Infantry Division	Asadabad, Asmar and Barikot	
11th Infantry Division	Jalalabad	
II Army Corps	Kandahar	
466th Commando Regiment	Kandahar	
12th Infantry Division	Gardez	
14th Infantry Division	Ghazni	
15th Infantry Division	Kandahar	
17th Infantry Division	Herat	
18th Infantry Division	Herat	
191st Artillery Regiment		
III Army Corps	Kandahar	
666th Commando Regiment	Khost and in the village of Nadir Shah Kot	
20th Infantry Division	Baghlan	
25th Infantry Division	Khost	
Other formations		
37th Commando Brigade	Kabul	
38th Commando Brigade	Khayr Kot	
444th Commando Regiment	Kabul	
66th Separate Air Assault Regiment	Khost	(identified by some sources)
203rd Special Forces Battalion	Kabul	
230th Independent AABn	Kabul	(identified by some sources)
7th Tank Brigade	Kandahar	Near the city, in cantonment
15th Tank Brigade	Pul-e Charkhi	
10th Engineer Regiment	Pul-e Charkhi	

degeneration of training for new military recruits; new recruits were being rushed into service because the Afghan government and the Soviet military feared a total collapse of the government.

All males between 19 and 39 were eligible for conscription; the only exceptions were certain party members, or party members in certain tasks, Afghans who studied abroad (mostly in the Eastern Bloc and the Soviet Union), and one-child families or low earners. Most people tried to evade conscription. Most soldiers were recruited for a three-year term, later extended to four-year terms in 1984. Each year, the Afghan Army lost an estimated 15,000 soldiers: 10,000 from desertion and 5,000 from casualties sustained in battle, and the government was forced to send army or police gangs to recruit civilians for service. Even so, some people carried fake papers so they could evade conscription. A side effect of the lack of recruits was that veterans were forced into longer service or re-recruited. A general amnesty was announced in 1980 to army draft deserters from previous administrations. In 1982, students who served in the military, and graduated 10th grade in high school, would pass 11th and 12th grade and be given a scholarship. People who were conscripted after the 12th grade, could, after military service, attend whichever higher education facility they wanted. To stop army desertions, soldiers were quickly promoted to higher ranks.

A view of the main runway of the Kabul International Airport in the 1980s. (Mark Lepko Collection)

Table 2: Democratic Republic of Afghanistan Air Force ORBAT, 1979–1986

Regiment	Base	Equipment
321st Fighter-Bomber Aviation Regiment	Bagram, then Shindand	24 Su-7BMK
322nd Fighter Aviation Regiment	Bagram	28 MiG-21FL/PFM/U
355th Fighter-Bomber Aviation Regiment	Bagram	30 MiG-17
335th Mixed Aviation Regiment	Shindand	24 Il-28
366th Fighter Aviation Regiment	Kandahar	30? MiG-17
373rd Transport Aviation Regiment	Kabul International	An-26
375th Separate Helicopter Regiment	Mazar-e Sharif	12 Mi-24A, 20 Mi-8T/MT
377th Separate Helicopter Regiment	Kabul International	12 Mi-25, 20 Mi-4 and Mi-8T/MT
382nd Transport Aviation Regiment	Kabul International	An-12
393rd Training Aviation Regiment	Mazar-e Sharif	?? L-39

The total number of the Afghan Armed Forces was between 55,000 and 105,000 soldiers and officers in 1979 and 400,000 servicemen in 1989. As of 1989 there were 1,568 tanks, 828 armoured fighting vehicles (AFVs), 4,880 artillery guns and mortars, 126 airplanes and 14 helicopters in service.

The major units of the Afghan Armed Forces were deployed as shown in Table 1.

The Afghan Air Force

The Afghan Air Force had, throughout its history, always been smaller than the Afghan Army. Many in the Afghan Air Force were given education and training in the Soviet Union. The majority of Air Force personnel were not considered politically reliable enough to fly strike missions against the Mujahideen and following the Soviet intervention, the Soviets grounded the Afghan Air Force. The Soviets did not allow Afghans into the security zones at Afghan airports. Afghans were generally not allowed to fly the airplanes of the Afghan Air Force, but the Soviets could. Afghan helicopters were assigned to tasks considered non-sensitive by the Soviets, and the majority of Air Force personnel were not told about missions beforehand, because the Soviets were afraid that they would contact the enemy. In Afghan helicopter flights a Soviet adviser was always present, and commanded the Afghan pilot who flew the helicopter.

Although the Afghan Air Force could deploy about 150 fixed-wing aircraft and 30 helicopters, the majority of airplanes and helicopters were grounded due to maintenance issues or the limited availability of crews. Among the fixed-wing aircraft in use were Mikoyan-Gurevich MiG-17 and MiG-21 fighters, Sukhoi Su-7 and Su-17 fighter-bombers, Ilyushin Il-18 and Il-28 bombers and Antonov An-2, An-24 and An-26 transport aircraft. Mil Mi-2, Mi-4, Mi-8 and Mi-24 helicopters were used by the Afghan Air Force. Other Soviet equipment and weapons were also used by the government. The Czech Aero L-39 Albatros jet trainer was the only non-Soviet equipment. Ground-based air defence systems included S-75 (ASCC/NATO reporting name 'SA-2 Guideline') and S-125

A MiG-21FL of the Bagram-based 322nd Fighter Aviation Regiment, seen in flight in the mid-1970s, armed with a pair of UB-16-57 pods for unguided rockets of 57mm calibre. (Mark Lepko Collection)

('SA-3 Goa') surface-to-air systems, primarily deployed for the defence of Kabul.

Finally, the Ministry of Interior Affairs of the Democratic Republic of Afghanistan controlled the *Sarandoy*, officially the 'Defenders of the Revolution', which was a militarised gendarmerie. The Ministry of Tribes and Frontiers of the Democratic Republic of Afghanistan, until 1983 under the authority of the Ministry of Defence of the Democratic Republic of Afghanistan, controlled the frontier troops and the tribal militia. The Afghan security service, KhAD, also controlled paramilitary formations. According to the Afghan government, the militia mustered an estimated 20,000 men. Those who worked in the *Sarandoy* were paid $162 a month, a wage which was higher than that of the Deputy Minister of National Defence of the Republic of Afghanistan before the Saur Revolution. However, there was a problem – the militia was even less disciplined and effective than the Afghan Army. Several journalists thought the government militia collaborated with the Mujahideen.[1]

Soviet Armed Forces in Afghanistan

The Soviet Army was also a conscript army; soldiers were conscripted for a two-year term. Everyone between 18 and 27 was eligible for conscription; the only exceptions were people with serious medical conditions, university students and those having two or more children. Many young men tried to evade conscription.

The Soviet troops, assigned for the invasion of Afghanistan, were combined into the 40th Army. It was formed in the Turkestan Military District and in the Middle Asia Military District of the Soviet Union and initially organised as listed in Table 3.

Table 3: 40th Army of the Soviet Ground Forces, ORBAT, 1979

Unit	Notes
Headquarters	
103rd Separate Signals Regiment	directly subordinated
186th Separate Motor Rifle Regiment	directly subordinated
345th Separate Guards Airborne Regiment	directly subordinated
2nd Anti-Aircraft Missile Brigade	equipped with 2K11 Krug ('SA-4 Ganef') SAMs
5th Guards Motor Rifle Division	
103rd Guards Airborne Division	
108th Motor Rifle Division	
56th Separate Guards Air Assault Brigade	
353rd Guards Artillery Brigade	
58th Motor Rifle Division	cadre only, reserve formation
68th Motor Rifle Division	cadre only, reserve formation
201st Motor Rifle Division	cadre only, reserve formation

Aviation support for the 40th Army was provided by the 34th Mixed Aviation Corps consisted of six aviation squadrons as shown in Table 4.

The 201st MRD, the 159th Separate Road Construction Brigade, the 860th Separate MRR, the 45th Separate Engineering Regiment, the 28th Rocket Artillery Regiment and the 459th Separate Spetsnaz Company were deployed to Afghanistan and included in the 40th Army, while the 59th Support Brigade was formed in Afghanistan and also included in the 40th Army.

The camp of Soviet troops deployed at Kabul International, seen here on the morning of 3 January 1980. (Efim Sandler Collection)

Table 4: Squadrons of the 34th Mixed Aviation Corps
Squadron
Aviation Squadron of the 115th Guards Fighter Aviation Regiment
Aviation Squadron of the 136th Fighter-Bomber Aviation Regiment
Aviation Squadron of the 217th Fighter-Bomber Aviation Regiment
Helicopter Squadron of the 181st Separate Helicopter Regiment
Helicopter Squadron of the 280th Separate Helicopter Regiment
302nd Separate Helicopter Squadron

Later on, two MRRs would be transformed into two Motor Rifle Brigades, and then two brigades would be deployed to the country in 1985: the 15th Separate Spetsnaz Brigade and the 22nd Separate Spetsnaz Brigade. Moreover, two other brigades would be formed within the 40th Army in Afghanistan: the 276th Pipeline Brigade in 1982 and the 278th Road Control Brigade in 1983, while the 353rd Guards Artillery Brigade and the 2nd Anti-Aircraft Missile Brigade were withdrawn from Afghanistan. The 58th MRD and the 68th MRD were never activated and deployed to Afghanistan.

Major Units of the 40th Army

Officially named 'The Limited Contingent of Soviet Forces in Afghanistan,' soon after the invasion major units of the 40th Army were deployed as shown in Table 5 and the remainder of this chapter.

Table 5: Locations of Headquarters and non-Divisional Units of the 40th Army

Unit	Garrison location
Headquarters of the 40th Army	Kabul
103rd Separate Signal Regiment	Kabul
28th Rocket Artillery Regiment	Shindand
59th Support Brigade	near Pul-e Khumri
159th Separate Road Construction Brigade	Bagram and Shindand

103rd Guards Airborne Division

The 103rd Guards Airborne Division was formed on 18 December 1944 as the 103rd Guards Rifle Division. It became the 103rd GAD on 3 June 1946 and by late 1979 comprised the elements shown in Table 6. Later on, the 62nd Separate Self-Propelled Artillery *Divizion*[2] of the 103rd GAD was transformed into the 62nd Separate Tank Battalion of the 103rd GAD. The division numbered about 6,000 officers and other ranks.

5th Guards Motor Rifle Division

The 5th Guards Motor Rifle Division was formed on 10 June 1945 as the 5th Guards Mechanised Division. It became the 5th Guards MRD on 11 January 1965 and by late 1979 comprised elements listed below in Table 7, including more than 10,000 officers and other ranks.

Table 6: 103rd Guards Airborne Division, ORBAT, 1979	
Unit	**Garrison location and notes**
Headquarters	Kabul
317th Guards Airborne Regiment	Kabul
350th Guards Airborne Regiment	near Kabul
357th Guards Airborne Regiment	Kabul
1179th Guards Artillery Regiment	Kabul
130th Separate Guards Engineering Battalion	Kabul
742nd Separate Guards Signal Battalion	
20th Separate Repair Battalion	
1388th Separate Support Battalion	
175th Separate Medical Battalion	
62nd Separate Self-Propelled Artillery *Divizion*	(later 62nd Separate Tank Battalion)
105th Separate Anti-Aircraft Missile *Divizion*	
80th Separate Guards Reconnaissance Company	

Table 7: 5th Guards Motor Rifle Division, ORBAT, 1979	
Unit	**Garrison location and notes**
Headquarters	Shindand
24th Guards Tank Regiment	Shindand
101st Motor Rifle Regiment	Herat
371st Guards Motor Rifle Regiment	Shindand
373rd Guards Motor Rifle Regiment	Adraskan
1008th Anti-Aircraft Artillery Regiment	Shindand
1060th Artillery Regiment	Shindand (later 1060th Guards Artillery Regiment)
1122nd Anti-Aircraft Artillery Regiment	Shindand
650th Separate Reconnaissance Battalion	Shindand
68th Separate Guards Engineering Battalion	Adraskan
388th Separate Signal Battalion	Shindand
177th Separate Repair Battalion	Shindand
375th Separate Support Battalion	Shindand
46th Separate Medical Battalion	Shindand
1377th Separate Anti-Tank Artillery *Divizion*	Shindand
307th Separate Missile *Divizion*	Herat

On 7 March 1985 the 12th Guards MRR was deployed to Afghanistan, assigned to the 5th Guards MRD and deployed to the city of Herat.

108th Motor Rifle Division

The 108th Motor Rifle Division was formed on 13 August 1941 as the 360th Rifle Division. It became the 108th MRD in May 1957 and by late 1979 comprised elements listed below, comprising more than 10,000 officers and other ranks (increased to over 14,000 by 1989). Notably, later on, the 186th Separate MRR was included into the 108th MRD and became 186th MRR of the 108th MRD.

Table 8: 108th Motor Rifle Division, ORBAT, 1979	
Unit	**Garrison location and notes**
Headquarters	Bagram
177th Motor Rifle Regiment	Jabal Saraj
180th Motor Rifle Regiment	Kabul
181st Motor Rifle Regiment	Kabul
186th Motor Rifle Regiment	near Kabul (formerly Separate)
234th Tank Regiment	Kabul (originally from 201st MRD)
1074th Artillery Regiment	Kabul
1049th Anti-Aircraft Artillery Regiment	Kabul
781st Separate Reconnaissance Battalion	Bagram
271st Separate Engineering Battalion	Bagram
808th Separate Signal Battalion	Bagram
1003rd Separate Support Battalion	Bagram
333rd Separate Repair Battalion	Bagram
100th Separate Medical Battalion	Bagram
738th Separate Anti-Tank Artillery *Divizion*	Jabal Saraj
646th Separate Missile *Divizion*	Bagram

201st Motor Rifle Division

The 201st Motor Rifle Division was formed on 25 May 1943 as the 201st Rifle Division. It became the 201st MRD in 1964 and by early 1980 comprised units listed below. During the division's deployment to Afghanistan, the 191st MRR was excluded from the 201st MRD and became 191st Separate MRR; the 234th Tank Regiment and the 285th Tank Regiment were also excluded from the 201st MRD and included into the 108th MRD. In total, the 201st numbered around 10,000 soldiers and officers.

Table 9: 201st Motor Rifle Division, ORBAT, early 1980	
Unit	**Garrison location**
Headquarters	near Kunduz
122nd Motor Rifle Regiment	Khulm
149th Guards Motor Rifle Regiment	near Kunduz
191st Motor Rifle Regiment (later Separate)	Ghazni
395th Motor Rifle Regiment	Pul-e Khumri
234th Tank Regiment (moved to 108th MRD)	Kabul
285th Tank Regiment	near Kunduz

998th Artillery Regiment	near Kunduz
990th Anti-Aircraft Artillery Regiment	Kunduz
783rd Separate Reconnaissance Battalion	Kunduz
541st Separate Engineering Battalion	near Kunduz
252nd Separate Signal Battalion	Kunduz
636th Separate Support Battalion	near Kunduz
340th Separate Repair Battalion	Kunduz
99th Separate Medical Battalion	Kunduz
370th Separate Anti-Tank Artillery *Divizion*	Kunduz
71st Separate Missile *Divizion*	Kunduz

56th Separate Guards Air Assault Brigade

The 56th Separate Guards Air Assault Brigade was formed on 11 June 1943 as the 7th Guards Airborne Brigade. It became the Separate Guards AABr on 1 October 1979 and by late 1979 comprised the elements listed below. During its deployment in Afghanistan, a tank platoon was added to the 56th Separate Guards AABr, reinforcing it from 2,833 officers and other ranks in 1979, to 2,452 servicemen in 1986.

Table 10: 56th Separate Guards Air Assault Brigade, ORBAT, 1979

Unit	Garrison location
Headquarters	Kunduz, later Gardez
1st Airborne Battalion	
2nd Airborne Assault Battalion	
3rd Airborne Assault Battalion	
4th Airborne Assault Battalion	
Artillery *Divizion*	
Reconnaissance Company	
Signals Company	
Repair Company	
Support Company	
Airborne Assault Company	
Medical Company	

860th Separate Motor Rifle Regiment

The 860th Separate Motor Rifle Regiment was formed on 18 December 1941 as the 376th Rifle Division. It became the 860th Separate MRR on 13 May 1966 and by late 1979 comprised the units listed below. At full strength, it counted more than 1,000 officers and other ranks.

Table 11: 860th Separate Motor Rifle Regiment, ORBAT, 1979

Unit	Garrison location
Headquarters	Fayzabad
1st Motor Rifle Battalion	
2nd Motor Rifle Battalion	
3rd Motor Rifle Battalion	
Tank Battalion	
Reconnaissance Company	
Medical Company	

345th Separate Guards Airborne Regiment

The 345th Separate Guards Airborne Regiment was formed on 30 December 1944 as the 345th Rifle Regiment. It became the 345th Separate GAR in 1979 and by late 1979 comprised elements listed in below. Later on, it received a howitzer artillery *divizion* and a tank company, and numbered up to 1,700 officers and other ranks.

Table 12: 345th Separate Guards Airborne Regiment, ORBAT, 1979

Unit	Garrison location
Headquarters	Bagram
1st Airborne Battalion	
2nd Airborne Battalion	
3rd Airborne Battalion	
Reconnaissance Company	
Engineering Company	
Signals Company	
Repair Company	
Regimental Aid Station	
Chemical Protection Platoon	
Commandant's Service Platoon	

45th Separate Engineering Regiment

The 45th Separate Engineering Regiment was formed on 10 February 1980 and by early 1980 comprised elements listed below. Later on, it was reinforced through the inclusion of the 1117th Separate Engineering Special Mine-Laying Battalion and the 2088th Separate Engineering Battalion, while the 274th Separate Water Supply Company was withdrawn from the 45th Separate Engineering Regiment.

Table 13: 45th Separate Engineering Regiment, ORBAT, 1979

Unit	Garrison location
Headquarters	Near Charikar
19th Separate Engineering Battalion	
92nd Separate Road Engineering Battalion	
274th Separate Water Supply Company	

Troops of the 783rd Separate Reconnaissance Battalion of the 201st MRD, the place and year are unknown. (ArtOfWar – Vladimir Shchennikov)

Some units of the Soviet Border Troops, also known as the KGB Border Troops, also participated in the Soviet-Afghan War. They operated in the northern and western parts of the country and numbered 8,000 soldiers and officers in 1981 and more than 11,000 servicemen in 1986.

The total number of the Soviet troops in Afghanistan was around 80,000 officers and men in 1979, around 120,000 in 1985 (according to other sources, in 1986) and around 70,000 in 1989; 600 tanks, 1,500 IFVs, 290 APCs, 900 artillery guns, 54 airplanes and 20 helicopters were in service as of 1979; 580 tanks, 2,888 IFVs and 388 APCs were in service as of 1988.

The Muslim Battalion

Before the official deployment of the Soviet troops to Afghanistan on 13 December 1979, the 154th Separate Special Purpose Detachment of the Main Intelligence Directorate of the General Staff of the Armed Forces of the USSR (commonly Separate Spetsnaz GRU Detachment, Separate Spetsnaz Detachment), was deployed to the country and stationed in the city of Kabul.[3] The Detachment was also known as the 'Muslim Battalion', because only Uzbeks, Tajiks and Turkmens served in it, and was supposedly assigned to guard the residence of Hafizullah Amin. On 2 January 1980 the 154th Separate Spetsnaz Detachment was withdrawn from Afghanistan.

66th Motor Rifle Brigade

On 1 March 1980 the 186th MRR of the 108th MRD was transformed into the 66th Separate MRBr. The composition of the 66th Separate MRBr is listed below: it comprised about 3,500 officers and other ranks.

Table 14: 66th Motor Rifle Brigade, ORBAT, 1979

Unit	Garrison location and notes
Headquarters	Jalalabad
1st Motor Rifle Battalion	Mehtar Lam
2nd Motor Rifle Battalion	Asadabad
3rd Motor Rifle Battalion	Jalalabad
Air Assault Battalion	Jalalabad (may have been 48th Separate AABn)
Tank Battalion	Jalalabad
Artillery *Divizion*	Jalalabad
Anti-Tank Battery	Jalalabad
Anti-Aircraft Missile Battery	Jalalabad
Reconnaissance Company	Jalalabad
Engineering Company	Jalalabad
Signals Company	Jalalabad
Repair Company	Jalalabad
Support Company	Jalalabad
Medical Company	Jalalabad

373rd Guards Motor Rifle Regiment

The 373rd Guards Motor Rifle Regiment of the 5th Guards MRD was the same day transformed into the 70th Separate Guards MRBr. Later on, the unit received the 4th MRBn and was bolstered to around 4,000 officers and other ranks.

Table 15: 373rd Guards Motor Rifle Regiment, ORBAT, 1979

Unit	Garrison location
Headquarters	Kandahar
1st Motor Rifle Battalion	
2nd Motor Rifle Battalion	
3rd Motor Rifle Battalion	
Air Assault Battalion	
Tank Battalion	
Artillery *Divizion*	
Anti-Tank Battery	
Anti-Aircraft Missile Battery	
Reconnaissance Company	
Engineering Company	
Signals Company	
Repair Company	
Support Company	
Medical Company	

In the summer of 1980, the 353rd Guards Artillery Brigade and the 2nd Anti-Aircraft Missile Brigade were withdrawn from Afghanistan, while on 1 September 1980 the 234th Tank Regiment of the 108th MRD was also withdrawn from Afghanistan.

Support- and Special Forces

On 29 October 1981 the 154th Separate Spetsnaz Detachment was deployed to Afghanistan and stationed near the town of Maymanah, capital of Faryab Province, 400km (249 miles) northwest of Kabul.

On 30 October 1981 the 154th Separate Spetsnaz Detachment was deployed to Afghanistan for the second time and cantoned near the town of Aqcha in Jowzjan Province, 380km (236 miles) northwest of Kabul.

On 1 December 1981 the 1049th Anti-Aircraft Artillery Regiment of the 108th MRD was withdrawn from Afghanistan. The same day the 1415th Anti-Aircraft Missile Regiment was deployed to the country and included into the 108th MRD.

On 1 April 1982 the 159th Separate Road Construction Brigade was transformed into the 58th Separate Troop Carrying Brigade. Its battalions were stationed in the city of Kabul, in the city of Pul-e Khumri, in the town of Shindand in Herat Province and in the town of Hairatan in Balkh Province, 340km (211 miles) north-west of Kabul.

On 28 August 1982 the 276th Pipeline Brigade was formed in the 40th Army. Its units were cantoned near and in the city of Pul-e Khumri, in the town of Hairatan, near the town of Aibak, capital of Samangan Province, 220km (137 miles) north-west of Kabul, and in the town of Dushi in Baghlan Province, 130km (81 miles) north of Kabul.

On 1 April 1983, the 278th Road Control Brigade was formed in 40th Army. Its units were quartered in the town of Chowgani in Baghlan Province, 120km (75 miles) north of Kabul, near the village of Salang-e Shamali in Baghlan Province, 90km (56 miles) north of Kabul, in the town of Jabal Saraj in Parwan Province and in the town of Hairatan in Balkh Province.

On 10 February 1984, the 173rd Separate Spetsnaz Detachment was deployed to Afghanistan and stationed in the city of Kandahar.

On 23 March 1984 the 285th Tank Regiment of the 108th MRD was transformed into the 682nd MRR of the 108th MRD stationed in the village of Rukhah in Parwan Province, 90km (56 miles) north-east of Kabul.

In September 1984 the 668th Separate Spetsnaz Detachment was deployed to Afghanistan and stationed in the town of Bagram in Parwan Province.

15th Separate Spetsnaz Brigade, 1985–1989

In March 1985 the 15th Separate Spetsnaz Brigade was deployed to Afghanistan. It comprised the 154th Separate Spetsnaz Detachment, the 177th Separate Spetsnaz Detachment, 334th Separate Spetsnaz Detachment and the 668th Separate Spetsnaz Detachment, with a total of 2,482 officers and other ranks as of 1988.

Table 16: 15th Separate Spetsnaz Brigade

Unit	Garrison location
Headquarters	Jalalabad
Special Radio Communication Detachment	Jalalabad
154th Separate Spetsnaz Detachment	Jalalabad
177th Separate Spetsnaz Detachment	Ghazni
334th Separate Spetsnaz Detachment	Asadabad
668th Separate Spetsnaz Detachment	Baraki Barak
Support Company	Jalalabad
Commander's Service Company	Jalalabad
Aid Station	Jalalabad

22nd Separate Spetsnaz Brigade, 1985–1989

Only a week later, on 15 March 1985, the 22nd Separate Spetsnaz Brigade was deployed to Afghanistan. It included the 173rd Separate Spetsnaz Detachment and comprised a total of around 2,500 officers and other ranks, organised as listed below. Unless stated otherwise they garrisoned in the city of Lashkar Gah, capital of Helmand Province, 550km (342 miles) southwest of Kabul.

Table 17: 22nd Separate Spetsnaz Brigade

Unit	Garrison location
Headquarters	Lashkar Gah
173rd Separate Spetsnaz Detachment	Kandahar
186th Separate Spetsnaz Detachment	Shah Joy
370th Separate Spetsnaz Detachment	Lashkar Gah
411th Separate Spetsnaz Detachment	Farah
Support Company	Lashkar Gah
Commander's Service Company	Lashkar Gah
Aid Station	Lashkar Gah

On 1 April 1986 the 28th Rocket Artillery Regiment was transformed into the 28th Artillery Regiment.

Soviet Military Aviation in Afghanistan

The Soviet Air Force entered the war with relatively few units actually deployed inside Afghanistan. It was significantly bolstered during the spring and summer of 1981, when the 34th Mixed Aviation Corps was transformed into the Air Force of the 40th Army. By then, this corps alone comprised 12 aviation regiments, four helicopter regiments, three aviation squadrons, six helicopter squadrons and one aviation detachment. Units *de facto* permanently assigned to the 34th Mixed Aviation Corps and then the Air Force of the 40th Army from 1981 until 1988 are listed in Table 18.

A view of Bagram Air Base in the 1980s, with a row of Soviet-operated An-26s in the background, a Mi-8 helicopter about to land, and an RSP-7 system in the foreground. The latter was a radar used to aid pilots during landing: the horizontal antenna was used to align the aircraft with the runway, while the vertically oriented one monitored the aircraft's altitude. The truck with two antennas to the right contained a weather station: its taller antenna was a goniometer. (Mark Lepko Collection)

Over the following years, 10 additional fighter aviation regiments – listed in Table 19 – were assigned to the Air Force of the 40th Army on a temporary basis. Additionally, the 302nd Fighter-Bomber Aviation Regiment, equipped with Su-17M-4s, was deployed at Kokayty Air Base in 1988–1989 and flew combat sorties inside Afghanistan during the last months of Soviet operations.

Trial Units

Of other notable deployments, in April 1980, the V-VS used its giant Antonov An-22 transports to send four Yakovlev Yak-38 vertical take-off and landing jets (borts 25, 53, 54, and 55) for operational testing to Afghanistan. Deployed at Shindand, they were flown by a team of naval aviators, led by chief test pilot Y. I. Mitnikov. Yak-38s flew their first sorties starting on 18 April 1980, and initially undertook only trial missions at altitudes between 150 and 3,000 metres. After collecting enough experience, the team flew 107 combat sorties: most of these in May 1980 and frequently in cooperation with Su-17s deployed at the same air base. Ending a month later, the deployment to Afghanistan revealed numerous weaknesses of the Yak-38 when operated in 'hot and high' conditions and resulted in the decision to launch the development of the Yak-38M variant,

The front section of a MiG-21bis (bort number 55) from the 115th Guards Fighter Aviation Regiment, parked in a revetment at Bagram Air Base. (Pit Weinert Collection)

Table 18: 34th Mixed Aviation Corps and the Air Force of the 40th Army in Afghanistan, 1981–1988		
Unit	**Base**	**Equipment and Notes**
50th Separate Mixed Aviation Regiment	Kabul	An-12, An-26, An-30, Mi-8, Mi-24
115th Guards Fighter Aviation Regiment	Kandahar and Bagram	MiG-21bis
143rd Guards Bomber Aviation Regiment	Qarshi and Sovetabad	Su-24M, based in Uzbek SSR
134th Fighter-Bomber Aviation Regiment	Shindand	MiG-27 and MiG-23UB
136th Fighter-Bomber Aviation Regiment	Kandahar and Shindand	MiG-21SM
149th Guards Bomber Aviation Regiment	Qarshi and Sovetabad	Su-24M, based in Uzbek SSR
156th Fighter-Bomber Aviation Regiment	Mary 2, Kandahar and Shindand	Su-17M3, distributed in Turkmen SSR and Afghanistan
166th Fighter-Bomber Aviation Regiment	Kandahar and Shindand	deployed in 1983; Su-17M-3
168th Fighter-Bomber Aviation Regiment	Sovetabad	MiG-23MLD, based in Uzbek SSR
217th Fighter-Bomber Aviation Regiment	Kyzyl-Arvat and Shindand	distributed in Turkmen SSR and Afghanistan
274th Fighter-Bomber Aviation Regiment	Bagram and Shindand	Su-17
735th Bomber Aviation Regiment	Qarshi and Sovetabad	Su-24M; deployed in Uzbek SSR from 1984
181st Separate Helicopter Regiment	Kunduz, Fayzabad, Maymanah	Mi-8T/MT, Mi-6, Mi-10PP, Mi-24
280th Separate Helicopter Regiment	Kandahar	Mi-6, Mi-8T, Mi-24
292nd Separate Helicopter Regiment	Kunduz and Jalalabad	Mi-8T, Mi-24A/V
335th Separate Combat Helicopter Regiment	Jalalabad, Ghazni, Gardez	Mi-8MT, Mi-24V/P, activated in 1984
200th Separate Assault Aviation Squadron	Bagram and Shindand	Su-25
263rd Separate Tactical Reconnaissance Aviation Squadron	Bagram and Shindand	
339th Separate Mixed Aviation Squadron	Kabul and Maymanah	
205th Separate Helicopter Squadron	Lashar Gah	Mi-8, Mi-24
239th Separate Helicopter Squadron	Ghazni	Mi-24
254th Separate Helicopter Squadron	Kunduz	
262nd Separate Helicopter Squadron	Bagram	
302nd Separate Helicopter Squadron	Shindand	13 Mi-8PP, Mi-24
320th Separate Helicopter Squadron	Kunduz and Kabul	
224th Separate Aviation Transport Detachment	Kabul	

Table 19: Fighter Aviation Regiments on temporary assignment to the Air Force of the 40th Army in Afghanistan, 1981–1988		
Unit	**Base**	**Equipment and Notes**
27th Guards Fighter Aviation Regiment	Bagram, Kandahar, Shindand	Su-24, 1981–1982
145th Fighter Aviation Regiment	Kandahar and Shindand	MiG-21bis, 1982–1983
927th Fighter Aviation Regiment	Kandahar and Shindand	MiG-21bis, 1983–1984
905th Fighter Aviation Regiment	Bagram and Shindand	MiG-23MLD, 1984–1985
982nd Fighter Aviation Regiment	Kandahar	MiG-23MLD, 1984–1986
655th Fighter Aviation Regiment	Bagram and Shindand	MiG-23MLD, 1985–1986
190th Fighter Aviation Regiment	Bagram and Shindand	MiG-23MLD, 1986–1987
168th Fighter Aviation Regiment	Bagram and Shindand	MiG-23MLD, 1987–1988
979th Fighter Aviation Regiment	Kandahar and Shindand	MiG-23ML, 1986–1988
120th Fighter Aviation Regiment	Bagram and Shindand	MiG-23MLD, 1988–1989

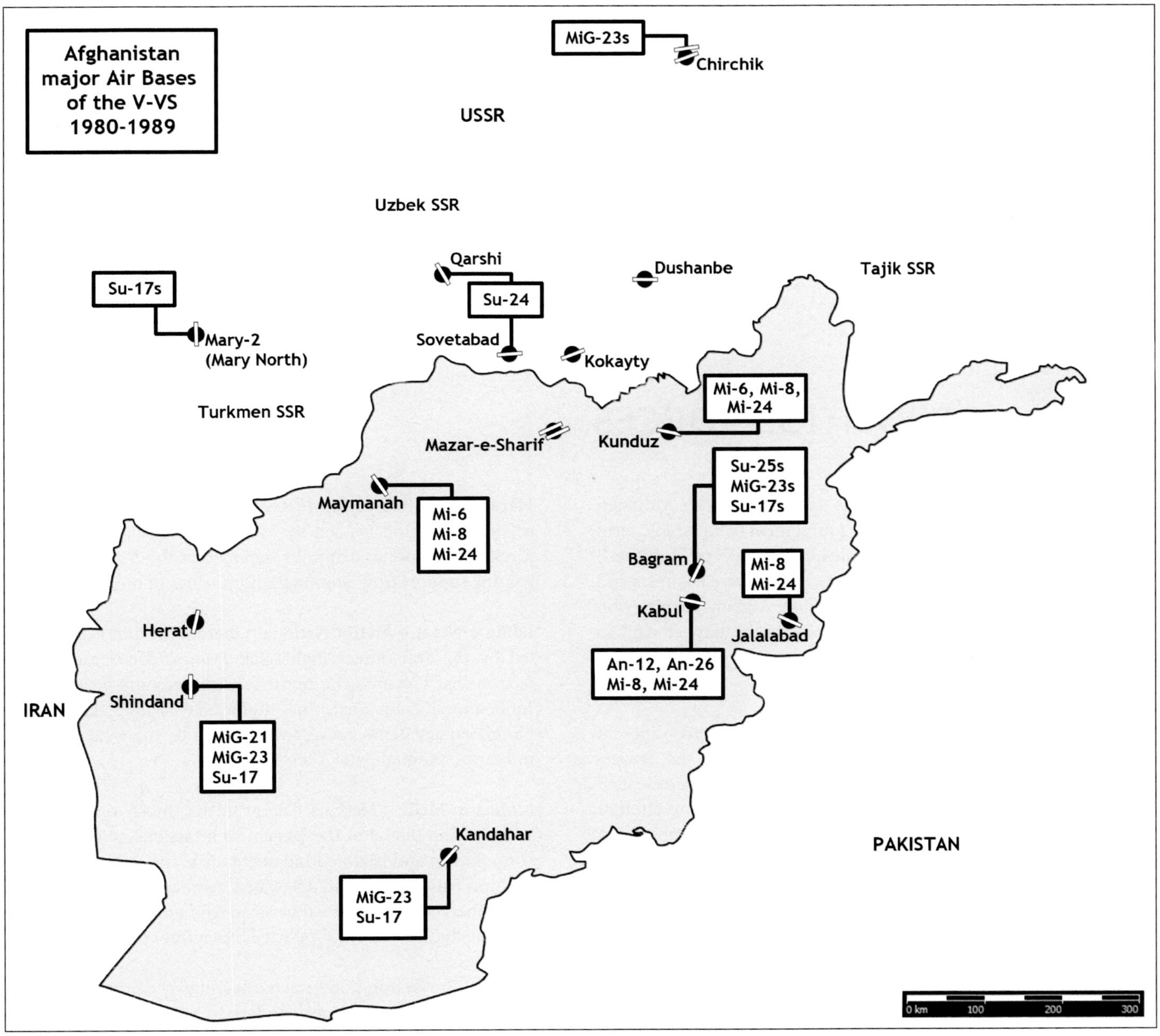

Afghanistan major Air Bases of the V-VS 1980-1989

MiG-23s
Chirchik
USSR
Uzbek SSR
Qarshi
Su-24
Sovetabad
Dushanbe
Tajik SSR
Su-17s
Mary-2 (Mary North)
Turkmen SSR
Kokayty
Mi-6, Mi-8, Mi-24
Kunduz
Mazar-e-Sharif
Su-25s
MiG-23s
Su-17s
Maymanah
Mi-6
Mi-8
Mi-24
Bagram
Mi-8
Mi-24
Kabul
Jalalabad
Herat
An-12, An-26
Mi-8, Mi-24
IRAN
Shindand
MiG-21
MiG-23
Su-17
Kandahar
PAKISTAN
MiG-23
Su-17
0 km 100 200 300

(Map by Tom Cooper)

A line-up of MiG-21bis of the 927th Fighter Aviation Regiment, V-VS (left side of the photograph), next to a line of MiG-21PFMs from 322nd Fighter Aviation Regiment of the Democratic Republic of Afghanistan Air Force, at Bagram Air Base on the Soviet unit's arrival in Afghanistan in 1983. (Pit Weinert Collection)

A Yak-38 seen while making a rolling take-off from Shindand Air Base in April 1980. (A. S. Yakovlev Collection)

powered by a more powerful engine, initiated in August 1981 (the Yak-38M entered service in 1984).

A year later, an even more important trial deployment began, when the V-VS sent a number of prototypes of the Sukhoi Su-25 to Afghanistan. As this type proved its mettle in combat beyond any doubt, and its series production was initiated, enough became available to establish the first Special Airborne Assault Squadron. The first such unit, the 200th Separate Assault Aviation Squadron equipped with Sukhoi Su-25s, arrived in November 1984. Later on, it was reorganised as the 378th Separate Assault Aviation Regiment, based at Bagram and Shindand air bases.[4]

2
AFGHAN OPPOSITION FORCES

The Mujahideen were the fighters of the Afghan resistance. Although the term 'Mujahideen' – which is the plural form of an Arabic term 'Mujahid', meaning 'one who wages jihad' ('struggle' or 'holy war') – is used in a religious context, not all guerrillas were Islamists and jihadists. Most of the rebels were common Afghan people, who decided to fight against the Soviet invasion and the 'puppet' Afghan government.

Peshawar Seven

In total, the Afghans are known to have formed 84 different resistance groups in Peshawar at the beginning of the Soviet-Afghan War. The coalition of the seven major rebel groups, called the 'Peshawar Seven', was created in 1985 (or according to another source, in 1982). They were often separated into the fundamentalist (Islamist) and traditional (moderate) factions.

The fundamentalist factions were:

Jamiat-e Islami ('Islamic Society'): a mostly Tajik faction headed by Burhanuddin Rabbani, a former Professor of Theology at Kabul University, advocating for a semi-democratic Islamic revolutionary state, one of the strongest of the Mujahideen factions.

Hezb-e Islami (Gulbuddin) ('Islamic Party'): a radical oppositionist faction led by Gulbuddin Hekmatyar who enjoyed the largest amount of ISI funding, Saudi intelligence funding, and US Central Intelligence Agency funding. This group, traditionally strongest in the Ghilzai Pashtun tribal regions in the south-east, aimed for a state similar to Khomeini Iran.

Hezb-e Islami (Khalis): a splinter faction headed by theologian Yunus Khalis, with its supporter base being Ghilzai Pashtuns, favoured cooperation with other factions.

Ittihad-e Islami ('Islamic Union'): a faction advocating for Wahhabism, led by fundamentalist Abdul Rasul Sayyaf and funded by Saudi Arabia. This group was smaller than the other parties, but influential in international recruitment for the jihad.

The traditional factions were:

Harakat-e Inqilab-e Islami ('Revolutionary Islamic Movement'): a Pashtun faction headed by Mohammad Nabi Mohammadi, a religious figure and former member of the parliament, and gaining support from among Pashtun tribes in the south.

Jabha-e Nejat-e Melli ('National Liberation Front'): the group led by the Sufi order Sibghatullah Mojaddedi, a monarchist faction that favoured the return of Afghanistan's ousted King, Mohammed Zahir Shah, in a traditional Islamic state with a parliamentary democracy. It was said to be the weakest group militarily, although with a respected leader.

Mahaz-e Melli ('National Front'): the most secular, pro-Western and liberal of the Mujahideen factions, rejecting both communism and Islamic fundamentalism, instead it adhered to Pashtun nationalism, and advocated democracy and a return of the monarchy. It was headed by Sayid Ahmad Gailani, an Islamic mystical figure, and was supported by a number of tribal leaders.

Not all of the faction leaders acted as military commanders. The most famous Mujahideen commanders in addition to Gulbuddin Hekmatyar and Yunus Khalis were Ahmad Shah Massoud, Ismail Khan and Mohammad Zabihullah of the Jamiat-e Islami, Abdul Haq and Jalaluddin Haqqani of the Hezb-e Islami (Khalis) and Amin Wardak of the Mahaz-e Melli.

Tehran Eight

There was a union of Shia Afghan Mujahideen, named the 'Tehran Eight', because it was supported by, and headquartered in, Iran and consisted of eight members. This union was formed in December 1987 and was made up mainly of ethnic Hazaras. The factions of the Tehran Eight were:

Afghan Hezbollah: headed by Karim Agmadi Yak Daste.

Nasr Party (also known as Islamic Victory Organisation of Afghanistan): led by Muhammad Hussein Sadiqi, Abdul Ali Mazari and Shaykh Shafak.

Corps of Islamic Revolution Guardians of Afghanistan: headed by Sheikh Akbari, Mokhsem Rezai and Sapake Pasdar.

The Islamic Movement of Afghanistan: led by Muhammad Asif Muhsini and Shaykh Sadeq Hashemi.

Committee of Islamic Agreement (also known as the Shura party): headed by Sayeed Ali Beheshti and Sayeed Djagran.

Islamic Revolution Movement: led by Nasrullah Mansur.

Union of Islamic Fighters: headed by Mosbah Sade, a Hazara leader of Bamyan Province.

Raad ('Thunder') party: led by Shaykh Sayeed Abdul Jaffar Nadiri, a future leader of Baghlan Province, and Mohammad Hazai Sayeed Ismail Balkhee.

There were also smaller resistance groups in Afghanistan connected to neither the 'Peshawar Seven' nor the 'Tehran Eight':

Sharafat Kuh Front: a faction headed by Mulawi Mohammad Shah, an Achakzai Pashtun, and based in Farah Province.

Harakat-e Mulawi: another rebel group.

Partisans of National Liberation of Afghanistan (also known as Front of Nimruz): a Baloch faction, founded in Nimruz Province, and led by Abdul Karim Brahui and Gul Mohammad Rahimi.

Settam-e Melli ('National Oppression'): a splinter faction of the People's Democratic Party of Afghanistan, headed by Tahir Badakhshi, an ethnic Tajik, and based in Badakhshan Province.

Afghan Social Democratic Party (also known as Afghan Millat Party): a Pashtun nationalist party led by Ghulam Mohammad Farhad.

Sazman-e Azadibakhsh-e Mardom-e Afghanistan ('Liberation Organisation of the People of Afghanistan'): a Maoist faction headed by Abdul Majid Kalakani and based in Parwan Province.

Shola-e Javid ('Eternal Flame'): another Maoist faction with a populist strategy, gaining support from university students, professionals, the majority Pashtuns and the Shia Hazaras.

Overall, despite appearances to the contrary, the Afghan Mujahideen were not a united movement. Actually, and despite internal and external pressures, they remained deeply divided along ethnic, ideological and personal lines. Throughout the years, there were various efforts to create a united front, but all of these were either not effective or failed in a short time. Indeed, it can be said that many of groups, especially the Pakistan-supported fundamentalist factions, were fighting a civil war against other factions as often as they fought the Soviets and the government.

A Mujahideen of the Hezb-e Islami (Khalis) faction in the Paktia Province of the mid-1980s. He is armed with a PKT machine gun. (Mark Lepko Collection)

Foreign Support

The disunity of Afghan armed opposition, as much as sensationalism in the media resulted in a situation where even today there is no clarity with regards to who supported the Mujahideen. The usual suspects are well-known: Pakistan, the United States of America, Saudi Arabia, the other Arab states of the Persian Gulf, India, China, the United Kingdom, Egypt and even the BND (*Bundesnachrichtendienst*, the West German intelligence agency). Actually, the seven major factions – the 'Peshawar Seven', which

A supply of AK-47/AKM assault rifles (or their Chinese copies, the Type 56) seized from the Mujahideen by the 317th GAR of the 103rd GAD in 1984. (Sergey Novikov)

were also receiving the majority (over 90 percent) of foreign financial and material aid – were all exclusively supported, and even guided into their major operations by Pakistan's ISI. The ISI took four years to properly organise this process and it was only once Brigadier General Mohammad Yousaf took over as the Chief of its Afghan Bureau in 1983 that the Peshawar Seven began operating in anything resembling a 'closely coordinated fashion'. Despite plentiful US efforts to wrest control, from that time on the ISI was the only body making decisions about the distribution of all sorts of aid, from money and relief support to all kinds of armaments, irrespective of their origins. Therefore, regardless of how much funding was provided by the US Congress and Saudi Arabia, or what kind of weapons were acquired from China and Egypt, it was only Yousaf's Afghan Bureau who organised the necessary logistic bases inside Pakistan, and who decided which of the Peshawar Seven was to receive what. Other parties received exactly nothing from the ISI, and thus nothing from the USA, Saudi Arabia, and their allies. For example, although his organisation was a part of Rabbani's Jamiat-e Islami, the most famous Afghan Mujahideen leader, Ahmad Shah Massoud, was regularly cut off from the ISI's logistic system by the activities of various warlords controlling the area between the Panjshir Valley and the border with Pakistan: usually for no other reason than competition and jealousy. Eventually, this caused such a massive rift between Rabbani, Massoud and successive governments in Islamabad, that during the 1990s Jamiat-e Islami began receiving the clandestine support of the Research and Analysis Wing – the primary intelligence service of India.

Another collection of trophies captured by the 317th GAR from the Mujahideen. This photograph shows two grenade launchers, several RPG grip-stocks, and anti-personnel mines. (Sergey Novikov)

Armament

Ironically, the primary supplier of arms for the Afghan armed opposition was the Afghan Army and the secondary supplier was the Soviet Army. In other words, most of the Mujahideen were armed with what they had captured on the battlefield, or what defectors

One of the most successful weapons deployed by the Mujahideen, even if under-recognised, were Chinese-made Type 85 single round rocket launchers of 107mm calibre. Based on the Soviet-designed BM-12, these were provided from 1984 by the ISI to a small number of hand-picked commanders. (Tom Cooper Collection)

A plume of smoke caused by a rocket strike on Asadabad in 1986. By that time, the ISI was supplying enough single-rail Type 85 launchers and 122mm calibre rockets to selected commanders for these to conduct semi-regular hit-and-run attacks on major Afghan and Soviet military bases and also against the bigger municipalities around the country. (ArtOfWar – Vladimir Lebedenko)

brought with them. This is why the majority of Mujahideen arms were of Soviet origin. Additionally, they were armed with a miscellany of arms left over from earlier times, such as British Lee-Metford and Lee Enfield rifles, or arms provided by different allies via the Afghan Bureau of the ISI. The latter included British Mk.7 anti-tank mines; Egyptian Maadi assault rifles; Chinese Type 56 semi-automatic carbines, Type 56 assault rifles, Type 54 12.7mm and Type 58 14.5mm heavy machine guns, Type 56 and Type 69 rocket-propelled grenades, Type 63 60mm mortars, Type 52 75mm, Type 65 82mm and Type 75 105mm recoilless rifles, Type 85 single round rocket launchers for 122mm calibre rockets (with an empty weight of 22.5kg), and Type 63 multiple rocket launchers of the same calibre; Italian VS-2.2, VS-3.6 and SH-55 anti-tank mines and TS-50 anti-personnel mines; US M18A1 Claymore anti-personnel mines, M16A1 assault rifles, M19 anti-tank mines and M72 LAW 66mm anti-tank rockets.

An ISI-trained team of Mujahideen with an FIM-92A Stinger MANPAD, photographed inside Afghanistan in the early 1988. (Mark Lepko Collection)

The underside of the rear fuselage of an Su-17M-3 of the V-VS after being peppered by shrapnel from a FIM-92A Stinger that proximity-fused behind and below the jet. Obviously, the pilot landed the aircraft safely, despite all the resulting problems. (Pit Weinert Collection)

Another controversy related to foreign aid for the Mujahideen surrounds their man-portable air defence systems (MANPADS). Especially in the West, legend has it that the war was decided by deliveries of the US FIM-92 Stinger MANPADS. In fact, for the first few years after the Soviet military intervention, the majority of such weaponry operated by the Mujahideen were 9K32 Strela-2s and 9K32M Strela-Ms of Soviet origin (ASCC/NATO reporting name 'SA-7 Grail') obtained through defectors. Large numbers of foreign MANPADS began arriving only in 1985, when the ISI began receiving Chinese HN-5s and Egyptian Ayn al-Sarqs. Both were copies of the Soviet Strela-M. British Blowpipe MANPADS followed a year later but were never really delivered to the Mujahideen: only a squadron of Pakistan Army soldiers sent to support the opposition during one of the Soviet offensives along the border with Pakistan brought them to the country. However, the Blowpipes proved much too troublesome in deployment, and the ISI discontinued their acquisition. Stingers only arrived later in 1985, within Operation Cyclone – an operation by the Central Intelligence Agency, aiming to arm and finance the Mujahideen. Even then, Stingers were distributed only to a handful of carefully selected Afghan field commanders, and after thorough training of their future operators in camps in Pakistan. In this regard, the logistics should be kept in mind too: the majority of arms, ammunition, food, and other equipment – ranging from blankets to radios (and batteries for radios) – for the Mujahideen had to be clandestinely carried by pack animals from ISI-operated depots in north-west Pakistan. The trails used by caravans carrying the logistics were heavily mined by the Soviets and, later on, regularly interdicted by their special forces. Thus, more often than

A group of mounted Mujahideen seen in 1984. (ArtOfWar – Vladimir Shchennikov)

not, it could take literally months for any kind of ammunition, as well as new arms such as Stingers, to reach their destinations and then be pressed into operational service.

Logistics

There was always a shortage of arms and ammunition despite all the foreign aid provided over the years. Early on, the primary weapon of the Mujahideen were old British rifles from the First World War, from around 1982 these were supplanted by different versions of assault rifles based on the design of the *Avtomat Kalashnikova 47* – the ubiquitous AK-47 or the later AKM. Although the Mujahideen became notorious for their 'hit-and-run' attacks made with single shot rocket launchers of Chinese origin, these were available in very small numbers and supplied by the ISI to less than a handful of favoured commanders. Unsurprisingly, it was only from 1987 that the Afghan opposition began deploying heavy artillery, recoilless guns, and large-calibre machine guns – and then, primarily, from its bases in the proximity of the border with Pakistan. Even then, the majority of these were of Soviet design, if not origin – whether because they were clandestinely bought from war-profiteers within the ranks of the Afghan and Soviet armed forces, or – though less often – captured in combat, or acquired from the People's Republic of China, or Egypt: indeed, the Mujahideen quickly learned that the quickest way of restocking with arms and ammunition was if they bought them from the stocks of the Soviet 40th Army.[1]

Despite their relatively poor armament, thanks to the rugged terrain of Afghanistan, and the Soviet emphasis on controlling only the major urban centres and communications to them, the Mujahideen controlled almost all of the countryside of Afghanistan as early as May 1980. Even then, the actual number of active combatants was relatively low: although rising from around 25,000 in 1980, to more than 140,000 in 1988, and over 250,000 a year later.

As of 1985, the Jamiat-e Islami faction controlled a huge swath of territory stretching from Herat Province through the north to Badakhshan Province. The Harakat-e Inqilab-e Islami group also held a large amount of territory in the southern provinces, stretching from Nimruz Province to Logar Province. The Hezb-e Islami (Khalis) faction had its stronghold in Nangarhar and Paktia Provinces, while the Hezb-e Islami (Gulbuddin) group held many pockets of territory throughout Afghanistan. The Mahaz-e Melli faction was prominent in Paktia and Paktika Provinces but also had territory in other parts of the country. As of 1987, the rebels were still in control of most of Afghanistan.

Soviet officers and soldiers named Afghan villages *kishlak* ('wintering place' in Turkic languages, a rural settlement of semi-nomadic Turkic peoples of Central Asia and Azerbaijan), and Afghan men – *bacha* ('boy' in Dari). They never called their enemy *Mujahideen*, instead they used *Dushmany* ('enemies' in Tajik), *Dukhi* (either a diminutive of 'Dushmany' or 'spirits' in Russian) or *Basmachi* ('bandits' in Uzbek, the term used by the Soviets for the Central Asia resistance fighters in the 1920s and 1930s). They also called British Lee Enfield rifles *bur* ('Boer' in Russian), in reference to the Anglo-Boer War. Afghan citizens, in their turn, called Soviet servicemen and military specialists *Shuravi* ('Soviet' in Dari).

3
1979–1980

Reportedly, from 1979 President Nur Mohammad Taraki of Afghanistan had made numerous appeals to Moscow for military intervention, but Moscow had refused. President Hafizullah Amin had also issued seven or eight such requests, but he too was turned down.[1] This is likely to prompt the question, why?

There are many different versions but something like the general consensus is that the Soviet leadership wanted their Afghan colleagues to sort out their problems on their own, without the direct involvement of large elements of the Soviet Armed Forces. It was only in late 1979 that the leaders in the Kremlin concluded that Amin was not in control of the situation and arrived at the decision in mid-December of that year to invade Afghanistan, to assassinate Hafizullah Amin, and to replace him with Babrak Kamal, the Ambassador of the Democratic Republic of Afghanistan to Czechoslovakia. The operation was scheduled for 25 December 1979. To their subordinate officers, Soviet Generals explained that they were carrying out an 'international duty' in Afghanistan. What was meant by an 'international duty' – nobody knew.

On 25 December 1979 the 40th Army under the command of Lieutenant General Yuri Tukharinov was officially deployed to Afghanistan. Units of the 108th MRD crossed the Soviet-Afghan border near the town of Termez in the Uzbek SSR (Soviet Socialist Republic), then advanced south and reached Kabul two days later. Units of the 5th Guards MRD entered Afghanistan on the night of 26/27 December and headed south from Kushka in the Turkmen SSR to Herat and Shindand, and then on to Kandahar. Units of the 103rd GAD were airlifted to Kabul and Bagram and by 27 December had taken control of the military bases and strategic installations in both cities. Later on, the 201st MRD was deployed to Afghanistan. It was supposed that Soviet troops would stay in garrison and secure important industrial and other objectives, to allow the Afghan Army to fight against opposition groups.

First Losses

On the first day of the invasion, 25 December 1979, an Ilyushin Il-76M heavy transport plane of the 128th Guards Military Transport

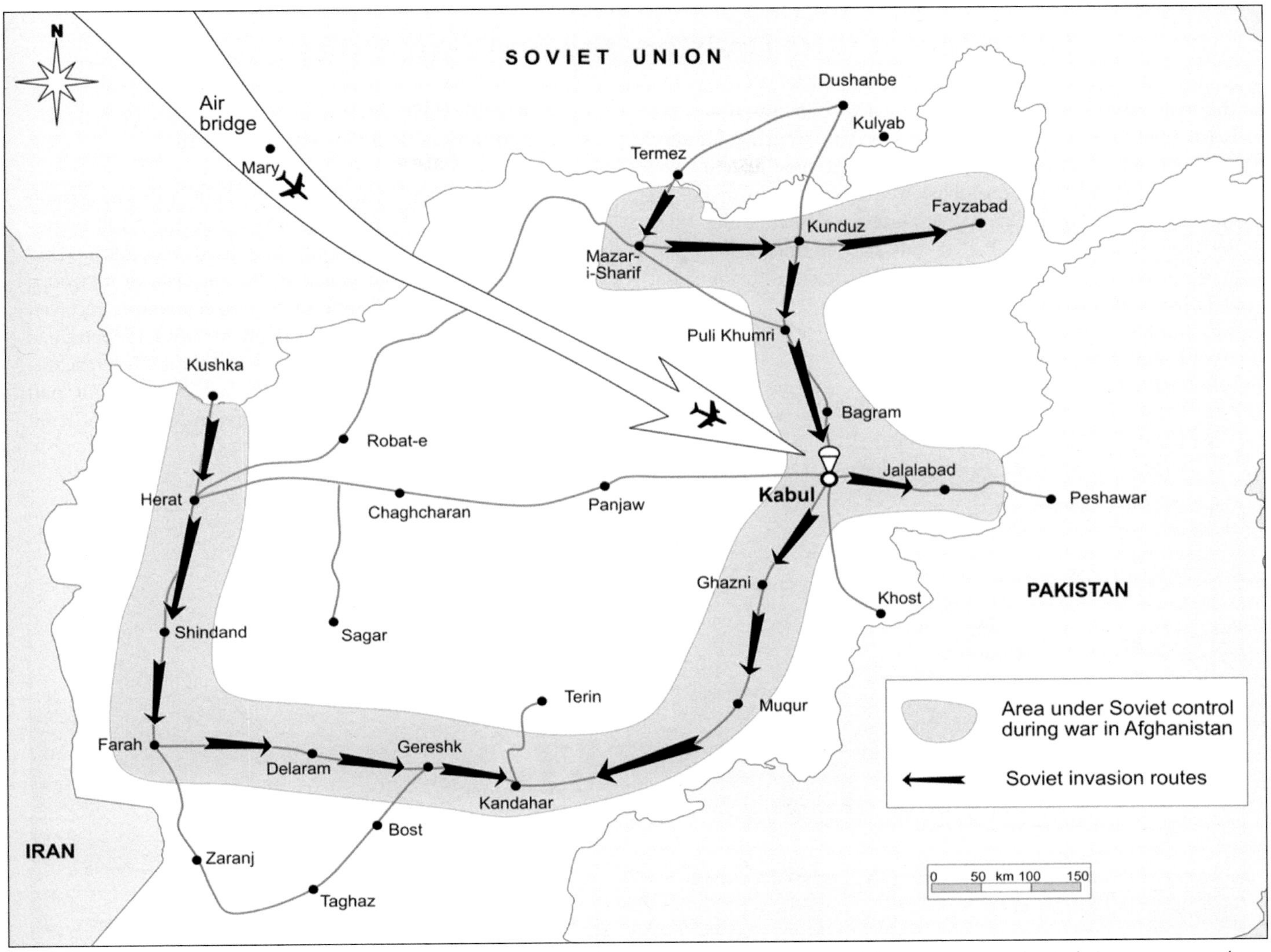

Map of Afghanistan with the major routes of Soviet advances during the intervention of December 1979, and the areas the 40th Army attempted to keep under control over the following years. (Map by Mark Thompson)

Tajbeg Palace seen on the morning after the attack by the KGB and the 154th Separate Spetsnaz Detachment on 27 December 1979. (Efim Sandler Collection)

Aviation Regiment, 18th Guards Military Transport Aviation Division, carrying soldiers and officers of the 103rd GAD from Tashkent Air Base to Bagram Air Base, was damaged by anti-aircraft artillery fire and crashed into a mountain near Kabul. According to various sources, between 43 and 67 Soviet officers and soldiers were killed.[2]

In the evening of 27 December 1979 two KGB special detachments, named *Grom* and *Zenit*, and the 154th Separate Spetsnaz Detachment stormed Tajbeg Palace in the outskirts of Kabul. The operation officially lasted for 40 minutes. As a result of the assault, the General Secretary of the Central Committee of the People's Democratic Party of Afghanistan and the Prime Minister of the Democratic

108th Motor Rifle Division: the first into Afghanistan

The first unit of the Soviet Army to enter Afghanistan was the 108th MRD. Originally, this was tasked with securing Kunduz. However, once the planners concluded that they had too few troops to secure Kabul, the division was ordered to march all the way to the Afghan capital! Its leading elements, the 781st Reconnaissance Battalion, had already crossed the border over a newly-constructed pontoon bridge near Termez on the morning of 25 December. It was followed by:

- 180th MRR, 108th MRD
- 234th Tank Regiment, 108th MRD
- 177th MRR, 108th MRD
- 1074th Artillery Regiment, 108th MRD
- 1049th Anti-Aircraft Artillery Regiment, 108th MRD
- 181st MRR, 108th MRD
- support units of the 186th MRR, 68th MRD

Ahead of the 108th, a battalion of the 56th Airborne Assault Brigade was deployed by helicopters to secure the 2,700-metre-long Salang Tunnel. Only recently mobilised, the 108th MRD found itself in a precarious situation: the majority of its troops had been re-activated only one or two weeks before, received no refresher training, were not trained for winter operations and could not even operate their radios and guns. Nevertheless, the 781st Reconnaissance Battalion and the 180th MRR had advanced along 570km of poor roads to reach Kabul as ordered by 27 December 1979.

BMP-1s of the 108th MRD outside Kabul, on 7 January 1980. (Efim Sandler Collection)

Republic of Afghanistan, Hafizullah Amin, and either his 5-year-old son, or both he and Amin's 11-year-old second son, and one woman were killed. Amin's daughter was wounded.[3] The Soviet Army lost seven soldiers and officers, the KGB – between seven and nine officers, the Afghan Army and National Guards lost between 150 and 348 people killed. Between three and 67 other servicemen of the Soviet Army and KGB officers, and either two or three Afghan civilians, were wounded. Kabul Radio announced that 'Amin had been sentenced to death at a revolutionary trial for crimes against the state and that sentence had been carried out.' Babrak Karmal became the General Secretary of the Central Committee of the People's Democratic Party of Afghanistan, Chairman of the Praesidium of the Revolutionary Council of the People's Democratic Party of Afghanistan, and Prime Minister of the Democratic Republic of Afghanistan.

Descent into Chaos

In January and February 1980, 130 members of the People's Democratic Party of Afghanistan were killed in the city of Kandahar and several neighbouring districts. Two Soviet soldiers were killed in two fights on 6 January 1980, and two further Soviet servicemen, belonging to the 12th Air Assault Company of the 4th AABn, 56th Separate Guards AABr, were killed in a fight in the town of Khinjan in Baghlan Province, 120km (75 miles) north of Kabul, on 8 January 1980.

On 9 January 1980, at least 10 Soviet soldiers (15, according to the *News from the USSR*, a periodical of the Soviet human rights movement) were reportedly shot and killed near Kabul, for disobeying orders, by servicemen from another unit.[4] The same day a Soviet convoy was ambushed near the village of Siyah Sang in Baghlan Province, 130km (81 miles) north-west of Kabul. Four soldiers of the 10th Air Assault Company of the 4th AABn, 56th Separate Guards AABr were killed in the ensuing clash. Such ambushes became quite common in the Soviet-Afghan War.

The mutiny in the town of Nahrin, in Baghlan Province, 170km (106 miles) north of Kabul, occurred on 9 January 1980 and was suppressed the next day. The 4th Artillery Regiment of the 20th Infantry Division of the Afghan Army, stationed there, refused to follow orders, and as a result a fight between renegade Afghan soldiers and the men of the 2nd MR Coy of the 1st MRBn, 186th MRR, 108th MRD and 2nd MRBn of the 186th MRR, 108th MRD took place with the use of artillery and aircraft. Between two and five Soviet soldiers and around 100 Afghan soldiers were killed, and two Soviet soldiers were wounded.

On 10 January 1980 a fight broke out near the village of Gul Khanah in Badakhshan Province, 300km (186 miles) north-east of Kabul. Three men of the Reconnaissance Company of the 860th Separate MRR were killed, one private was taken prisoner and later also killed, several other soldiers were wounded.

Murdered Afghan citizens, the place and year is not known. Tragically, such scenes became much too common in this war. (Afghan-war-soldiers.ru)

A Soviet convoy was ambushed on 13 January 1980 near the city of Taluqan, capital of Takhar Province, 250km (155 miles) north of Kabul. Nine men of the 186th MRR, 108th MRD, including three officers, were killed in the ensuing fight and in the explosion of a mortar, killing its crew.

On 14 January 1980, the United Nations General Assembly passed a resolution protesting against the Soviet invasion of Afghanistan. The same day two Soviet servicemen were killed in clashes, and another soldier, belonging to the Reconnaissance Company of the 860th Separate MRR, died in a road accident when a BRDM amphibious armoured scout car fell off a cliff in Badakhshan Province.

Another ambush took place on 16 January 1980 near the town of Dushi in Baghlan Province. The Mujahideen shot-up a truck and killed 12 Soviet soldiers, mostly from the 3rd MRBn of the 177th MRR, 108th MRD.

On 20 January 1980 three servicemen of the 860th Separate MRR were killed in a fight in Badakhshan Province, and two soldiers of the 4th AABn, 56th Separate Guards AABr were killed in a clash near the village of Salang-e Shamali in Baghlan Province.

In late January/early February of 1980 the first *known* massacre of the Soviet-Afghan War took place. On 25 January 750 Afghan civilians were killed in several villages of Chahar Dara District in Kunduz Province. On 10 February 250 Afghan men and women were killed in another district of the same province, Dasht-e Archi.

Five Soviet servicemen died in two accidents on 26 January 1980. A private from the 357th GAR, 103rd GAD died in the city of Kabul when a fellow soldier mishandled his assault rifle. Two officers and one private from the 186th MRR, 108th MRD died at Kunduz Air Base, when they were hit by a helicopter blade. Four Soviet servicemen, including one officer, died in two fights and two accidents on 30 January 1980. Eight Soviet soldiers died on 9 February 1980 in two skirmishes, an explosion, a fire and three accidents.

First Soviet Offensives

From 11 to 15 February 1980 the Command of 40th Army carried out an operation in Paktia Province, involving the 56th Separate Guards AABr. One Soviet soldier was killed and a lieutenant colonel, a military adviser, died in an accident; more than 70 were wounded.

On 12 February 1980 a fight broke out near the village of Khwajah Ghar in Takhar Province, 270km (168 miles) north of Kabul. Six men of the 1st Airborne Company of the 1st ABn, 56th Separate Guards AABr were killed. Two Soviet soldiers of the 191st MRR, 201st MRD died that day near the city of Kunduz and one other, belonging to the 2nd Reconnaissance Company of the 781st Separate Reconnaissance Battalion, 108th MRD, died in Kabul.

Four officers of the Soviet Army, including another lieutenant colonel, who was a military adviser, and one KGB officer, were killed on 13 February 1980 when rebels shot down a Mi-24 attack helicopter of the 1st Helicopter Squadron, 292nd Separate Helicopter Regiment near the city of Jalalabad. One officer of the 177th MRR, 108th MRD was killed the same day in a fight in the Salang Pass.

On 16 February 1980 four servicemen of the 1st Helicopter Squadron, 280th Separate Helicopter Regiment, including three officers, died when a Mil Mi-6A heavy transport helicopter crashed in Baghlan Province. Two soldiers of the Soviet Army and one soldier of the Soviet Border Troops were killed in two clashes. One Private of the 636th Separate Support Battalion, 201st MRD died near the town of Khulm in Samangan Province. One soldier of the 1060th Guards Artillery Regiment, 5th Guards MRD was killed when he reportedly tried to defect to the Mujahideen in Herat Province.

On 22 February 1980 Senior Lieutenant Alexander Vovk, a political officer of the 103rd GAD, was killed with a single shot near the Green Market in Kabul. Soon after, a group of officers of the 357th GAR, 103rd GAD, headed by the deputy commander of the regiment, Major Vitali Zababurin, arrived at the market and started to shoot at the people in the streets and throw grenades into houses. Dozens of Afghan civilians were killed. Sometime later several hundreds of thousands of people took to the streets of Kabul, shouting and demanding an end to the Soviet aggression. After that the Soviet Command ordered the Afghan Army and KhAD to fire at the demonstrators. As a result, during 22 and 23 February between 50 and 800 more Afghan civilians were killed, five Afghan soldiers, one Soviet soldier and an unknown number of Afghan civilians were wounded.

On 23 February 1980, which is the main holiday of the Soviet Army, an accident occurred in the Salang Tunnel, located at the Salang Pass in the Hindu Kush Mountains, 100km (62 miles) north of Kabul, and connects northern and southern parts of the country. The military convoys of the 2nd Anti-Aircraft Missile Brigade and of the 186th MRR, 108th MRD stopped because of a stalled truck. Tens of vehicles were standing in the narrow tunnel for a few hours with running engines. According to official sources, 16 Soviet soldiers

A destroyed ZSU-23-4 Shilka self-propelled anti-aircraft gun of the 181st MRR, 108th MRD, sometime in 1980. (181msp.ru)

A convoy of the 3rd Support Company of the 636th Separate Support Battalion of the 201st MRD, the place and year are not known. (ArtOfWar – Vladimir Shchennikov)

died of carbon monoxide poisoning.[5] According to unofficial sources, the casualties were around 80.[6]

The same day several hundred people organised a rally in the village of Mir Bacha Kot in Kabul Province, 25km (16 miles) north of Kabul. They reportedly attacked a Soviet checkpoint and wounded an officer of the 2nd MR Coy of the 1st MRBn, 181st MRR, 108th MRD. After that, Soviet soldiers started shooting at the crowd and killed 22 people.

On 25 February 1980 one Soviet officer was killed when a helicopter was shot down, two soldiers died in two accidents, and one more serviceman died in hospital from wounds.

In late February to mid-March 1980 the Soviet Command carried out an operation in Kunar Province. The 180th MRR of the 108th MRD, the 317th GAR and the 350th GAR of the 103rd GAD, with an infantry battalion of the 66th Infantry Regiment of the 11th Infantry Division of the Afghan Army were tasked to destroy the enemy in the village of Shigal, 200km (124 miles) north-east of Kabul, and to destroy the Mujahideen logistic base in the village of Dangam. During this operation Soviet servicemen killed an unknown number of Afghan civilians, including children, in several villages of Kunar Province. Between 49 and 53 Soviet soldiers and officers, including a lieutenant colonel, reportedly up to 1,500 Mujahideen and a lot of Afghan civilians were killed, between 26 and 40 further Soviet soldiers were wounded and a Soviet soldier went missing.

Servicemen of the 4th MR Coy of the 2nd MRBn, 149th Guards MRR, 201st MRD and prisoner. The place and year are unknown. (ArtOfWar – Vladimir Shchennikov)

During this offensive, one of the major battles of the Soviet-Afghan War took place near the village of Shigal. Soldiers and officers of the 3rd ABn of the 317th GAR, 103rd GAD under the command of Major Vasili Kustrio landed near the settlement in the morning of 29 February and, according to the official version, soon after that were engaged in a skirmish with Afghan rebels that lasted until the evening.[7] Between 33 and 37 Soviet servicemen and a number of Mujahideen were killed in this fight. According to the unofficial version, most of the Soviet conscripts killed that day were killed by their fellow soldiers.[8]

The same day, the 2nd MRBn of the 180th MRR, 108th MRD fought near the neighbouring village of Shin Koruk Darah and 16 Soviet soldiers were killed.

A private from the tank battalion of the 149th Guards MRR, 201st MRD was killed by an Afghan civilian on 1 March 1980 near the city of Kunduz, reportedly as a result of a domestic dispute.

Between five and 10 servicemen of the 3rd MRBn, of the 191st MRR, 201st MRD were killed in a skirmish near the town of Baghlan on 5 March 1980.

On 8 March 1980 a Soviet private from the 4th MR Coy of the 2nd MRBn, 860th Separate MRR, deserted from his unit in the city of Fayzabad. He was reportedly later found dead. Seven Soviet servicemen, including one officer, died on 12 March 1980.

On 14 March 1980 a group of soldiers of the 2nd MRBn of the 191st MRR, 201st MRD hit an improvised explosive device near the town of Nahrin, Baghlan Province. Three soldiers were killed and one officer was badly wounded; he died in a hospital the next day.

A warrant officer from the 70th Separate Guards MRBr was killed on 15 March 1980 by a fellow officer near the town of Shindand in Herat Province, reportedly as a result of a drunken brawl.

On 18 March 1980 Soviet servicemen killed 25 people near the village of Giru in Ghazni Province, 215km (134 miles) southwest of Kabul. Six Soviet servicemen, including one officer, died on 20 March 1980.

Five Soviet servicemen, including the commander of the 45th Separate Engineering Regiment, Lieutenant Colonel Anatoli Abdeyev, and another lieutenant colonel, died on 24 March 1980. Lieutenant Colonel Abdeyev was killed by his subordinate in the village of Deh-e Miskin in Parwan Province, 50km (31 miles) north of Kabul, reportedly as a result of the negligent handling of a weapon.

From 26 to 30 March 1980 the Soviet Command carried out an operation in Badakhshan Province. Heavy fighting broke out on 26 March 1980 near the town of Jurm, 300km (186 miles) north-east of Kabul. Servicemen of the 860th Separate MRR and the 24th Infantry Regiment, 20th Infantry Division of the Afghan Army reportedly killed 60 Mujahideen and took 40 others prisoner. On 30 March 1980 the 860th Separate MRR plus air support fought with a rebel group near the town of Baharak, 320km (199 miles) north-east of Kabul, and lost four soldiers killed and seven more wounded. A pilot from the 3rd Helicopter Squadron, 181st Separate Helicopter Regiment was wounded during the evacuation and later died. One hundred and seventy guerrillas were reportedly killed and eight more were taken prisoner.

In late March 1980 Soviet troops carried out an operation in Kunar Province. On 29 March 1980 a clash erupted near the village of Seray, 160km (99 miles) east of Kabul. Six servicemen, including an officer, of the 7th MR Coy of the 3rd MRBn, 66th Separate MRBr were killed. Four more Soviet servicemen died that day in other parts of the country. Between six and 16 men of the 66th Separate MRBr were killed and one soldier went missing in two separate actions on 31 March 1980. In April 1980 Soviet servicemen killed around 2,000 Afghan civilians in Laghman Province.

Defections and Atrocities

On 1 April 1980 a private from the 371st Guards MRR, 5th Guards MRD deserted from his unit and surrendered to Mujahideen near Shindand Air Base. Later he was reportedly released with the help of international organisations and emigrated to the United States of America.

From 2 to 11 April 1980 Soviet troops carried out an operation in the Surkh Rud District of Nangarhar Province. Nine servicemen of the 66th Separate MRBr were killed in action and two more were killed by a soldier of the Afghan Army, three others died in an accident, one soldier died of wounds and one more went missing.

On 4 April 1980 Soviet troops killed 30 people in the city of Fayzabad. The same day Soviet officers and men killed 30 people in Baharak, Badakhshan Province.

On 8 April 1980 the Soviet Air Force carried out several strikes near the city of Kandahar and killed 150 people, mostly civilians, who were identified as 'mutineers' in official Soviet Army reports. This situation was to repeat itself many times until the end of the war. The same day Soviet jets conducted a strike near the village of Deh Rawud in Uruzgan Province, 400km (249 miles) south-west of Kabul, 15 people were killed.

Six soldiers of the Reconnaissance Company of the 70th Separate Guards MRBr and two pilots from the 3rd Helicopter Squadron,

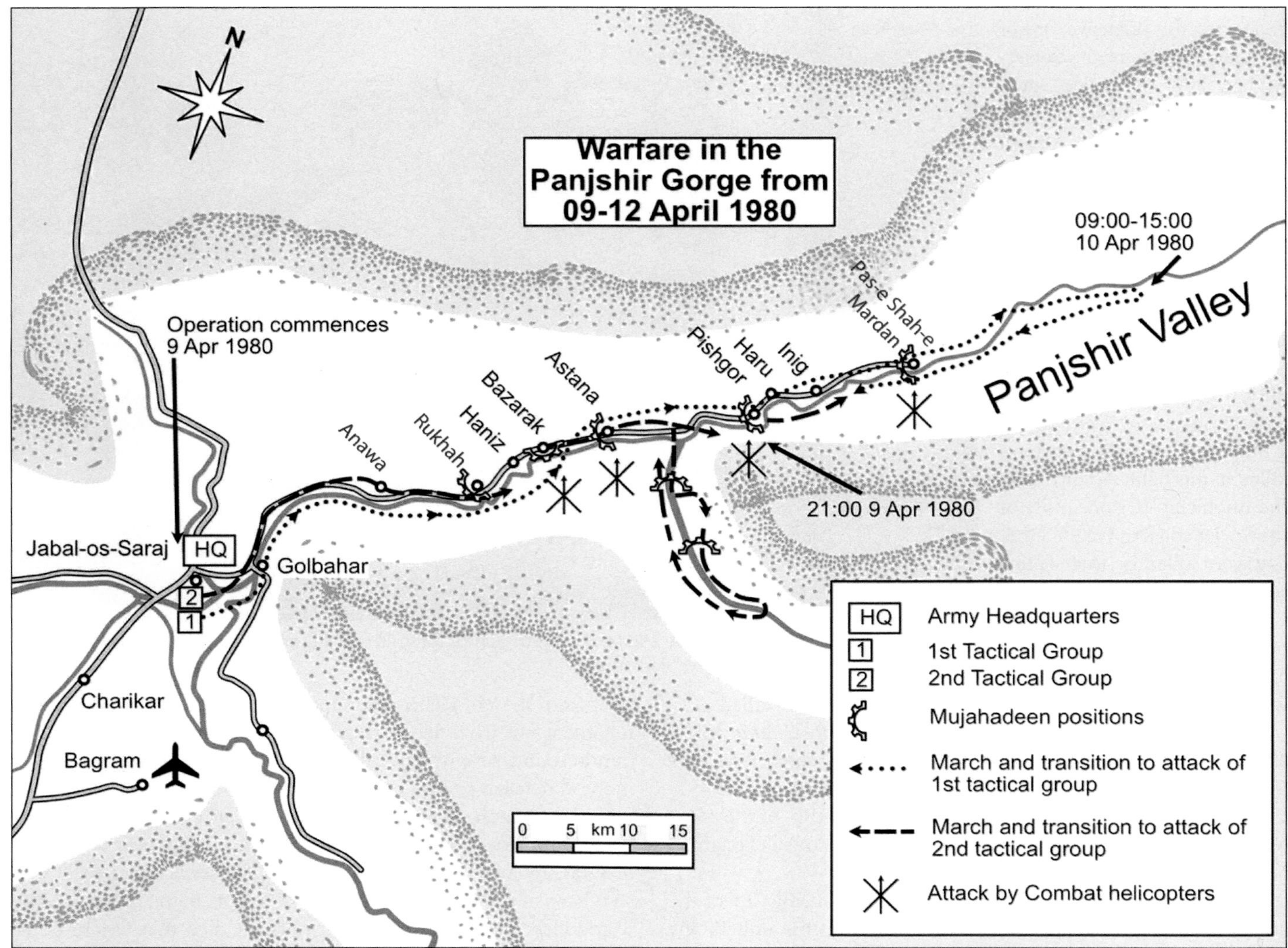

Map of the Soviet Army's Panjshir I. (Map by Mark Thompson)

280th Separate Helicopter Regiment died on 9 April 1980 in a Mil Mi-8 helicopter crash at Kandahar Air Base.

Panjshir I

From 9 to 12 April 1980 the Soviet Command carried out their first Panjshir offensive, or 'Panjshir Operation' in Soviet military parlance, in the strategic Panjshir Valley (also known as the 'Panjshir Gorge').[9] This valley lies in the Hindu Kush Mountains close to the Salang Pass: it stretches from a point about 70km (43 miles) north of Kabul and is more than 100km (62 miles) long. In 1980 it was located in Parwan Province of Afghanistan (nowadays the Panjshir Province). The 4th AABn of the 56th Separate Guards AABr, the 2nd ABn of the 345th Separate GAR and one MRBn of the 177th MRR, 108th MRD, with two infantry battalions of the Afghan Army advanced, trying to eliminate Mujahideen units. Soviet troops reportedly captured the headquarters of Ahmad Shah Massoud. Sixteen servicemen were killed in action and two officers were wounded. The rebels lost four men killed.

After this operation Ahmad Shah Massoud negotiated a truce with the Soviet Command through intermediaries. He committed not to attack Soviet and Afghan troops. The Soviet Command committed to provide him air and artillery support, if his groups would fight the groups of the Hezb-e Islami (Gulbuddin) Mujahideen faction.

On 10 April 1980 Soviet aircraft conducted several strikes on the city of Kunduz and killed more than 150 people, including a Soviet soldier. At least one more Soviet serviceman was wounded.

On 11 April 1980 rebels shot down a Mil Mi-6 helicopter of the 1st Helicopter Squadron, 181st Separate Helicopter Regiment near the town of Shindand in Herat Province, killing five Soviet servicemen, including three officers.

Seven paratroopers, including one officer, of the 103rd GAD were killed on 14 April 1980, when a BMD airborne infantry fighting vehicle hit a landmine in the Chawkay Valley in Kunar Province, 160km (99 miles) east of Kabul.

Twelve Soviet soldiers died on 18 April 1980, six of them belonging to the 4th MR Coy of the 2nd MRBn, 860th Separate MRR when they got caught in a mudflow in the city of Fayzabad.

The same day the Soviet Air Force again bombed the vicinity of Kandahar and killed 150 Afghan citizens. Soviet servicemen that day killed 50 people in the city of Jalalabad. On the same day, Soviet soldiers killed 45 people near the village of Khwajah Ghar in Takhar Province. On 20 April 1980 150 Afghan guerrillas were reportedly killed in a fight near the city of Ghazni. Between six and 11 men of the 70th Separate Guards MRBr were killed on 26 April 1980 in a fight in Uruzgan Province.

Anti-Government Protests

From late April to early June 1980 students at various institutes in Kabul held a protest in the capital. They demonstrated against the Afghan government and demanded the withdrawal of Soviet troops from Afghanistan. Afghan security forces and, according to some reports Soviet troops, broke up the rallies, beating the demonstrators

Soldiers of the 3rd Mortar Battery of the 3rd MRBn of the 181st MRR, 108th MRD in the town of Surobi, Kabul Province, 1980. The writing on the banner reads *Resheniya XXVI siezda KPSS odobryayem i podderzhivayem* (*We welcome and support the decisions of the 26th congress of the CPSU*). (181msp.ru)

and firing into them.[10] Between 72 and 200 students were killed and between 400 and 2,000 were arrested. In the first half of June over 500 people, students and teachers from more than 10 Kabul schools, were poisoned and hospitalised – there were no fatalities.

During May 1980 between 10 and 12 members of the People's Democratic Party of Afghanistan were killed in the city of Herat every day. On 3 May 1980 a corporal from the tank battalion of the 149th Guards MRR, 201st MRD went missing in Badakhshan Province. The next day five men of the 541st Separate Engineering Battalion, 201st MRD, including one officer, were killed in a fight in the same province, when they were sent to find the missing man. Nine Soviet servicemen, including one officer, died on 5 May 1980, eight of them died in road accidents. Between three and 11 servicemen of the 5th Guards MRD were killed on 8 May 1980 in a fight in the Lur Kuh Mountains in Farah Province.

On 10 May 1980 five soldiers of the 56th Separate Guards AABr went absent without leave from their unit in the city of Kunduz. Later three of them were found dead, the other two were not found.

On 11 May 1980 another major engagement between Soviet troops and Afghan guerrillas took place near the village of Kharah in Kunar Province, 220km (137 miles) north-east of Kabul. Units of the 1st MRBn and of the mortar platoon of the AABn, both of the 66th Separate MRBr, were marching from the village of Bar Kanday, 170km (106 miles) north-east of Kabul, to Kharah and were ambushed. Between 31 and 46 Soviet soldiers and 36 rebels were killed, at least 25 more Soviet soldiers and at least 65 insurgents were wounded, five other Soviet soldiers went missing. Some of these men were taken prisoner during clashes with the Afghan resistance and subsequently killed, but some of them deserted from their units and even defected to the rebels. A number of such young men moved to European and North American countries, where they told a lot about what was really happening during the Soviet-Afghan War.

Between 12 and 13 Soviet servicemen, including a lieutenant colonel, died on 13 May 1980.

A fire occurred at Kabul Air Base on 21 May 1980. One soldier of the 446th Separate Troop Carrying Battalion of the 59th Support Brigade died during the extinguishing of it, one officer and two more soldiers suffered burns and later died in hospitals. Fifteen Soviet servicemen, mostly from the 181st MRR, 108th MRD, were killed and an officer was wounded on 24 May: 12 of them died in a single engagement in Kunar Province.

The long, first summer

In late May 1980 the Soviet Command carried out an operation in Ghazni Province. During this offensive, in the town of Waghiz Soviet troops killed at least 30 Afghan civilians with chemical agents. In June 1980 Soviet helicopters dropped chemical bombs on a village in Paktia Province, one Afghan civilian was killed.

In early June 1980 Soviet artillery shelled villages in Koh Daman, Gul Darah, Farza, Nijrao and Ghorband Valleys near Kabul. Later, ground units entered several villages in these valleys, and Soviet servicemen killed an unknown number of Afghan civilians.

On 3 June 1980 a convoy of the 650th Separate Reconnaissance Battalion of the 5th Guards MRD was ambushed near the town of Delaram in Nimruz Province, 600km (373 miles) south-west of Kabul. Soviet servicemen fought back and lost between nine and 11 men killed, including an officer, at least one further Soviet soldier was wounded. The Mujahideen lost five fighters. At least two BRDM vehicles were destroyed.

Four days later, on 7 June 1980, during a crossing of the Kokcha River near the city of Fayzabad by the 2nd MRBn, 149th Guards MRR of the 201st MRD, a PTS-2 amphibious vehicle stalled and then capsized. The bodies of three soldiers were found and identified, seven more Soviet servicemen, including one officer, were swept away by the current and officially went missing, but it is likely that they also died.

On 9 June 1980 Soviet aircraft conducted a strike near the town of Jurm in Badakhshan Province, killing 180 people.

Eleven Soviet servicemen, including five officers, died on 12 June 1980. The same day the Soviet Air Force conducted a strike near Fayzabad and 200 Afghan citizens were killed.

Six Soviet servicemen, including one officer, died on 19 June – five of them, belonging to the 181st MRR, 108th MRD, died as a result of the explosion at the ammunition depot in Pul-e Charkhi prison near the city of Kabul.

From 22 to 28 June 1980 the Soviet Command carried out an operation in Kandahar and Helmand Provinces in South Afghanistan. Fourteen servicemen were killed in clashes. On 23 June 1980 two soldiers of the 9th MR Coy of the 3rd MRBn, 860th Separate MRR died and three more went missing during a crossing of the Vardudzh River in Badakhshan Province.

A soldier of the 9th MR Coy of the 3rd MRBn, 181st MRR, 108th MRD, and an Afghan soldier, in front of the wreckage of a downed Mi-25 of the Afghan Air Force. (181msp.ru)

On 25 June 1980 Soviet troops killed hundreds of Afghan citizens in different parts of the country. Soviet jets conducted a strike on the town of Jangal in Badakhshan Province, 250km (155 miles) north of Kabul, killing 80 people. Soviet servicemen killed 60 people near the village of Shin Koruk Darah in Kunar Province. Fifty people were killed near the city of Khost in Paktia Province. Fifty people were killed near the town of Sar-e Pul in Jowzjan Province, 350km (217 miles) north-west of Kabul. Fifty people were killed near the village of Margar in Kapisa Province, 60km (37 miles) north-east of Kabul. Eighteen people were killed near the town of Kotah-ye Ashro in Wardak Province, 40km (25 miles) west of Kabul.

During the first half of July 1980 Soviet troops entirely or partially destroyed between 50 and 60 villages in several districts around Kabul.

A serviceman of the 9th MR Coy of the 3rd MRBn, 181st MRR, 108th MRD, standing atop a BTR-60PB, at the entrance to the Salang Tunnel. (181msp.ru)

On 1 July 1980 a soldier from the 3rd ABn of the 357th GAR, 103rd GAD suddenly started firing a machine gun at his fellow soldiers at the battalion's location near the city of Jalalabad. Five Soviet soldiers were killed and many others were wounded. Later these five soldiers were declared killed in action. Four more Soviet servicemen, including a colonel, a military adviser, died that day in other regions of the country.

Twenty-seven Soviet servicemen died on 5 July 1980 in five fights, four explosions, an ambush and in the shooting down of a helicopter. Seventeen of them were paratroopers of the 345th Separate GAR.

Two privates were killed in fights and one colonel died in a road accident in Kabul on 7 July 1980.

On 10 July 1980 fighting broke out in the town of Qara Bagh in Kabul Province, 35km (22 miles) north of Kabul. Later that day Soviet servicemen killed an unknown number of Afghan civilians in this settlement. According to some sources, they killed a large number of people and the survivors started to flee Qara Bagh.[11]

Eight Soviet soldiers were killed in three clashes on 14 July 1980.

Eleven servicemen of the Soviet Army and a KGB officer died on 20 July.

Ten Soviet servicemen died on 23 July 1980. Eight of them were officers: three pilots of the 262nd Separate Helicopter Squadron died in a Mi-24 helicopter when it was shot down near the town of Bagram in Parwan Province, and three pilots of the 4th Helicopter Squadron, 280th Separate Helicopter Regiment with two GRU officers were killed, when rebels shot down a Mil Mi-8 helicopter in Kandahar Province.

Eight Soviet servicemen, including one officer died on 24 July. Five of them, belonging to the 177th MRR of the 108th MRD, were killed in a single action in Parwan Province.

From 24 to 28 July 1980 the Soviet Command carried out an operation in Wardak

A rare photograph of a BMD-1 from the 345th Separate GAR, modified though the installation of the barbette from a Mi-24D helicopter, including the Yak machine gun. (Efim Sandler Collection)

Province, eastern Afghanistan – 15 servicemen were killed and at least one more was wounded.

At around the same time the Soviet Air Force killed an unknown number of Afghan civilians and destroyed several villages in Dai Mirdad District of Wardak Province.

At about the same time Soviet aircraft conducted strikes on several villages near the city of Maidan Shahr, the capital of Wardak Province, 30km (19 miles) south-west of Kabul, and killed up to 500 people. According to some sources, a regiment of the Afghan Army fought the Soviet units in Wardak Province because of these bombardments.[12]

On 27 July 1980 a high-ranking officer of the Soviet Ministry of Internal Affairs was killed in Kabul, reportedly near the embassy of the USSR.

On 28 July 1980 a Soviet convoy was ambushed near the village of Turani in Baghlan Province, 185km (115 miles) north of Kabul. In retaliation, the next day Soviet aircraft conducted a strike on Turani, and Soviet servicemen killed around 50 people in the town of Baghlan.

From 29 July to 4 August 1980 the Soviet Command conducted the Yavarzan Offensive in Badakhshan Province. The 2nd MRBn and the Engineering Company of the 149th Guards MRR, 201st MRD fought for four days, lost five soldiers killed, and then retreated. On 2 August the 2nd MRBn of the 149th Guards MRR, 201st MRD was cut off near the settlement of Qara Deh, 260km (162 miles) north-east of Kabul. Soviet servicemen organised a perimeter defence. In the evening of 2 August, the 783rd Separate Reconnaissance Battalion, under the command of Major Alibek Kadyrov and units of the 3rd MRBn of the 149th Guards MRR, all of the 201st MRD were sent out to reinforce it, but in the morning of 3 August they were ambushed between Qara Deh and the neighbouring village of Yavarzan. This fight lasted for about 24 hours. Between 45 and 49 Soviet soldiers and officers and an unknown number of Mujahideen were killed, between 46 and 49 more Soviet soldiers were wounded.

Six Soviet servicemen died on 31 July 1980. A sergeant from the Reconnaissance Company of the 395th MRR, 201st MRD defected on that day to the guerrillas in Kunduz Province.

In late July 1980, Soviet helicopters conducted strikes on the town of Islamabad in Laghman Province, 90km (56 miles) east of Kabul, and on the neighbouring villages of Sabrabad and Shamaram, partially destroying both of them.

In August 1980 a Soviet soldier, probably looking for money or marijuana in a house in the village of Samar Khel in Nangarhar Province, 130km (81 miles) east of Kabul, began firing at random at those who were in the house, killing several people and wounding one more, who later died in a hospital. Later the Afghan authorities stated that this crime was carried out by the Mujahideen.

Eight Soviet servicemen died on 5 August 1980.

In early August 1980 insurgents pushed the Afghan troops from several villages near the city of Kabul. On 7 August either Soviet, or Afghan aircraft conducted strikes on these villages, killing an unknown number of people.

From 6 to 11 August 1980 Soviet troops carried out an operation in Kapisa Province, involving the 345th Separate GAR, and the 181st MRR of the 108th MRD. Between 26 and 32 officers and men were killed in the action.

In mid-August 1980 Soviet artillery shelled several villages, believed to be the hideouts of rebels, around the city of Mehtar Lam.

On 14 and 15 August 1980 the 191st Separate MRR lost five soldiers and two officers killed in several clashes in Ghazni Province.

A soldier of the Reconnaissance Company of the 181st MRR, 108th MRD, the location is unknown, 1980. The writing on the vehicle reads *'Mama! Ya hochu domoy...'* (*'Mom! I want to go home...'*). (181msp.ru)

On 16 August 1980 Soviet troops heavily shelled Herat, killing around 3,000 people. After that Soviet troops entered the city and looted many shops, particularly those that sold gold and silver items.

On 19 August 1980 Soviet artillery shelled several villages in the Alishang Valley in Laghman Province.

Eleven Soviet soldiers were killed on 23 August 1980. Six of them, belonging to the 70th Separate Guards MRBr, died in a single fight near the village of Deh-e Masus in Kandahar Province, 460km (286 miles) southwest of Kabul. Ten Soviet servicemen, including five officers, died on 25 August 1980.

Panjshir II

From 28 August 1980 to 18 September 1980 Soviet and Afghan troops carried out Panjshir II. The 180th MRR, the 181st MRR and the 271st Separate Engineering Battalion, all of the 108th MRD were involved in the operation. They lost around 500 men killed, while the rebels lost 25 combatants. Several helicopters were shot down.

From 4 to 16 September 1980, the Soviet Command carried out an operation in Herat Province, involving the 101st MRR, 24th Guards Tank Regiment and 1060th Guards Artillery Regiment, all of the 5th Guards MRD. Ten or 11 soldiers were killed in clashes and in a friendly fire incident, at least three others were wounded and one went missing.

On 6 September 1980 two tanks and several other vehicles got separated from a Soviet convoy in the Alishang Valley in Laghman Province and then were ambushed and destroyed by Mujahideen. In reprisal, on the night of 6/7 September Soviet artillery shelled several neighbouring villages and the town of Maskurah, 95km (59 miles) east of Kabul, killing and wounding an unknown number of people.

In mid-September 1980 Soviet helicopter gunships conducted a strike on a wedding party in the village of Ganjabad in Farah Province, 660km (410 miles) west of Kabul. Around 150 Afghan civilians were killed and many others were wounded.

Seven Soviet soldiers were killed in six clashes on 25 September 1980.

Seven more Soviet soldiers were killed on 27 September 1980 in a friendly fire incident, when a Mil Mi-8 helicopter of the 3rd Helicopter Squadron, 50th Separate Mixed Aviation Regiment conducted a strike near the village of Jalala in Kunar Province, 210km (130 miles) northeast of Kabul.

Eleven Soviet servicemen, including an officer, died on 29 September 1980.

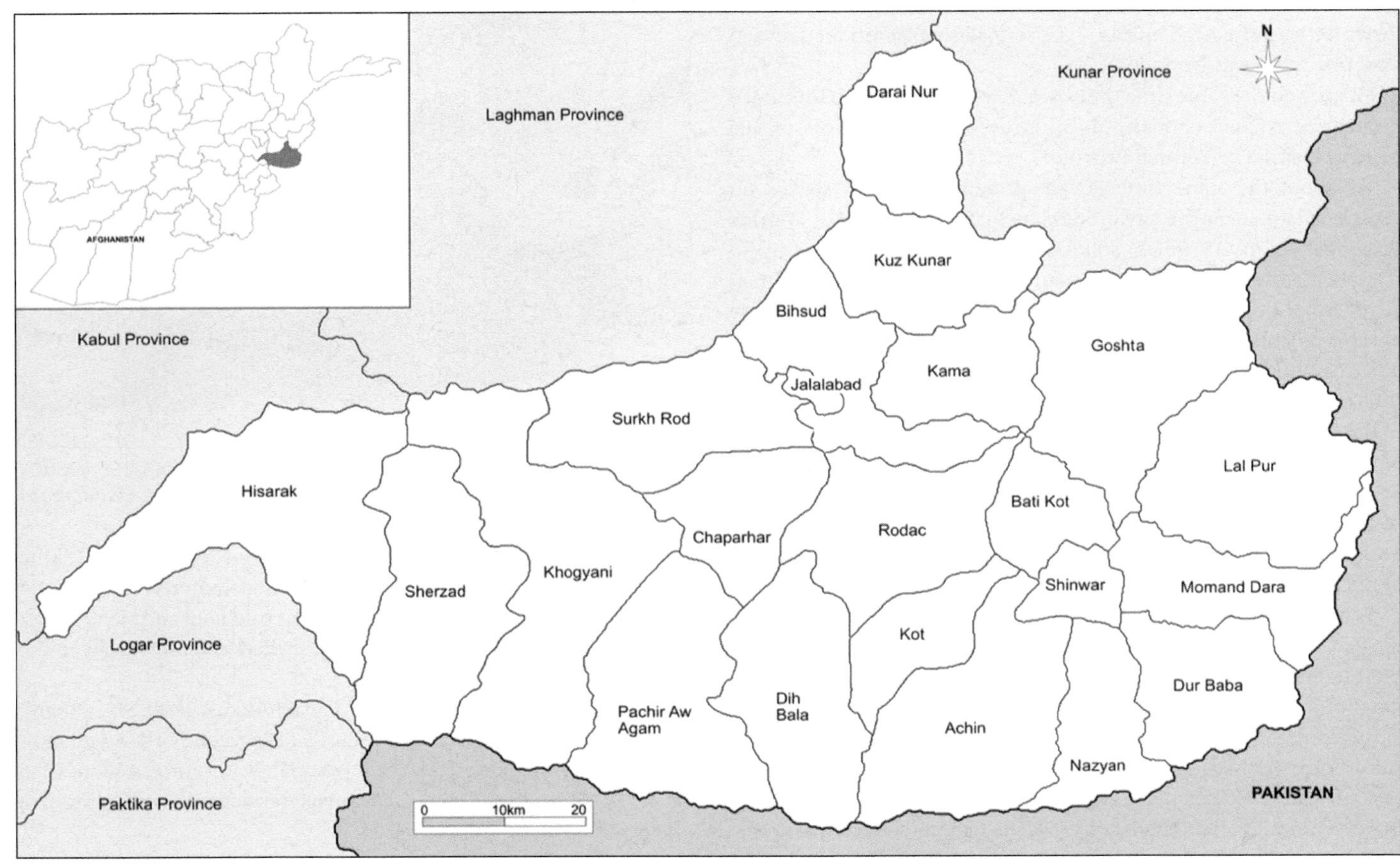

A map of Nangahar Province, in eastern Afghanistan, on the border with Pakistan. (Map by Mark Thompson)

According to some reports, in October 1980 Soviet servicemen killed 500 people in the town of Baghlan.[13]

Tora Bora

In October and November 1980 Soviet troops for the first time conducted a local offensive against Mujahideen bases in the Tora Bora area in Nangarhar Province, 105km (65 miles) south-east of Kabul. Many of these were already heavily fortified by the time.

On 2 October 1980 a fight between Soviet troops and Mujahideen erupted in Logar Province. In retaliation, on 5 October Soviet soldiers and officers killed and wounded an unknown number of people on the Kabul to Gardez road.

On 4 October 1980 a senior lieutenant of the Soviet Army, the deputy commander of the Reconnaissance Company of the 317th GAR, 103rd GAD, was killed in Kabul, when a KGB officer tried to arrest him. The senior lieutenant was suspected of selling army issued items to rebels.

The next day a convoy of the 177th MRR, 108th MRD, was ambushed near the village of Galiyan in Parwan Province, 70km (43 miles) north-west of Kabul. Six or seven Soviet soldiers were killed and three others were wounded in the ensuing fight. Three more Soviet soldiers died that day in other parts of the country.

From 6 to 13 October 1980 Soviet troops carried out an operation in Helmand Province, involving the 70th Separate Guards MRBr. Eight soldiers were killed and at least one more was wounded.

On 9 October 1980 Soviet soldiers killed 40 people on the Kabul to Gardez road.

On 10 October 1980 Soviet soldiers and officers killed several dozen people in the village of Katah Khel in Kabul Province, 20km (12 miles) north-east of Kabul.

On 13 October 1980 between seven and nine soldiers of the 181st MRR, 108th MRD were killed in a fight and a BMP IFV explosion in Kapisa Province.

Nine Soviet servicemen, including a lieutenant colonel, died in five clashes and one explosion, and one more soldier went missing on 14 October 1980.

Another Atrocity in Laghman

In mid-October 1980 Soviet troops again committed a massacre in Laghman Province. At first a fight between a Soviet unit and three Mujahideen broke out near the village of Shamangal in the Alishang Valley, 100km (62 miles) east of Kabul. Soviet soldiers caught the rebels and burnt one of them alive. Then they killed between 350 and 1,200 civilians in several neighbouring villages. Sometime later Soviet helicopters conducted a strike on a group of nomads near the village of Dewah, 90km (56 miles) east of Kabul, killing eight of them and wounding an unknown number.

On 17 October, a major of the Soviet Army, the Chief of Staff of the 1496th Separate Troop Carrying Battalion of the Air Force of the USSR, was killed, reportedly with a sabre, in a shop in the town of Shindand in Herat Province. Soviet servicemen used to go shopping in Afghan towns and cities; they called Afghan shops *dukan* ('shop' or 'store' in Arabic).

Six Soviet civilian pilots died on 28 October 1980 in a plane crash in Kabul Province.

During November 1980 three members of the People's Democratic Party of Afghanistan were killed in the city of Kabul every day.

On 6 November 1980 a captain of the Soviet Border Troops died in Badakhshan Province, when he hit a Soviet mine.

On 8 November 1980 Soviet soldiers shot-up passenger buses near the Salang Tunnel and killed two bus drivers.

From 14 November 1980 to 5 December 1980 the Soviet Command carried out Operation Udar ('Strike' in Russian) in Kabul, Parwan and Bamyan Provinces, involving the 177th MRR, 108th MRD and the 14th Separate Pipeline Battalion. Three or four Soviet soldiers died and reportedly more than 500 Mujahideen were killed, 736 other rebels were taken prisoner.

Twelve Soviet servicemen, including a lieutenant colonel, died in several clashes and a road accident on 19 November 1980.

In December 1980 Soviet soldiers, for no apparent reason, fired on a passenger bus on the Kabul – Jalalabad Road, killing 11 people and wounding many others.

The commander of the 2nd Motor Rifle Platoon of the 5th MR Coy, 2nd MRBn, 395th MRR, 201st MRD was killed by a Soviet sentry near the town of Nahrin in Baghlan Province on 7 December 1980.

On 8 and 9 December 1980 the Soviet Command carried out an operation in the village of Dasht-e Qala in Takhar Province, 270km (168 miles) north of Kabul. The 56th Separate Guards AABr and some units of the Afghan Army were involved. Two Afghan soldiers and 23 insurgents were killed and an Afghan soldier was wounded. Twenty-one guerrillas were taken prisoner.

Two soldiers of the 1049th Anti-Aircraft Artillery Regiment of the 108th MRD were killed in a shop in Kabul on 12 December 1980.

Panjshir III

From 12 to 29 December 1980 the Soviet Command conducted Panjshir III. The 177th MRR and 181st MRRs, both of the 108th MRD, were involved in the operation. The Soviet Air Force heavily bombed the settlements located in the valley. Between 12 and 15 Soviet servicemen, 15 Mujahideen and around 100 Afghan civilians were killed.

In mid-December 1980 rebels destroyed a Soviet tank near the town of Alishang in Laghman Province, 90km (56 miles) east of Kabul, and killed a Soviet officer. In retaliation, Soviet troops bombed Alishang, the town of Islamabad and one of the nearby villages, killing at least 16 people.

A private from the 1st MRBn of the 181st MRR, 108th MRD died as a result of a drug overdose in the town of Bagram in Parwan Province on 16 December 1980.

In late December 1980, the Soviet Command carried out an operation in Kandahar Province. The 70th Separate Guards MRBr and the 317th GAR of the 103rd GAD were involved. According to the official version, on 20 December 1980, during this offensive, heavy fighting broke out in the village of Sutian, 490km (304 miles) southwest of Kabul,[14] according to another source, near the village of Mullayan, 445km (277 miles) southwest of Kabul.[15] Eight soldiers of the 3rd ABn of the 317th GAR, 103rd GAD were killed and 14 others were wounded. One hundred and sixty-two Mujahideen were also reportedly killed. According to unofficial reports, Soviet artillery that day at first started heavily shelling Sutian. The villagers tried to hide in the fields near the settlement, but Soviet servicemen saw that and shot at them with rifles and from AFVs. After that Soviet soldiers and officers entered the village and killed those who survived the shelling. Around 3,000 Afghan civilians, including an unknown number of women and children, were killed.[16] Six Soviet soldiers died on 30 December 1980, five of them in hospital.

Therefore, the first year of the Soviet military intervention ended in same fashion as it began: widespread atrocities against any kind of opposition. The principal difference was that the armed opposition continued growing in numbers and had begun improving its organisation.

4
1981

The commander of the 1st ABn of the 345th Separate GAR, Captain Alexander Lebed, a future lieutenant general and Secretary of the Security Council of the Russian Federation, took part in the Soviet-Afghan War from 1981 to 1982. During that period his superior was the commander of the 345th Separate GAR, Lieutenant Colonel Pavel Grachyov, a future General of the Army and Minister of Defence of the Russian Federation (in 1985–1988, Pavel Grachyov was the commander of the 103rd GAD).

Bloody Winter

Fighting in that year began on 9 January 1981, with a clash between Soviet troops and Mujahideen near the town of Khanabad in Kunduz Province, 240km (149 miles) north of Kabul. Two Soviet soldiers were killed. In retaliation, Soviet soldiers later that day massacred around 200 Afghan civilians, including children, in several villages near Khanabad. Fifteen Soviet soldiers, including three officers, died on 22 January 1981: 11 of them, belonging to the 395th MRR of the 201st MRD, were killed in a single action in Baghlan Province. Eight Soviet soldiers, mostly from the 6th Airborne Company of the 2nd ABn, 345th Separate GAR, were killed on 24 January 1981.

In early February 1981, 25 members of the People's Democratic Party of Afghanistan were killed in the city of Kabul in one day. A few days later, Soviet troops shelled a fort in Qara Bagh District of Kabul Province and killed nine people. On 14 February 1981 a Soviet unit entered a village near the city of Jalalabad with the intention of plundering it. In one of the houses soldiers and officers saw two (according to another source, three) young women, two old men and either four or seven small children. Soviet servicemen raped the women in front of their relatives, then they killed them and everyone else, and then burnt the bodies. A 12-year-old boy, a brother of one of the women, was able to hide and later identified the criminals. They were arrested and an investigation began. At first Soviet commanders in Afghanistan and, according to some sources, even Soviet leaders in Moscow tried to make the case go away and claimed that the crime was committed by a group of rebels, dressed in Soviet uniforms, but then for some reason the case went to trial, and the perpetrators were convicted. According to some reports, some of them were even sentenced to death.[1]

War on Afghan Civilians

In spring 1981 the Soviet Air Force heavily bombed numerous villages in Baraki Barak District of Logar Province. Seven Soviet servicemen, including one officer, died on 5 April 1981. Nine Soviet soldiers, including one officer, mostly from the AABn of the 70th

Servicemen of the 3rd MR Company, 1st MRB, 181st MRR, 108th MRD inspecting an Afghan lorry near the city of Jalalabad, August 1981. (181msp.ru)

Separate Guards MRBr, were killed on 6 April. Between 14 and 23 Soviet men, including two officers, died, and one soldier went missing, on 15 April 1981. Between nine and 18 of them were killed in a single fight near the town of Bagram in Parwan Province. In May 1981 Soviet officers and soldiers killed almost every resident of one of the villages north of Kabul, and then they completely destroyed the settlement. At about the same time Soviet servicemen killed 31 Afghan civilians in the village of Kochkin in Kabul Province, 20km (12 miles) north-west of Kabul. In early May 1981 Soviet servicemen killed several children in the village of Kalakan in Kabul Province, 30km (19 miles) north of Kabul. According to some sources, the soldiers said, 'When the children grow up they would take up arms against us.'[2]

Eleven men of the 180th MRR of the 108th MRD, including one officer, were killed on 3 May 1981. Four days later, a Soviet-Afghan convoy was ambushed by the Mujahideen in Logar Province. Many Afghan soldiers and KhAD officers were killed in the ensuing fight, while Soviet troops lost about 30 AFVs. In retaliation, Soviet soldiers and officers killed an unknown number of people in the neighbouring villages.

In summer 1981 Soviet soldiers killed 137 people in several districts of Kandahar Province. On 18 and 19 June 1981 Soviet troops stormed the Tora Bora fortress in Nangarhar Province. The 66th Separate MRBr with the 11th Infantry Division of the Afghan Army was involved in the assault. On 23 June 1981 Soviet aircraft bombed Kandahar and killed more than 100 Afghan civilians. Eleven Soviet soldiers were killed on 26 June 1981. On 3 July 1981 Soviet artillery heavily shelled the city of Kabul. From 7 to 18 July 1981 the Soviet Command carried out an operation in Kunar Province, involving the 66th Separate MRBr and the 357th GAR of the 103rd GAD. Between eight and 13 Soviet officers and men and 22 insurgents were killed, at least three Soviet soldiers were wounded. Eleven Soviet servicemen, including two officers, died, and one more soldier went missing on 14 July 1981. Eleven more Soviet servicemen, including a lieutenant colonel, a military adviser, died the next day.

In August 1981 Soviet helicopters conducted a strike on a wedding party in the village of Jalrez in Wardak Province, 60km (37 miles) south-west of Kabul. Thirty Afghan civilians were killed and 75 were wounded. At about the same time a Soviet convoy was passing by the town of Jabal Saraj in Parwan Province and was fired upon, in retaliation the Soviets entered a neighbouring village and burnt 13 old people alive.

1st Marmul Offensive

In August 1981 the Soviet Command carried out the 1st Marmul Offensive in Balkh Province, involving the 149th Guards MRR of the 201st MRD and some units of the Soviet Border Troops.

During this operation, on 31 August 1981, between six and 12 men of the 149th Guards MRR of the 201st MRD, including the deputy commander of the regiment, Lieutenant Colonel Vyacheslav Barynin, and one other officer, were killed in a fierce fight near the village of Yek Kowtal in Balkh Province, 275km (171 miles) north-west of Kabul.

On 7 August 1981 four soldiers of the 1st MRBn of the 191st Separate MRR, according to official sources, deserted from their unit near the village of Babus in Logar Province, 50km (31 miles) south of Kabul.[3] According to unofficial reports, these servicemen were drunk, got separated from a Soviet convoy and went missing.[4] However, in retaliation Soviet troops destroyed the neighbouring village of Dado Khel with aircraft and artillery, killing around 45 Afghan civilians.

Between 14 and 16 August Soviet officers and soldiers were killed in four separate engagements near the cities of Herat and Kandahar, near the town of Bagram in Parwan Province and near the town of Khinjan in Baghlan Province. On 18 August 1981 the head of a group of Soviet geologists in the Democratic Republic of Afghanistan, Yevgeni Okhrimyuk, was abducted by insurgents in Kabul. According to some sources, they wanted to exchange him for 50 rebels, held by the Afghan authorities. Okhrimyuk was at first brought to the village of Shewaki in Kabul Province, 10km (6 miles) south-east of the capital, and then to the city of Peshawar in Pakistan. Soon after the guerrillas left Shewaki with the prisoner, the settlement was bombed by the Afghan Air Force. Okhrimyuk was reportedly killed in June 1982.

In September 1981 high school students organised a demonstration in Kabul, protesting against the enlistment in the army. They also demanded the withdrawal of Soviet troops from Afghanistan. Soviet troops shot into the rally, killing six girls. The first Soviet general died in Afghanistan on 5 September 1981. Soviet helicopter gunships conducted a strike near the city of Farah. One of the helicopters belonging to the 302nd Separate Helicopter Squadron, with the deputy commander of the Air Force of the Turkestan Military District Major General Vadim Khakhalov, three Soviet soldiers and two Afghan soldiers on board, was shot down by the Mujahideen. All of the servicemen were killed. During the next four days, seven more Soviet soldiers were killed in several fights around Farah, while trying to evacuate the general's body.

Panjshir IV

From 6 to 22 September 1981 the Soviet Command carried out Panjshir IV. Around 100 servicemen were killed in action. Two Soviet officers, military advisers, including a colonel, were wounded in an ambush near the city of Ghazni on 6 September 1981. From 14 to 28 September 1981 Soviet and Afghan troops carried out an operation in Badghis Province, north-west Afghanistan. At least three Soviet soldiers and several Afghan soldiers were killed. An unknown number of Soviet and Afghan servicemen were wounded.

Ten Soviet soldiers, mostly from the 2nd MRBn of the 181st MRR, 108th MRD, were killed on 16 September 1981. Twelve Soviet servicemen, including one officer, died on 17 September 1981. On 18 September 1981 a large Mujahideen group entered Kabul and abducted three officials of the Afghan government. Ten Soviet servicemen, including one officer, died on 22 September 1981.

Hepatitis Epidemic

From October to December 1981 more than 3,000 soldiers and officers of the 5th Guards MRD, including the commander of the division, Major General Boris Gromov, contracted hepatitis from substandard food. Fourteen Soviet servicemen, including four officers, died, and one more soldier went missing on 17 October 1981. From 19 to 28 October 1981 the Soviet Command carried out an operation in Kandahar Province involving the 70th Separate Guards MRBr and the 317th GAR of the 103rd GAD. Ten or 11 Soviet soldiers and officers were killed.

On 24 October 1981, the 1st MRBn of the 371st Guards MRR, 5th Guards MRD and Afghan Army lost 14 servicemen killed in a clash near the village of Khak-e Mulla in Ghor Province, 350km (217 miles) west of Kabul. Two more Soviet soldiers were wounded.

On 25 October 1981 10 servicemen of the Soviet Border Troops, including three officers, were killed, and nine other soldiers were wounded in a five-to-six-hour fight near the village of Chashm Darah in Badakhshan Province, 350km (217 miles) northeast of Kabul. Five more Soviet servicemen were killed that day in other regions of the country.

In November 1981 Soviet aircraft bombed a hospital in Waras District of Bamyan Province. On 4 November 1981 Soviet jets and helicopters conducted a strike on a hospital in the Panjshir Valley. On 5 November 1981 Soviet helicopters destroyed a hospital in Jaghori District of Ghazni Province. On 6 November 1981 Soviet helicopters destroyed a hospital in Nangarhar Province.

From 7 to 9 November 1981 the Soviet Command carried out an operation in Jowzjan Province, involving the 122nd MRR of the 201st MRD, and the 154th Separate Spetsnaz Detachment. Twenty Mujahideen were killed, one Soviet soldier went missing, seven rebels were taken prisoner.

Thirteen Soviet servicemen, including two officers, died on 12 November 1981. On 17 November 1981 Soviet servicemen killed 150 people near the village of Farghamiru in Badakhshan Province, 290km (180 miles) northeast of Kabul. On 20 November 1981 a Soviet convoy was ambushed near the village of Timurak in Balkh Province, 340km (211 miles) north-west of Kabul, six servicemen of the 154th Separate Spetsnaz Detachment, including one officer, were killed. During the week after that the 154th Separate Spetsnaz Detachment carried out an operation around Timurak, reportedly several dozen guerrillas were killed. On 26 November 1981 the 154th Separate Spetsnaz Detachment carried out an operation in the Khanaqah District of Jowzjan Province; 25 insurgents were killed and 21 more were taken prisoner. On 27 November 1981 Soviet servicemen killed 38 people near the city of Kabul. Seventeen Soviet soldiers and officers, mostly from the 177th MRR of the 108th MRD, were killed, and one more was captured in three fights on 2 December 1981.

Between 17 and 29 Soviet servicemen were killed and 27 others were wounded in some isolated clashes that took place on 6 December 1981 in the town of Charikar, near the town of Baghlan, near the town of Surobi in Kabul Province, 55km (34 miles) east of Kabul, and near the city of Pul-e Khumri.

From 6 to 8 December 1981 Soviet and Afghan troops stormed a Mujahideen base, located in the village of Jar Kuduk in Jowzjan Province, 440km (273 miles) north-west of Kabul. The 122nd MRR of the 201st MRD and the 154th Separate Spetsnaz Detachment were involved in the assault. Five Soviet soldiers and reportedly 290 rebels were killed, four more Soviet soldiers were wounded. On 17 December 1981 the 154th Separate Spetsnaz Detachment carried out an operation in the village of Khanaqah in Jowzjan Province, 380km (236 miles) north-west of Kabul. On 19 December 1981 servicemen of the 154th Separate Spetsnaz Detachment killed around 25 people in a village in Jowzjan Province. Twenty Soviet servicemen, including two officers, died on 24 December 1981.

Sixteen Soviet servicemen, including three officers, died on 25 December 1981. Nine of them, belonging to the 19th Separate Engineering Battalion of the 45th Separate Engineering Regiment, were killed in a single explosion near the village of Deh-e Miskin in Parwan Province.

5
1982

Reportedly, between 1979 and 1982 Soviet troops perpetrated 47 chemical weapons attacks in Afghanistan, killing at least 3,000 people.[1] During the winter of 1981–1982, the Mujahideen significantly decreased their activity: nevertheless, 11 Soviet servicemen, including two officers, died in six clashes and two accidents, and one more soldier went missing on 9 January 1982, while three other soldiers were killed in four different firefights three days later.

Servicemen of the 181st MRR of the 108th MRD and Afghan citizens, reportedly draft dodgers, in Tagab District, Kapisa Province, in 1982. (181msp.ru)

Operation Darzab

From 15 to 20 January 1982 the Soviet Command carried out an operation in Jowzjan Province. The 149th Guards MRR of the 201st MRD, the 1074th Artillery Regiment of the 108th MRD, the 350th GAR of the 103rd GAD, the 154th Separate Spetsnaz Detachment and the 154th Separate Spetsnaz Detachment were to destroy a Mujahideen base in the town of Darzab, 380km (236 miles) northwest of Kabul. Six or seven Soviet soldiers and officers and 25 rebels were killed, two other Soviet soldiers were wounded. One Mil Mi-8 helicopter of the 3rd Helicopter Squadron, 181st Separate Helicopter Regiment either crashed or was shot down. According to another source, the operation was carried out on one day, 15 January, and only the 154th Separate Spetsnaz Detachment was involved. The losses were two servicemen killed and two wounded.[2]

On 16 January 1982, 19 Soviet servicemen, including four officers, died in six skirmishes, one explosion and two accidents; seven men of the 181st MRR of the 108th MRD were killed in a single fight in Kabul Province. Three days later, on 19 January 1982, the second Soviet general died: a Mil Mi-8 helicopter of the Afghan Air Force with the Deputy Chief Military Adviser in the Democratic Republic of Afghanistan, Chief of the Operations Control Group of the Ministry of Defence of the Democratic Republic of Afghanistan, Lieutenant General Pyotr Shkidchenko, was shot down near the city of Khost in Paktia Province. Four or five occupants were killed.

Operation Parwan

From 28 January to 6 February 1982 the Soviet Command carried out an operation in Parwan Province. The 59th Support Brigade, the 345th Separate GAR, and the 180th and 181st MRRs and 1415th Anti-Aircraft Missile Regiment of the 108th MRD, the 317th GAR and the 350th GAR of the 103rd GAD were involved. Twenty-two Soviet officers and soldiers were killed, one soldier went missing, and a rebel was taken prisoner.

On 29 January 1982 troops of the 154th Separate Spetsnaz Detachment killed three people in the village of Arab Kho in Balkh Province, 330km (205 miles) north-west of Kabul, and then fought with Mujahideen near one of the villages in Jowzjan Province. A Soviet soldier and 15 rebels were killed. Nine more Soviet soldiers and officers died in six clashes and one road accident that day in other parts of the country.

Twelve Soviet servicemen, including two officers, died on 31 January 1982. One of them, a lieutenant colonel from the 70th Separate Guards MRBr, was killed when a Soviet tank fired on his BTR APC in the city of Kandahar.

Bloody Winter in Panjshir

On 1 February 1982 a Soviet convoy was ambushed by a rebel group in the Panjshir Valley. On 11 February Mujahideen ambushed another Soviet convoy in the Panjshir Valley and destroyed 33 AFVs. In retaliation, from 14 to 19 February Soviet soldiers killed between 1,000 and 2,000 Afghan civilians, including women, children and old people, in several villages in the valley.

On 2 February 1982 servicemen of the 154th Separate Spetsnaz Detachment killed eight people in a village in Jowzjan Province.

Nine Soviet servicemen, including one officer, died on 5 February 1982. Five of them, belonging to the 181st MRR of the 108th MRD, were killed in a mortar attack in the Nijrab Valley in Kapisa Province.

On 7 February 1982 Soviet troops killed 31 Afghan civilians, elderly people, with chemical weapons near the village of Rabat in Ghazni Province, 115km (71 miles) south of Kabul.

A tragic accident happened in the city of Kabul on 9 February 1982. A group of young soldiers of the 1074th Artillery Regiment of the 108th MRD was cooking dinner in a large army tent. One of them decided to pour gasoline onto the stove. A fierce fire started. The soldiers tried to escape from the tent, but the fire exit had been boarded up by the top sergeant in order to prevent thefts of the company's equipment. As a result, between 22 and 25 Soviet servicemen died from burns.

On 10 February 1982 an explosion occurred in the city of Herat. Several Soviet civilians were killed.

From 14 to 21 February 1982 the 154th Separate Spetsnaz Detachment carried out an operation in Balkh and Jowzjan provinces. An unknown number of people were killed. Eight Soviet soldiers died on 17 February 1982. From 25 February to 12 March 1982 the Soviet Command carried out an offensive in Kapisa Province. The 345th Separate GAR, and the 177th, 180th and 181st MRRs and the 285th Tank Regiment of the 108th MRD were involved in the operation. Between 13 and 23 soldiers and officers were killed in action, at least one other soldier was wounded and one more went missing. Ten Soviet soldiers were killed in several clashes on 11 March 1982, while three days later the V-VS conducted a strike on a hospital in Jaghori District of Ghazni Province.

From 29 March to 9 April 1982 the 154th Separate Spetsnaz Detachment and some units of the Afghan Army carried out an operation in the Sang Charak District of Jowzjan Province, one Soviet officer was killed. On 30 March 1982 a private from the 5th Guards MRD was killed by a fellow soldier in the town of Shindand in Herat Province 'for some unknown reason,' according to an official source.[3]

In April 1982 the Soviet Command carried out an operation in Kandahar Province, involving the 70th Separate Guards MRBr and the 191st Separate MRR. Twenty-one soldiers and officers were killed in clashes and two friendly fire incidents and at least one more soldier was wounded. Three Mujahideen were taken prisoner, one of them, a former Soviet serviceman, was killed. One BTR-D airborne armoured personnel carrier was destroyed.

At about the same time either around 200 or around 2,000 Afghan civilians were killed by Soviet soldiers and officers in a village between the town of Khulm in Samangan Province and the city of Mazar-e Sharif, capital of Balkh Province, 310km (193 miles) northwest of Kabul, in retaliation for the death of four Soviet servicemen.

Incident with Iran

On 5 April 1982 Soviet troops stormed the Rabat-e Jali fortress in Nimruz Province. The 70th Separate Guards MRBr, the 317th GAR of the 103rd GAD and the 459th Separate Spetsnaz Company were involved in the assault. During this operation several Soviet helicopters that were providing close air support, entered Iranian airspace, conducted an air strike on the asphalt plant near the town of Khormek, and then landed at the airfield near the settlement. Soon after that, several F-4 Phantom II fighters of the Iranian Air Force launched an air strike on the airfield, destroying two Mil Mi-8 helicopters.

On 15 April 1982 Soviet servicemen killed 20 people near the village of Yangi Shaghasi in Faryab Province, 460km (286 miles) west of Kabul. On 21 April 1982 a convoy of the 56th Separate Guards AABr was passing by the village of Nari in Paktia Province, 115km (71 miles) southeast of Kabul. Suddenly one of the BMD-1 airborne infantry fighting vehicles hit a mine. Nine Soviet soldiers were killed. Right after that a fight started, and five more soldiers were killed.

1st Khulm Offensive

In late April to May 1982 the Soviet Command carried out the 1st Khulm Offensive in Samangan Province, northern Afghanistan. The 122nd MRR of the 201st MRD and some units of the Soviet Border Troops with the units of the 18th and 20th Infantry Divisions of the Afghan Army were involved in the operation. Soviet and Afghan troops reportedly eliminated the rebel groups in Khulm and destroyed their infrastructure around the town. Between one and four soldiers of the Soviet Army and one soldier of the Soviet Border Troops were killed.

Five men of the 56th Separate Guards AABr, including two officers, were killed, and two more soldiers were wounded on 2 May 1982, when an artillery tractor hit a landmine in Logar Province.

Nine Soviet servicemen died the next day. Six of them, belonging to the 3rd MRBn of the 101st MRR, 5th Guards MRD, were killed, when rebels shot-up a BTR APC in the city of Herat.

From 4 to 7 May 1982 Soviet troops carried out an operation in Helmand Province. The 70th Separate Guards MRBr, the 191st Separate MRR and the 24th Guards Tank Regiment of the 5th Guards MRD were involved. Eleven soldiers and officers were killed in action and at least three more soldiers were wounded.

Fourteen Soviet servicemen, including one officer, died, and one soldier was taken prisoner and later killed on 5 May 1982.

Panjshir V

From 15 May to 2 June 1982 the Soviet Command carried out Panjshir V. Soviet troops were to destroy Mujahideen bases in the Panjshir Valley and blockade the main routes of their groups. The territory of the valley was divided into three zones. Forces were allocated to the zones as follows:

First zone

- 191st Separate MRR
- 177th MRR, 108th MRD
- 180th MRR, 108th MRD
- 181st MRR , 108th MRD
- 1074th Artillery Regiment, 108th MRD
- 781st Separate Reconnaissance Battalion, 108th MRD
- 58th Infantry Regiment of the 8th Infantry Division, Afghan Army
- 72nd Infantry Regiment of the 8th Infantry Division, Afghan Army
- 332nd Infantry Regiment of the 8th Infantry Division, Afghan Army

Second zone

- 66th Separate MRBr
- 149th Guards MRR, 201st MRD
- 783rd Separate Reconnaissance Battalion, 201st MRD
- 66th Infantry Regiment, 11th Infantry Division, Afghan Army
- 10th Infantry Regiment, 20th Infantry Division, Afghan Army

Third zone

- 345th Separate GAR
- 317th GAR, 103rd GAD
- 357th GAR, 103rd GAD
- 1179th Guards Artillery Regiment, 103rd GAD
- 37th Commando Brigade, Afghan Army
- 444th Commando Regiment, Afghan Army

The offensive officially lasted for two and a half weeks, but these units and formations advanced for two months and reportedly eliminated all enemy groups in the Panjshir Valley. Either 117 or around 1,000 officers and men were killed in action and up to 2,000 more were wounded. One Mikoyan-Gurevich MiG-21bis fighter, one Mi-24 helicopter and two Mil Mi-8 helicopters were shot down.

On 17 May 1982, during this offensive, two Mil Mi-8 helicopters of the 3rd Helicopter Squadron, 50th Separate Mixed Aviation Regiment were shot down. A fight between Mujahideen and servicemen of the 1st MRBn, 191st Separate MRR and the 1074th Artillery Regiment of the 108th MRD erupted near the village of Rukhah in Parwan Province. Between 14 and 29 Soviet servicemen were killed.

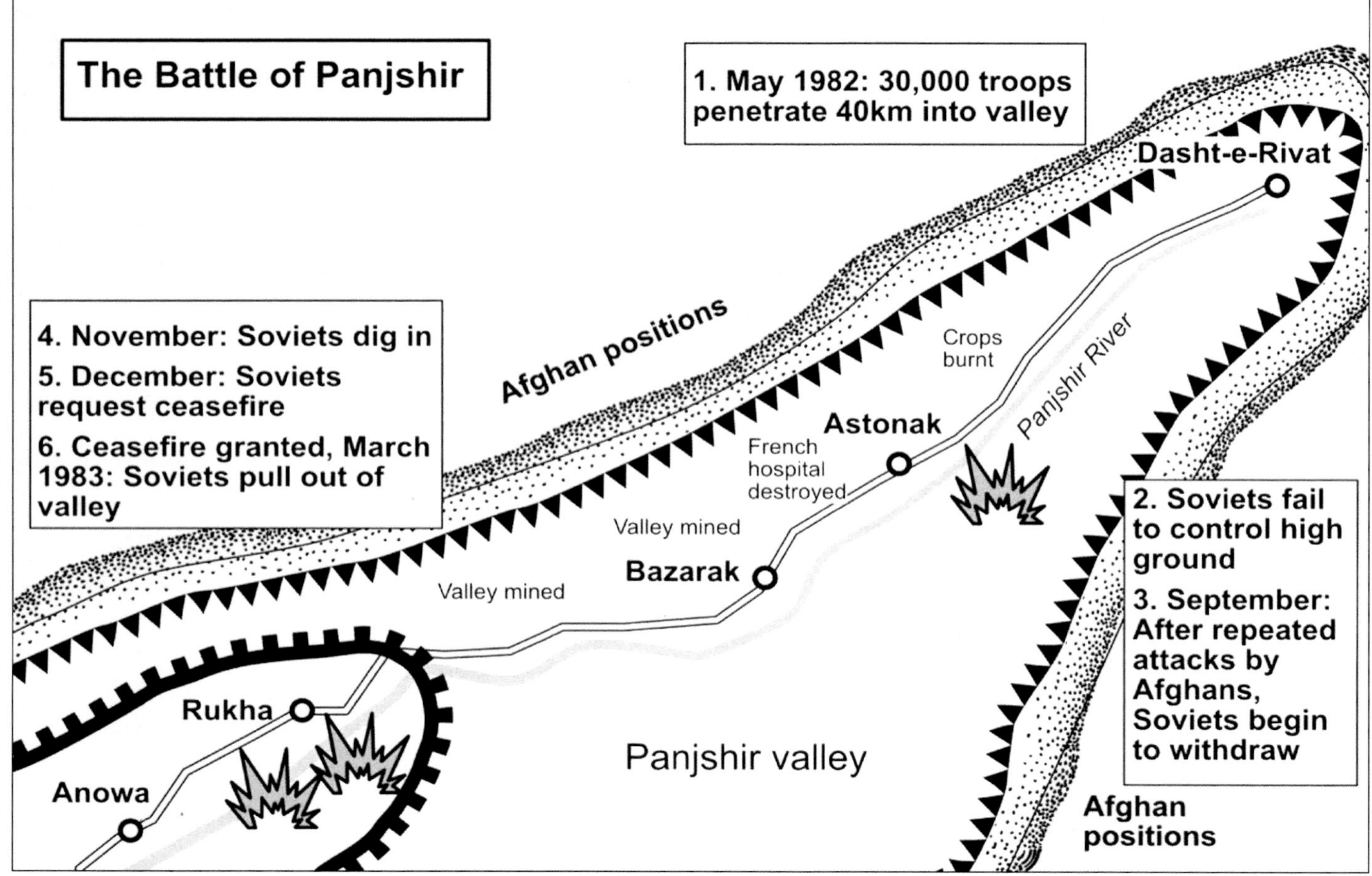

The Soviet Army's advance into the Panjshir Valley, in May 1982.

On 24 May 1982 eight or nine soldiers of the 201st MRD were killed and one more serviceman went missing in Baghlan Province.

On 29 May 1982 the Soviet Air Force carried out a strike near the city of Kandahar and killed 48 people.

On 2 June 1982 Soviet troops stormed a Mujahideen base, located near the town of Nangabad in Herat Province, 695km (432 miles) west of Kabul. The 101st MRR of the 5th Guards MRD was involved in the assault. Three Soviet soldiers and reportedly more than 200 rebels were killed.

On 6 June 1982 six or seven servicemen of the 3rd Spetsnaz Company of the 154th Separate Spetsnaz Detachment were killed and one more soldier was wounded in a fight near the town of Aqcha in Jowzjan Province.

Fourteen soldiers of the 70th Separate Guards MRBr and 12 Afghan guerrillas were killed on 14 June 1982 in a fierce fight near the village of Regi in Kandahar Province, 460km (286 miles) southwest of Kabul.

Negotiations in Geneva

On 16 June 1982 the Geneva talks on Afghanistan began. They lasted intermittently until early 1988.

In the second half of June 1982 the Soviet Command carried out an operation in Baraki Barak District of Logar Province, involving the 56th Separate Guards AABr. Four Soviet soldiers and officers were killed. During this offensive several villages were bombed and as a result of this between 203 and 208 insurgents and between 90 and 95 Afghan civilians, including 25 children, were killed.

On 23 June 1982 Soviet jets conducted a strike near the village of Dasht-e Qala in Takhar Province. As a result, at least 60 people, mostly civilians, were killed, and more than 100 others were wounded.

On 25 and 26 June 1982 Soviet troops carried out an operation in Ghazni Province, involving the 191st Separate MRR and the AABn of the 66th Separate MRBr. Five men were killed in action and at least one more was wounded.

In late June 1982 the Soviet Command carried out an offensive in the Khak-e Safed Mountains in Farah Province. The 101st MRR, the 24th Guards Tank Regiment and the 650th Separate Reconnaissance Battalion of the 5th Guards MRD, and the 3rd ABn of the 350th GAR, 103rd GAD unsuccessfully fought with rebels for a few days and lost around 30 men killed.

On 24 July 1982 a convoy of the 1074th Artillery Regiment of the 108th MRD was ambushed near the town of Surobi in Kabul Province. Eight Soviet soldiers and one officer were killed, one private went missing.

From 24 to 31 July 1982 the Soviet Command carried out an offensive in Kapisa Province. The 177th and 180th MRRs of the 108th MRD were involved in the operation. Ten soldiers were killed and one was taken prisoner.

On 29 July 1982 Soviet servicemen killed 120 Afghan civilians in several villages of Dahana-ye Ghuri District in Baghlan Province.

In August 1982 the Soviet Air Force bombed at least four villages in Muhammad Agha District of Logar Province.

On 2 August 1982 a private from the Engineering Company of the 70th Separate Guards MRBr entered the grounds of the villa of the Soviet military advisers in the city of Kandahar, killed one of them, and then he was shot dead by another Soviet serviceman.

Twelve Soviet soldiers died on 10 August 1982.

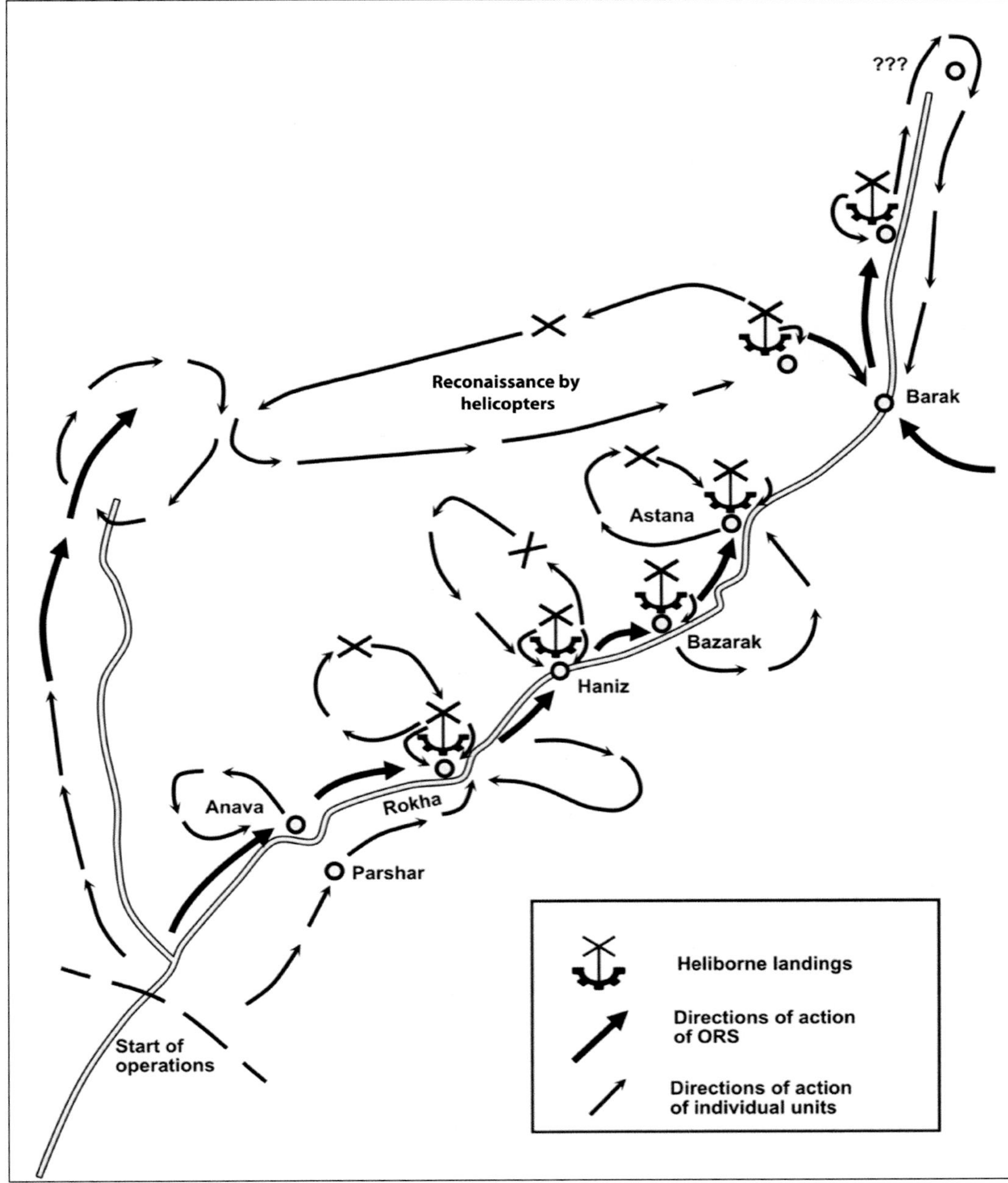

A reconstruction of the Soviet Army's Panjshir V Offensive. (Map by Mark Thompson)

Motor rifle and airborne units conducted *zachistkas*,[4] and aircraft again bombed villages containing civilians, many of whom fled the valley. Between 47 and 60 officers and men of the Soviet Army and one KGB officer were killed in action and died in accidents, at least seven other servicemen were wounded and later died of wounds and one soldier went missing. One Mil Mi-8 helicopter of the 262nd Separate Helicopter Squadron was shot down.

On 21 August 1982 a BMP IFV of the Reconnaissance Company of the 149th Guards MRR of the 201st MRD hit a landmine near the town of Kishim in Badakhshan Province, 270km (168 miles) north of Kabul. Between six and 11 men, including the commander of the Reconnaissance Company, were killed, two more soldiers were wounded.

On 23 August 1982 Soviet troops killed 17 people and wounded eight others in Muhammad Agha District of Logar Province.

On 30 August 1982 a Soviet unit surrounded the village of Abchakan in Logar Province, 70km (43 miles) south of Kabul. The troops collected the villagers but did not kill anybody on this occasion – instead they stripped every single person. After that the soldiers looted the houses and took all of the grain and all of the cattle.

In late August – early September 1982 the Soviet Command carried out an operation in Bamyan Province, involving the 2nd ABn of the 357th GAR, 103rd GAD. Nine Soviet servicemen and three insurgents were killed, 24 more Soviet soldiers were wounded.

In Autumn 1982 Soviet soldiers killed seven elderly people in the town of Bazarak in Parwan Province, 90km (56 miles) east of Kabul.

Ten Soviet servicemen, including one officer, were killed on 12 August 1982 in a single fight in Kandahar Province.

On 18 August 1982 Soviet helicopter gunships carried out a strike near the city of Kandahar and killed an unknown number of people.

Panjshir VI

From 18 August to 30 September 1982 the Soviet Command carried out Panjshir VI. This operation involved:

- 345th Separate GAR
- 177th MRR, 108th MRD
- 180th MRR, 108th MRD
- 181st MRR, 108th MRD
- 285th Tank Regiment, 108th MRD
- 317th GAR, 103rd GAD
- 357th GAR, 103rd GAD
- 154th Separate Spetsnaz Detachment

Massacre in Pad Khwab-e Shanah

A massacre took place on 13 September 1982: 105 people, including 11 or 12 children, were killed in the town of Pad Khwab-e Shanah in Logar Province, 60km (37 miles) south of Kabul. Soviet troops were searching for 'bandits' and surrounded the settlement. There was a group of resistance fighters in the town and they and 61 civilians with children hid in an underground irrigation canal, called a *karez*. The Soviet soldiers saw them and asked two other inhabitants of the town, elders, to tell them to come out of the canal. The people below refused to leave their shelter. Then the soldiers brought two tanker

A destroyed BMP-2 IFV of the 149th Guards MRR, 201st MRD, the location and year are unknown. (Kunduz.ru)

A clandestinely taken photograph of a Su-17M-3 of the V-VS, in the process of diving low for an air strike on Mujahideen positions in the Urgun area. (Central Intelligence Agency)

trucks to the openings of the *karez*, poured some liquid into it and added some white powder. After that they set the combination of liquid and powder alight, and the people in the canal were burnt alive. The townspeople were removing the bodies from the *karez* for a week.

On 16 September 1982 five or six soldiers of the 276th Pipeline Brigade were killed near a village in Samangan Province.

In early October 1982 the 154th Separate Spetsnaz Detachment and some units of the Afghan Army carried out an operation in Samangan Province. One Soviet soldier and an unknown number of Mujahideen were killed. Several Soviet soldiers were wounded. Many rebels were taken prisoner.

On 12 October 1982 a colonel of the Air Force of the 40th Army was killed when a Mil Mi-8 helicopter was shot down in Kabul Province.

Ten Soviet servicemen were killed in several clashes and explosions on 17 October 1982.

Twelve Soviet servicemen, including two officers, died on 25 October.

Thirteen Soviet servicemen, including one officer, died on 2 November 1982.

The next day, 3 November 1982, the largest road accident of the Soviet-Afghan War occurred in the Salang Tunnel. Soviet military convoys caused a traffic jam again; in addition, there were an unknown number of Afghan civilian cars in the tunnel. Soldiers and officers began to repair the stalled vehicles. Sometime later one of the tanker trucks exploded and a huge fire started. According to official sources, between 56 and 64 Soviet servicemen and 112 Afghan soldiers and civilians died.[5] According to unofficial data, around 700 Soviet soldiers and officers and up to 2,300 Afghan servicemen and Afghan civilians burnt to death or were killed by smoke and by carbon monoxide.[6]

From 25 November to 9 December 1982 the Soviet Command carried out an offensive in Kandahar Province, involving the 70th Separate Guards MRBr. Eleven or 12 soldiers and officers were killed in action. One Sukhoi Su-17M3 fighter-bomber of the 136th Fighter-Bomber Aviation Regiment was shot down.

In early December 1982 servicemen of the 56th Separate Guards AABr killed several Afghan civilians in a shop near the city of Gardez.

On 5 December 1982 Soviet helicopters and artillery conducted strikes on the village of Namazgah in Badakhshan Province, 260km (162 miles) north of Kabul, and on the neighbouring village of Kangurchi.

Fourteen servicemen of the Soviet Border Troops died and two more soldiers were wounded on 13 and 14 December 1982 in an explosion and a friendly fire incident.

A fight broke out in Logar Province on 16 December 1982. Eight soldiers of the 1st Airborne Company, 1st ABn, 56th Separate Guards AABr were killed and one officer went missing.

Twelve Soviet servicemen, including three officers, were killed on 17 December.

On 22 December 1982 Soviet servicemen killed one person in the village of Zara Qala in Logar Province, 40km (25 miles) south of Kabul.

From late 1982 into early 1983 negotiations between the Soviet Command and Ahmad Shah Massoud took place, and a truce in the

Panjshir Valley was negotiated. Soviet troops had to be withdrawn from the village of Rukhah. Ahmad Shah Massoud committed not to fight against the Soviet and Afghan troops.

6
1983

In January 1983 the Soviet Command carried out an offensive in Logar Province. During this operation Soviet servicemen killed four elderly people and wounded an unknown number of others.

On 2 January 1983, 16 Soviet civilian engineers were kidnapped and one was killed by Mujahideen in the city of Mazar-e Sharif. A month later, on 2 February, they were found by a Soviet unit in the village of Vakhshak in Baghlan Province, 160km (99 miles) north-west of Kabul. Soviet and Afghan troops stormed the village, lost 10 Soviet servicemen, 22 Afghan servicemen and five or six of the civilians killed and three more Soviet soldiers with three civilians wounded during the assault. Three helicopters were shot down and five BTR APCs were destroyed. After that Soviet aircraft destroyed the entire village.

On 14 January 1983 a colonel from the 5th Guards MRD died of disease in the town of Shindand in Herat Province.

Fourteen Soviet servicemen and one civilian contractor died on 15 January 1983. Ten Soviet soldiers died and one more went missing on 17 January; seven of them, belonging to the 66th Separate MRBr, were killed in a single fight in Kunar Province. On 5 February 1983 three Soviet soldiers were killed in clashes and a colonel, the Deputy Chief Medical Officer of the 40th Army, died of a heart attack. Ten Soviet servicemen, including two officers, died, and two more soldiers were wounded on 14 February 1983; seven of them were killed in clashes in Nangarhar Province. On 15 February 1983 the rebels shot down an Antonov An-12 transport airplane of the 1st Aviation Squadron, 111th Separate Mixed Aviation Regiment near Jalalabad Air Base, killing 11 Soviet servicemen, including five officers amongst whom was the commander of the squadron, Major Nikolai Samylin. Three more Soviet soldiers were killed that day in fights in other regions of the country. During 26 and 27 February 1983 servicemen of the Soviet Border Troops and Afghan troops killed 25 people in the town of Khulm in Samangan Province. Six KhAD officers were also killed when an explosion happened in the town.

Seven Soviet servicemen, including a lieutenant colonel, died on 22 February 1983.

2nd Marmul Offensive

From 11 to 22 March 1983 the Soviet Command carried out the 2nd Marmul Offensive in Balkh Province. The 122nd and 395th MRRs of the 201st MRD, the 154th Separate Spetsnaz Detachment and some units of the Soviet Border Troops with some units of the Afghan Army were involved in the operation. Six Soviet soldiers and officers were killed.

Ten Soviet soldiers died, 25 more Soviet soldiers were wounded and one officer was taken prisoner on 31 March 1983.

On 4 April 1983, a car with a senior lieutenant and a private from the 3rd Pipeline Battalion of the 276th Pipeline Brigade was ambushed near the village of Surkhian in Baghlan Province, 120km (75 miles) north of Kabul. The officer was killed in the ensuing shootout, and the soldier was taken prisoner. The next day, five more soldiers of the 3rd Pipeline Battalion of the 276th Pipeline Brigade, including one officer, were killed in a skirmish near the same settlement when they tried to rescue the private from captivity, and the private was also killed.

From 8 to 15 April 1983 the Soviet Command carried out an offensive in Kapisa Province. The 180th and 181st MRRs and 1074th Artillery Regiment of the 108th MRD were involved. Between seven and 14 servicemen were killed in action and 63 soldiers were wounded.

Seventy Afghan civilians were killed on 14 April 1983, when the Soviet Air Force conducted a strike near the village of Surkhakan in Laghman Province, 100km (62 miles) east of Kabul.

On 26 and 27 April 1983 a series of explosions occurred in Kabul. One Soviet serviceman and five Afghan civilians were killed, several dozen Afghan civilians were injured.

In late April to early May 1983 the Soviet Command carried out an operation in Kandahar Province, involving the 70th Separate Guards MRBr. Eighteen soldiers were killed and between five and eight were wounded.

In May or June 1983 Soviet soldiers killed two children, a five-year-old boy and an eight-year-old girl, and 21 elderly people in two settlements in Laghman Province.

On 16 May 1983 a fierce fight erupted near the village of Donai in Kunar Province, 200km (124 miles) east of Kabul. Between 16 and 18 servicemen of the 3rd MRBn of the 66th Separate MRBr, including two officers, and reportedly 70 rebels were killed. The same day two Soviet military advisers, including a lieutenant colonel, went missing near the town of Urgun in Paktika Province, 180km (112 miles) south of Kabul.

Eleven Soviet soldiers died and two more servicemen were wounded on 17 May 1983.

On 25 May 1983 Soviet aircraft bombed the village of Nazar Khel in Logar Province, 30km (19 miles) south of Kabul.

In June or July 1983 Soviet servicemen carried out a *zachistka* of the village of Karez-e Mir in Kabul Province, 20km (12 miles)

Black Tulip

The Antonov An-12 was nicknamed 'Black Tulip' by Soviet military personnel in Afghanistan. According to one version, it was named that because it was the most common plane used for carrying the bodies of officers and other soldiers home from Afghanistan to the Soviet Union, and the compartments for coffins were decorated by wreaths of black tulips. According to a second version, the funeral home in Tashkent, capital of the Uzbek Soviet Socialist Republic, that made those coffins, was named 'A Black Tulip.'[1] According to the third version, a zinc coffin looks like the unopened flower of a black tulip.

The bodies were known as 'Cargo 200,' and there are also a few versions of the origin of this expression. According to one, a zinc-lined coffin with a body weighed about 200 kilograms.[2] According to another, the Minister of Defence of the USSR's Order No. 200 regulated the procedure of military transportation, including the transportation of deceased soldiers.[3]

north-west of Kabul, and killed eight Afghan civilians, two children and six elderly people.

On 3 June 1983 between 10 and 13 Soviet servicemen, including a colonel and three other officers, were killed in a heavy fight in Kandahar Province. One Soviet soldier died the same day at Kabul Air Base from electrocution; this soldier, a corporal from the 2nd ABn of the 350th GAR, 103rd GAD, was later declared killed in action, which was typical of the Soviet military statistics.

Ten Soviet servicemen, including one officer, were killed on 8 June 1983. Nine of them, belonging to the 180th MRR of the 108th MRD, were killed in a single fight in Kabul Province.

Eight Soviet servicemen, including one officer, died on 9 June. Thirteen Soviet servicemen, including three officers, died on 11 June 1983. Ten of them, belonging to the 860th Separate MRR, were killed and more than 60 other servicemen were wounded in a fierce fight near the village of Sakhay-e Malang Ab in Badakhshan Province, 320km (199 miles) northeast of Kabul. The commander of the 860th Separate MRR, Lieutenant Colonel Lev Rokhlin, a future lieutenant general and the chief of the 1995 storming of Grozny operation, was dismissed for this fight and appointed the deputy commander of the 191st Separate MRR.

On 14 June 1983 a woman civilian contractor was killed in an apartment in Kabul. On 16 June 1983 a private from the Headquarters of the 40th Army deserted from his unit in the capital and surrendered to the rebels. Later he was, as with many soldiers before him, released with the help of international organisations and emigrated to the West, but 18 months later he reportedly returned to the USSR.

Massacre in Rauza

On the night of 30 June 1983, a Soviet unit surrounded the village of Rauza in Ghazni Province, 120km (75 miles) south-west of Kabul. A few hours later Soviet soldiers started a *zachistka*. There was only one Afghan resistance fighter in the village, an 18-year-old man, who hid in a well near his house, but the Soviet patrol found him. A brief shootout took place, one Soviet officer and the rebel were killed, and another Soviet soldier was wounded. Soviet soldiers immediately shot four men in the house, relatives of the young man, they then began beating and robbing all the men they could find in the neighbourhood, after that they collected them near one of the houses and killed them. A total of 23 unarmed people were murdered.

In early July 1983 Soviet helicopters conducted a strike on the village of Bagh-e Shah in Badakhshan Province, 300km (186 miles) north-east of Kabul. Sixteen Afghan civilians were killed and 40 more people were wounded. Most of the settlement was destroyed.

In July 1983 Soviet troops used chemical weapons during the storming of a Mujahideen base in Kunduz Province.

Twelve Soviet soldiers died on 1 July 1983.

Thirteen Soviet servicemen died the next day. Eight of them, including a lieutenant colonel and five other officers, were killed, when insurgents shot down an Antonov An-12 airplane, belonging to the 1st Aviation Squadron, 50th Separate Mixed Aviation Regiment, near Jalalabad Air Base.

From 22 to 29 July 1983 Soviet troops stormed the Tora Bora fortress in Nangarhar Province. The 66th Separate MRBr, and the 181st MRR, 271st Separate Engineering Battalion and 808th Separate Signal Battalion of the 108th MRD were involved in the operation. Eleven or 12 soldiers and officers were killed in action or died from heat exhaustion. One Mil Mi-8 helicopter of the 2nd Helicopter Squadron, 335th Separate Combat Helicopter Regiment was shot down.

Eleven Soviet servicemen, including the commander of the 459th Separate Spetsnaz Company, commander of the Reconnaissance Company of the 180th MRR of the 108th MRD and three pilots of the 3rd Helicopter Squadron, 280th Separate Helicopter Regiment, died on 23 July 1983, one other soldier was wounded and one more went missing.

In late July 1983 Soviet jets bombed the village of Khwajah Kalan in Ghazni Province, located near the village of Rauza, in retaliation for the rebel attack on a convoy. The villagers saw that there was a fight, and fled the settlement: nevertheless, one Afghan civilian was killed. The village was partially destroyed.

Siege of Urgun

In August 1983 the Mujahideen laid siege to the town of Urgun in Paktika Province. On 6 August 1983 five soldiers of the Reconnaissance Company of the 345th Separate GAR were killed in a friendly fire incident in Parwan Province. From 8 to 19 August 1983 the Soviet Command carried out an operation in Herat Province, involving:

- 101st MRR, 5th Guards MRD
- 371st Guards MRR, 5th Guards MRD
- 24th Guards Tank Regiment, 5th Guards MRD
- 1060th Guards Artillery Regiment, 5th Guards MRD

Twelve Soviet servicemen were killed in action. On 13 August 1983 some rebels reportedly attacked the residence of the Prime Minister of the Democratic Republic of Afghanistan in Kabul. One private from the 317th GAR of the 103rd GAD was wounded repulsing this attack and later died in hospital.

On 18 August 1983 the Soviet Air Force carried out an air strike near the city of Kandahar and killed an unknown number of people. Afghan guerrillas shot down a Sukhoi Su-17M3 fighter-bomber of the 156th Fighter-Bomber Aviation Regiment during this attack, killing one Soviet officer.

Another Soviet soldier defected to the rebels on 28 August 1983, and he is reportedly still living in Afghanistan. From 5 to 23 September 1983 the Soviet Command carried out an offensive in Paktia and Logar Provinces. The 56th Separate Guards AABr, the 357th GAR of the 103rd GAD and the 154th Separate Spetsnaz Detachment were involved in the operation. Twenty-seven Soviet officers and men and at least three rebels were killed in action, at least three Soviet servicemen were wounded. During this offensive, on 13 September 1983, Soviet servicemen killed eight people, including four women and one child, in the Muhammad Agha District of Logar Province. During this offensive, on 14 September 1983, between 11 and 14 soldiers of the 1st ABn of the 56th Separate Guards AABr were killed in an AFV explosion near the village of Ali Khel in Paktia Province, 80km (50 miles) south-east of Kabul. This place became infamous because of the numerous clashes around it in the following years and a high number of Soviet casualties.

From 9 to 12 September 1983 the Soviet Command carried out an operation in Laghman Province. The 66th Separate Guards MRBr, and the 180th and 181st MRRs of the 108th MRD were involved, 17 or 18 Soviet servicemen and eight Mujahideen were killed. During this offensive, on 11 September 1983, nine Soviet soldiers were killed in a fight near the city of Mehtar Lam. Eight servicemen of the Soviet Army and two KGB officers died on 13 September 1983.

On 16 September 1983 an Antonov An-12 airplane of the 194th Guards Military Transport Aviation Regiment collided with a Mil Mi-6 helicopter at Shindand Air Base. Ten Soviet servicemen, including eight officers, died in this crash. A fight between Afghan Army and rebels broke out on 18 September 1983 near the town of Urgun in Paktika Province. Guerrillas stormed the Nek Mohammed Kala fortress, located 4km (2.5 miles) from the town using a captured tank and took 243 servicemen prisoner. Fourteen Soviet servicemen, including one officer, were killed, and two more were wounded in seven clashes on 22 September 1983. In early October 1983 the Soviet Air Force bombed a village in Tani District of Paktia Province. On 2 October 1983 a bomb exploded in Kabul, killing 13 Soviet civilians and wounding 12 more. Twenty-one Soviet servicemen were killed in five skirmishes the same day: 10 near the village of Sur Pul in Wardak Province, 70km (43 miles) south-west of Kabul, seven others near the village of Duranay, located next to it, two more Soviet soldiers died near the town of Ziarat Jah in Herat Province, 650km (404 miles) west of Kabul, another one near the city of Kandahar, and one more near the town of Surobi in Kabul Province.

The same day Soviet jets and helicopters bombed a village in Muhammad Agha District of Logar Province.

Troublesome Kandahar

Ten Soviet officers and soldiers, including three pilots of the 262nd Separate Helicopter Squadron, were killed when a Mi-24 helicopter was shot down in Parwan Province on 3 October 1983. Eleven Soviet servicemen, including three officers, died on 9 October. On 10 October 1983 the Mujahideen ambushed a Soviet unit near the city of Kandahar, and several men were killed. On 11 October another Soviet convoy was ambushed in the same place, several more officers and soldiers were killed. The next day Soviet servicemen carried out an act of retaliation. They killed between 160 and 170 Afghan civilians (including three children) in the village of Kulchabat, Kandahar Province, 500km (311 miles) south-west of Kabul. Then they killed 100 more Afghan men and women in Mushkizi, a neighbouring village. And 100 more Afghan villagers were slaughtered in a third nearby settlement, Bala Karz.

Soviet troops continued to operate in Kandahar Province. From 12 to 23 October 1983 the 70th Separate Guards MRBr lost 16 men killed and at least one more wounded.

On 14 October 1983, 12 servicemen of the 3rd MRBn of the 395th MRR, 201st MRD, including two officers, were killed in a fierce fight with a rebel group near the village of Dahana-ye Ghuri in Baghlan Province, 145km (90 miles) north-west of Kabul. On 18 October 1983 a Mil Mi-8 helicopter of the 3rd Helicopter Squadron, 280th Separate Helicopter Regiment came under fire, was damaged and then landed near the Kajaki Dam in Helmand Province. Three Soviet officers were taken prisoner by the rebels and later killed.

On 19 October 1983 an unknown number of people were killed by Soviet servicemen near the town of Siyah Darah in Bamyan Province, 250km (155 miles) west of Kabul. The same day Soviet helicopters bombed a village of Nazar Khel in Logar Province over a period of 10 hours. Two privates of the 2nd ABn of the 357th GAR, 103rd GAD died on 21 October 1983 in the town of Bamyan, the capital of the province of the same name, 130km (81 miles) west of Kabul, when a grenade exploded during an exercise. Four pilots of the 3rd Helicopter Squadron, 181st Separate Helicopter Regiment, including the commander of the squadron, Lieutenant Colonel Edmund Shefer, died in a Mil Mi-8 helicopter crash near Fayzabad Air Base on 25 October 1983. On 26 October 1983 Soviet servicemen killed 50 people in the city of Bala Murghab in Badghis Province, 550km (342 miles) west of Kabul. On 28 October 1983 a colonel of the Soviet Army hit a mine in Kabul Province and was killed.

On 3 November 1983 a Soviet colonel died of disease in the quarters of the 14th Infantry Division of the Afghan Army in the city of Ghazni. The same day one woman, a civilian contractor, was killed and another was wounded by a Soviet soldier in the city of Pul-e Khumri, as a result of a dispute.

Six soldiers of the 3rd Spetsnaz Company of the 154th Separate Spetsnaz Detachment died on 4 November 1983 in a road accident in Parwan Province.

Mutiny in Paktia

On 11 November 1983 men of the 38th Commando Brigade of the Afghan Army mutinied in Paktia Province and killed a Soviet lieutenant colonel, a military adviser.

From 13 to 30 November 1983 the Soviet Command carried out an offensive in Kabul Province. The 285th Tank Regiment and the 781st Separate Reconnaissance Battalion of the 108th MRD, and the 317th GAR and the 350th GAR of the 103rd GAD were all involved in the operation. Ten Soviet soldiers and officers were killed.

On 14 November 1983 rebels shot down a Mil Mi-8 helicopter of the Afghan Air Force near the city of Kabul and killed three Soviet military advisers, including two lieutenant colonels.

Pistols captured by troops of the 40th Army from dead or captured Mujahideen in December 1983. (ArtOfWar – Vladimir Shchennikov)

Men of the 2nd MRBn of the 149th Guards MRR of the 201st MRD, the location of the photograph and year it was taken are not known. (ArtOfWar – Vladimir Shchennikov)

when a self-propelled gun hit a landmine near the town of Muhammad Agha in Logar Province, 40km (25 miles) south of Kabul.

Eleven Soviet servicemen, including two officers, died on 3 December 1983. Six of them, belonging to the 66th Separate MRBr, were killed in a single action in Kunar Province.

The same day Soviet servicemen wounded 16 people, including five women and three children, in the village of Darah in Logar Province, 50km (31 miles) south of Kabul.

On 6 December 1983 Soviet servicemen tied three people to a tank and then blew them up in the village of Kutub Khel in Logar Province, 30km (19 miles) south of Kabul.

Six Soviet servicemen, including a lieutenant colonel, died, one other soldier went missing and one private defected to the Mujahideen on 15 November 1983.

Two Soviet military advisers, including another lieutenant colonel, died on 29 November 1983, when a Mil Mi-8 helicopter of the Afghan Air Force crashed at Muqur Air Base in Ghazni Province, 240km (149 miles) south-west of Kabul.

Five servicemen of the 4th AABn of the 56th Separate Guards AABr, including one officer, were killed on 2 December 1983,

Between 15 and 18 Soviet servicemen, including one officer, were killed in 10 clashes on 14 December 1983.

On 23 and 24 December 1983 between 350 and 400 people were killed by the Afghan authorities in Pul-e Charkhi prison. On 28 December 1983 the Tajbeg Palace in Kabul was reportedly shelled with mortars, one Soviet soldier was killed. Four Soviet soldiers, including a lieutenant colonel – the commander of the 2nd MRBn of the 371st Guards MRR, 5th Guards MRD, died on 29 December 1983.

7
1984

The year 1984 was the period of the highest official number of Soviet losses in the whole Afghan War. These began on 1 January, when a private from the 1st Tank Company of the Tank Battalion, 191st Separate MRR, died from noxious liquid poisoning in Ghazni Province. A few days later, two Soviet tanks were destroyed by the Mujahideen near the village of Kulchabat in Kandahar Province. In reprisal, Soviet and Afghan servicemen killed an unknown number of Afghan civilians in this settlement, including elderly people.

3rd Marmul Offensive

From 8 January to 29 February 1984 the Soviet Command carried out the 3rd Marmul Offensive in Balkh Province. Some units of the Soviet Border Troops were involved in the operation. Four soldiers and officers were killed and at least one soldier was wounded.

On 10 January 1984 another Soviet general, Lieutenant General Anatoli Dragun, the Chief of one of the Directorates of the Soviet General Staff, died in Kabul – officially of acute heart failure.

On 13 January 1984 12 to 14 soldiers of the 3rd Spetsnaz Company of the 154th Separate Spetsnaz Detachment were killed in a fight with the Mujahideen near the village of Wakah in Kabul Province, 55km (34 miles) east of Kabul.

In January 1984 the rebels tried to force the Afghan Army garrison out of the town of Urgun in Paktika Province, but failed, and on 16 January the siege of Urgun was lifted. Six-hundred guerrillas had been reportedly killed since August 1983. Soviet troops, including the 56th Separate Guards AABr, the 191st Separate MRR and the 345th Separate GAR, also fought in Paktika Province and from 11 to 26 January 1984 lost between 11 and 15 soldiers and officers, including the commander of the 200th Separate Assault Aviation Squadron, Lieutenant Colonel Pyotr Ruban, killed when his new Sukhoi Su-25 attack airplane was shot down on 16 January near Urgun.

On 18 January 1984 rebels shot down an Antonov An-12 transport of the 930th Military Transport Aviation Regiment near the city of Mazar-e Sharif. Between eight and 11 servicemen, including a colonel and a lieutenant colonel, were killed.

Three Soviet soldiers and another lieutenant colonel died on 24 January 1984.

Nine Soviet servicemen, including another lieutenant colonel, died on 29 January.

During the Cold War, the General Staff of the Soviet Armed Forces sought for ways to mechanise all branches of the ground forces, including the, nominally 'light', Airborne Assault troops. In the late 1960s, its requirement for a lightly armoured fire-support vehicle that could be transported by Mi-6 helicopters and An-12 transport aircraft, or even dropped by a parachute from Il-76 transports that were under development, led to the emergence of the BMD-1: an entirely new vehicle, with a turret similar in design and carrying the same armament as that of the contemporary BMP-1 IFV, mounting a low-pressure 73mm gun with 28 rounds (derived from the rockets used by the RPG-7), a co-axial PKT 7.62mm calibre machine gun and an anti-tank missile system (the Malyutka 9M14 (AT-3 Sagger), or in the BMD-1P, the Fagot 9K111 (AT-4 Spigot) anti-tank guided missile system (neither system is shown here as they were rarely deployed in Afghanistan). The vehicle had a crew of three (commander, gunner, and driver), and could accommodate five additional troops positioned around the interior in very cramped conditions (in practice, troops often preferred to ride exposed on the rear deck). Large numbers of BMD-1s were deployed by all Airborne Assault units early during the Soviet military intervention in Afghanistan. (Artwork by David Bocquelet)

The primary infantry fighting vehicle of the Soviet Army at the time of the military intervention in Afghanistan of late 1979 and early 1980, was the BMP-1 – the first vehicle of this kind in the world to enter service. While earlier armoured personnel carriers were only meant to transport infantry across the battlefield, the IFV had the added advantage of providing the crew and passengers with options to fight from under armour. The hull was lightly armoured and the engine installed in the front, in an attempt to improve protection and create a large compartment for up to eight passengers in the rear. The crew of three had a 2A28 GROM 73mm main gun and a PKT 7.62mm calibre machine gun. Though not shown here, in other theatres most BMP-1s also carried a launch rail above the gun for the Malyutka anti-tank missile, or an attachment point for the Fagot 9K111 (AT-4 Spigot) on top of the turret in the BMP-1P version. The smoke grenade dischargers mounted on the turret rear in this example were a feature of the BMP-1P standard from the later 1970s and were later retrofitted to other models. Together with BTR-60s and BTR-70s, BMP-1s formed the backbone of Soviet motor rifle formations early during the war in Afghanistan. (Artwork by David Bocquelet)

Since the late 1960s, the primary short-range air defence weapon in all mechanised formations of the Soviet Army was the ZSU-23-4 Shilka. Based on the chassis of the PT-76 light tank, it had a spacious hull and turret of welded steel, with four water-cooled ZU-23 23mm calibre guns, with a cyclic rate of fire of 800 to 1,000 rounds per minute. The vehicle carried a total of 2,000 rounds of ammunition (500 for each barrel), including armour piercing, incendiary, and high explosive incendiary. The maximum effective range was 2,500 metres (2,734 yards) and aiming was aided by a fire control radar. The crew consisted of four: commander, gunner, loader, and driver, and a battery of four was assigned to every tank or motor rifle regiment. In Afghanistan, Shilkas soon proved a powerful fire-support vehicle, capable of pouring immense volumes of shells upon ground targets and with the ability to elevate the guns to high angles being particularly useful in the valleys and gorges of Afghanistan. (Artwork by David Bocquelet)

Quite early in the war, the Soviet Army learned the lesson about the inability of most of its fighting vehicles to elevate their guns to the levels necessary to shoot at Mujahideen ambushing its columns from above while inside narrow gorges. Based on experience with ZSU-23-4s, one of the quickest solutions was what have become termed 'technicals' in the West: the installation of a ZU-23 gun on the flat bed of the Ural 375, or similar, medium trucks. Although providing no protection for the crew, this proved a highly popular solution and the mass of Soviet motor rifle battalions received batteries of suitably modified Urals. This vehicle (probably using a 'licence plate' in the form of '31-76' in large lettering on the rear side of its flatbed), was assigned to a VDV unit in the mid-1980s. (Artwork by David Bocquelet)

Experience from the 1973 war in the Middle East had demonstrated the shortcomings of the basic BMP-1 design and proposed improvements were soon on the drawing board. There was much debate as to whether to retain the 73mm gun or adopt another calibre. Experience in Afghanistan soon showed that a weapon capable of high-angle elevation would be useful and thus the 30mm cannon was adopted. The hull of the base model BMP-2 remained broadly similar in layout to that of the BMP-1 while the new, larger, welded steel turret of the BMP-2 now accommodated both a commander and gunner. The 2A42 30mm calibre autocannon had a selectable rate of fire, from slow, at 200–300 rounds per minute, to fast at 550 rounds per minute, though the latter rate quickly exhausted ammunition and filled the turret with fumes. The gun was installed on a stabilised mount and was capable of near-vertical elevation but was cumbersome to reload. The co-axial armament included the usual PKT 7.62mm calibre machine gun. A launch system for the 9M113 Konkurs anti-tank guided missiles (ASCC/NATO reporting name 'AT-5 Spandrel') was fitted to the base model BMP-2 but rarely used in Afghanistan. This BMP-2D was assigned to the 317th Guards Airborne Regiment of the 103rd Guards Airborne Division, where it replaced old BMD-1s. (Artwork by David Bocquelet)

The first BMP-2s were deployed to Afghanistan in 1982 and the BMP-2D was a further modification to suit local conditions, the most obvious being the addition of side-skirts to resist 12.7mm machine gun fire. Some vehicles may also have had additional mine protection for the crew. This artwork shows one of four BMP-2Ds assigned to a company of the 860th Separate Motor Rifle Regiment in the Faizabad area around 1984–1985: their known hull numbers were 242, 243, 244, and 246. All four have had their original dark green overall colour largely repainted with brown or dark sand colour, and splotches of dark green then 'outlined' in light grey. Notably, like all BMP-2Ds, they had storage boxes on the rear of the turret, and a bank with three smoke mortars on either side. In comparison, and with a handful of exceptions, most of the BMP-2Ds assigned to the 108th MRR of the 108th Motor Rifle Division as of 1986–1987, usually wore a camouflage pattern in two shades of green, which tended to bleach under the sun, dust, mud and wear into various shades of light green and light brown. (Artwork by David Bocquelet)

While keeping more advanced T-64s, T-72s, and T-80s based in Eastern Europe and the Ukraine, for deployment in Afghanistan the Soviet Army called upon older T-62s. Developed in the late 1950s as a successor to the highly-successful T-54/55 series, these mounted a 115mm calibre high-velocity smoothbore gun, for which the vehicle carried 40 rounds. A PKT 7.62mm calibre machine gun was installed coaxially, while a much heavier DShK 12.7mm calibre machine gun was usually positioned atop the commander's hatch. The mass of T-62s deployed by the Soviets in Afghanistan were of the M version with additional turret armour (variously referred to in the West as 'brow' or 'horseshoe' armour) and a reinforced glacis (upper hull front), but initially were fielded in their original form as shown in these two artworks. In the light of constantly growing losses, crews used spare track sections and other means of improving their protection. As far as is known, they never wore any livery other than overall dark green. (Artwork by David Bocquelet)

The MT-LB was a multi-purpose tracked vehicle that was developed as a lightly armoured version of the MT-L artillery tractor. It had a small turret at the front right, fitted with a PKT 7.62mm calibre machine gun. This MT-LB of the 180th MRR carries a 2S9B Vasilek 82mm calibre gun-mortar on its rear deck. Capable of direct or indirect fire, the Vasilek was loaded with clips of ammunition and could fire at up to 100 rounds per minute, significantly bolstering the firepower of the unit. (Artwork by David Bocquelet)

The 2S5 Giatsint-S 152mm calibre self-propelled gun was one of the heaviest artillery pieces deployed by the Soviet Army in Afghanistan. Developed in the early 1970s to replace older, towed pieces, it was mounted on the same chassis as the 2K11 Krug (ASCC/NATO reporting name 'SA-4 Ganef') medium range surface-to-air missiles and possessed good cross-country mobility. The vehicle could carry 30 152mm calibre shells, each of which could reach a range of 28km, or 33–40km with rocket-assisted projectiles. Self-defence armament consisted of a single PKT 7.62mm calibre machine gun. A single vehicle had a crew of five, could go into action within three minutes of stopping and had a rate of fire of 5–6 rounds per minute. (Artwork by David Boquelet)

One of perhaps the most under-recognised helicopter types deployed by the Soviets in Afghanistan was the Mil Mi-6. With a rotor diameter of 35 metres, maximum take-off weight of 44,000kg (97,003lbs) and capable of lifting up to 12,000kg (26,455lbs), this heavy-lift transport helicopter was heavily involved in all major operations; hauling troops, ammunition, supplies and lighter vehicles all over the country. Usually operated by a crew of five, it had seating for 65 armed troops. It was not usually armed, but an Afanasev A-12 12.7mm calibre machine gun (with 270 rounds) was often installed in the observer's cabin, low in the nose. This is a reconstruction of one of the examples photographed early in the Soviet intervention, and probably operated by the 181st Separate Helicopter Regiment in the Kunduz area. (Artwork by Luca Canossa)

Many units of the 40th Army started the Soviet military intervention in Afghanistan filled with poorly-trained reservists, equipped with obsolete equipment, and ill-prepared for a prolonged war. The same was the situation with many of the V-VS units tasked with deploying to the country and providing support. It was only once the Kremlin decided to strengthen its troops in the country in 1981 that the first generation of modifications resulting from early experiences began to appear. A good example for this was this Mi-8MT from one of about a dozen helicopter regiments forward deployed in Afghanistan by 1983–1984. While still wearing its old camouflage pattern in dark green over light grey, the helicopter has already received a hoist winch above the cabin door, and flare dispensers strapped to the bottom of the boom. Nevertheless, this example is known to have been forced down by small arms fire in the winter of 1984: the crew was evacuated by another helicopter and the wreckage abandoned. (Artwork by Tom Cooper)

By 1985, the second generation of upgrades for Soviet ground vehicles and aviation in Afghanistan became available. One of the good examples of it was this Mi-8MTV-1: this variant received not only better navigational systems (important for operations in the high mountains, as was usual in Afghanistan), but also a 7.62mm machine gun installed in the nose, armour plates along the lower sides of the cockpit and cabin seats, the rescue winch and, most importantly, improved flare dispensers on the rear of the fuselage, and exhaust diffusers. By then, most of the older Mi-8MTs had been upgraded to a similar configuration, while newly-built Mi-8MTV-1 had received slightly different versions of this camouflage pattern in Soviet made colours similar to sky (BS381C/210), and aircraft grey green (BS381C/283) or camouflage beige (BS381C/389) on upper surfaces and sides. Undersides were usually painted in light admiralty grey (BS381C/697). Underslung armament usually included B-8V30 pods for 80mm calibre unguided rockets. (Artwork by Tom Cooper)

Ever since the delivery of the first Mi-24As and Mi-25s to Afghanistan in the late 1970s, this attack helicopter saw massive use in this conflict. The V-VS initially deployed its Mi-24Ds and Mi-24Vs – with a six-barrel 12.7mm machine gun in a barbette under the forward cockpit – gradually increasing their total to about 250 examples by 1985–1987. Around the same time, the significantly improved Mi-24P appeared, mounting a twin 23mm gun on the right side of the forward fuselage, exhaust diffusers, and flare dispensers added on the rear of the fuselage. Due to the type's relatively weak performance in 'hot and high' conditions, the external load was usually limited to a pair of B-8V pods, sometimes accompanied by a pair of 9K114 Shturm (ASCC/NATO reporting name 'AT-6 Spiral') anti-tank guided missiles. Alternatively, general purpose bombs (up to 500kg), and even massive and laser-guided S-25-0 rockets are known to have been used in combat in Afghanistan by Soviet Mi-24s. (Artwork by Tom Cooper)

The old MiG-21 still formed the backbone of both the Soviet and Afghan air forces in the early 1980s. Although originally designed as a point defence interceptor, it was simple to maintain and easy to fly, and relatively adaptable, which is why both air forces deployed it as a fighter-bomber armed with free-fall bombs and unguided rockets, as well. Early on during the Soviet military intervention in Afghanistan, the 115th Guards Fighter Aviation Regiment was deployed to Bagram Air Base, to stand quick reaction alert and fly escort for vulnerable transport aircraft. However, before long, the MiG-21bis of this unit were armed with free-fall bombs like FAB-250M-62s (inboard pylon) and RBK-250s (outboard pylon) and joined other types in the battle against the Mujahideen. Eventually, MiG-21s flew more combat sorties than any other aircraft type deployed in this war. (Artwork by Tom Cooper)

Over time, MiG-21bis of the 115th Guards Fighter Aviation Regiment wore a number of very different liveries. The earliest was actually meant for interception purposes and included an overall livery in the Soviet colour coded RC336, and simply called 'grey'. Later, some of the aircraft were painted in beige or light stone, dark brown and black-green, as shown above, or even in this version of the 'horns' camouflage pattern, usually applied on MiG-21MFs exported abroad in the 1970s: this camouflage pattern consisted of beige (BS381C/388) and dark green (IBS381C/641) on upper surfaces and sides, and light admiralty grey (BS381C/697) on undersides. Furthermore, this jet received the Guards patch underneath the cockpit and an inscription in Cyrillic, indicating the pilot was from the Latvian SSR. The jet is shown armed with R-13M (inboard pylon) and R-60M air-to-air missiles, and carrying a drop tank with capacity of 800 litres under the centreline. (Artwork by Tom Cooper)

This MiG-23MLD was one of about 40 of the 168th Fighter Aviation Regiment: a unit that saw lengthy involvement in the Soviet military intervention in Afghanistan. Initially, the 168th was home-based at Sovetabad Air Base, in the Uzbek SSR as of 1983–1984: in 1986–1987, it was also forward deployed at Bagram and Shindand air bases. The MiG-23MLD was foremost an interceptor, and the task for the regiment was both quick reaction alert and flying escort for fighter-bombers operating close to the border with Pakistan. However, the regiment also flew hundreds of air strikes, deploying a miscellany of unguided bombs. This jet is shown decorated with a total of 27 small red stars, applied on the left forward fuselage marking over 270 combat sorties flown. (Artwork by Tom Cooper)

This is a reconstruction of 'white 55' – the MiG-23MLD from the 120th Fighter Aviation Regiment flown by Captain Sergey Privalov on 12 September 1988, when it was damaged by a proximity-fusing AIM-9L fired by a Pakistani F-16A. The jet is shown in the configuration at the time of its sortie, with an R-24R semi-active radar homing, medium range-air-to-air missile under the wing (the infrared homing variant, R-24T, was also deployed by the V-VS in Afghanistan but rarely photographed). Secondary armament consisted of either two or four R-60M infrared homing, short-range air-to-air missiles, and internally installed twin 23mm calibre GSh-23 autocannon. (Artwork by Tom Cooper)

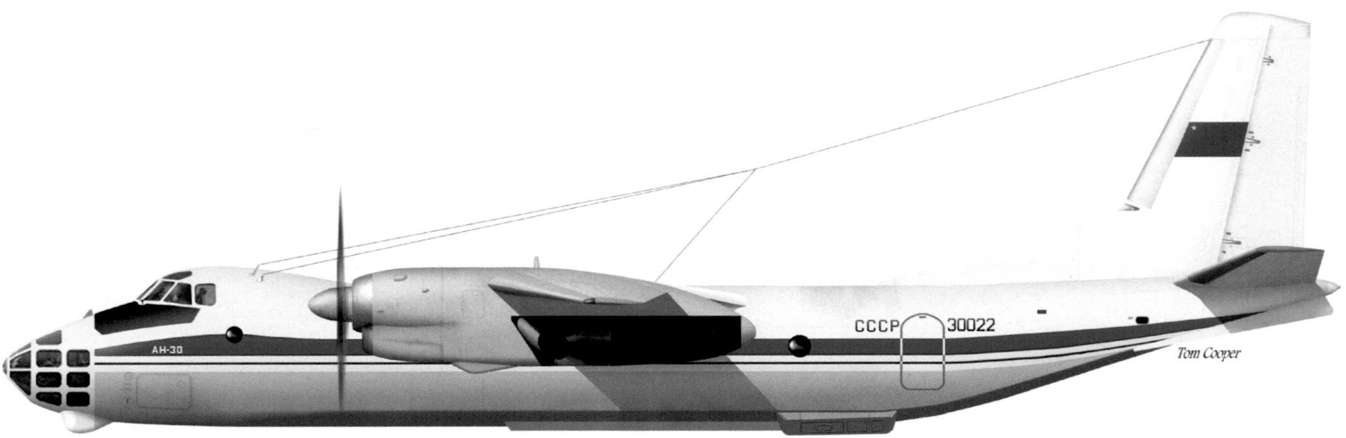

The An-30 was a version of the An-24, custom-tailored for aerial cartography, reconnaissance, and mapping purposes. It received an optical sight for ensuring accuracy of aerial photography, computer flight-path-control equipment, and five camera windows in the floor of the rear cabin, each of which could be closed to protect the glass panels. Of the cameras, three were mounted vertically, and two pointing at an angle of 28° each side of the aircraft (for oblique photography). The rear fuselage also contained working stations for two camera operators, and a crew rest area. During the 1980s in Afghanistan, the only unit operating An-30s was the 50th Separate Long Range Reconnaissance Squadron of the 50th Mixed Aviation Regiment, which had two examples permanently based at Kabul International. They were deployed very intensively, including to guide bombers into attacks on selected targets, and to collect post-strike reconnaissance. (Artwork by Tom Cooper)

One of the unsung heroes of the Soviet military intervention in Afghanistan were the fighter-bombers of the Sukhoi Su-17 family. Prior to the appearance of the Su-25, Su-17s were the primary fighter-bombers of the V-VS in this campaign, and units operating them flew thousands of combat sorties. This Su-17M-2 was operated by the 166th Fighter-Bomber Regiment from Kandahar and Shindand, while this unit was deployed inside Afghanistan in the 1983–1985 period. It is shown armed with a FAB-500M-62 general purpose bomb on the inboard underwing pylon, and carrying a 800-litre drop tank. The jet is shown wearing one of the camouflage patterns in mid-stone (BS381C/362), middle brown (BS381C/411) and light Brunswick green (BS381C/225) on top surfaces and sides, and light admiralty grey on undersides: somewhat ironically, back in the 1950s, the Soviets decided to use the British Standard colours as the basis for standardisation of their own colours. (Artwork by Tom Cooper)

Sukhoi Su-24s of the V-VS saw rather limited action in Afghanistan. While a small testing unit was around earlier in the conflict, no operational units were ever deployed in the country. The type only flew its first combat operations in 1984, during one of the Panjshir offensives, and then again in 1988–1989 during the Soviet withdrawal. Soviet Su-24s were also the first V-VS aircraft to deploy laser-guided bombs in anger. While the type proved quite problematic to fly, and experienced a high attrition rate even in peacetime, none was lost over Afghanistan. This early Su-24M of the 143rd Bomber Aviation Regiment is shown together with two of its heaviest weapons (FAB-1500M-54 to the left, and the laser-guided KAB-1500L to the right), and markings indicating 40 combat sorties, all from the 1988–1989 period, when the unit was forward deployed at Mary-2. (Artwork by Tom Cooper)

The Su-25 was still in the process of research and development when the USSR launched its military intervention in Afghanistan. The working up of the series production and application of different modifications on the basis of operational testing in the country resulted in a situation where the first regiment completely equipped with the type only came into being in 1985, in the form of the 378th Separate Assault Aviation Regiment. Proving a massive success, the Su-25 was soon much in demand, but the majority of newly-manufactured aircraft were necessary to bolster V-VS units in Eastern Europe. Thus, even two years later – by when the 378th was reorganised and its aircraft received bort numbers applied in red, outlined in black, as shown here – there were only enough Su-25s available for one regiment in Afghanistan. All Soviet Su-25s had already received their camouflage painting at the factory in Tbilisi, which developed some five or six different versions, some of which consisted of only two, but others up to four, different colours. (Artwork by Rolando Ugolini)

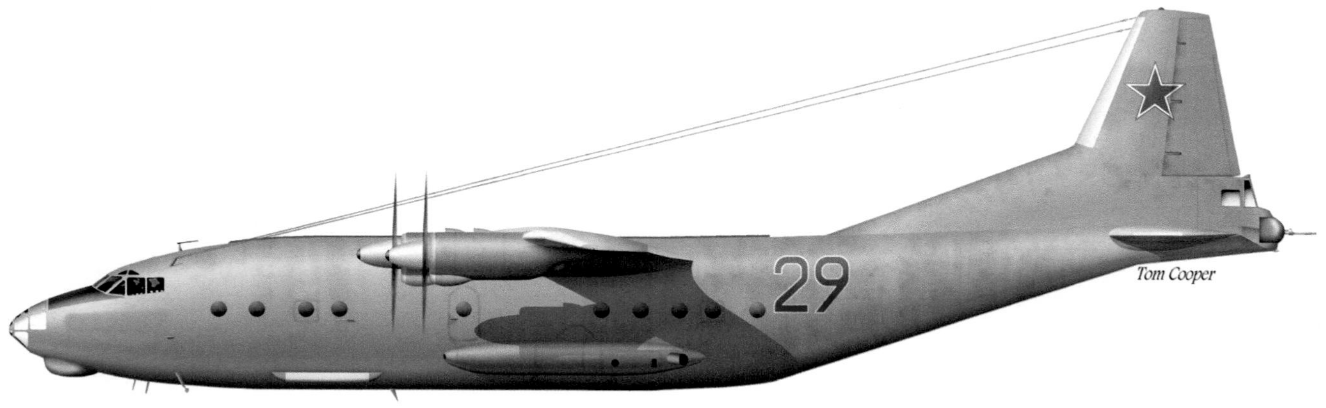

This An-12BK is from the 134th Transport Regiment, one of the units of the Transport Aviation branch of the Soviet Air Force, which made regular flights to Afghanistan in support of the 40th Army. Like almost all An-12s in military service in the 1980s, it was painted in grey overall, with spinners and the leading edge of engine nacelles left in bare metal. The long add-on pod installed on the lower forward fuselage contained a chaff and flare dispenser. The unusually large number was applied on the rear fuselage in red and outlined in white: An-12s from the 50th Mixed Aviation Regiment of the 40th Army, and the 194th Transport Regiment are known to have worn them applied in almost exactly the same fashion – often making unit identification hard. (Artwork by Tom Cooper)

The Il-76 transport aircraft was still relatively new in service with the V-VS in the late 1970s, and the Soviet military intervention in Afghanistan was the first major enterprise to see its involvement. Nevertheless, an Il-76 became the first Soviet aircraft lost in this conflict, when a jet from the 128th Guards Transport Aviation Regiment carrying troops of the 103rd GAD was hit by anti-aircraft artillery and then crashed into a mountain near Kabul on 25 December 1979. By 1987, Il-76s from four additional units are known to have been regularly involved in Afghanistan, including the 194th, 339th and 708th Transport Aviation Regiments. The fourth was the 25th Guards Transport Aviation Regiment, home-based at Melitopol, in Ukraine, to which this example – manufactured in 1987 – is known to have belonged: it was sighted on several occasions at Bagram and Kabul International through 1988 and in early 1989. (Artwork by Rolando Ugolini)

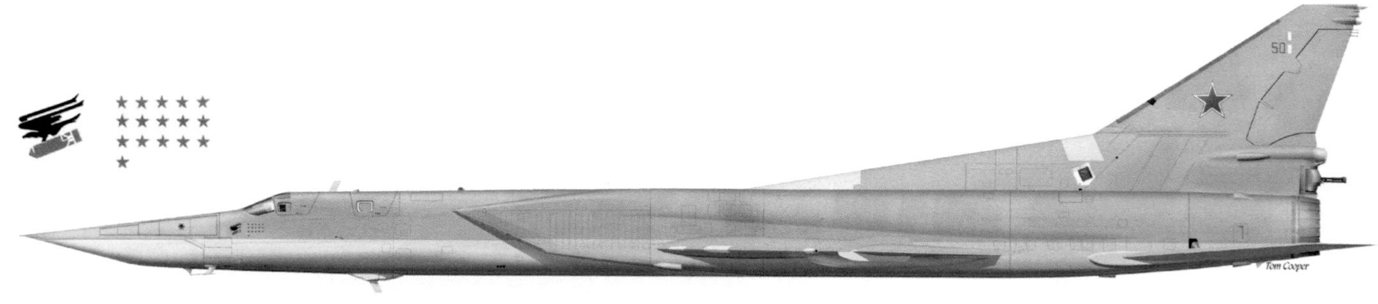

Based at Tartu, in the Estonian SSR, the 326th Heavy Bomber Aviation Division of the 46th Air Army of the High Supreme Command was one of the units operating Tu-22M-3 bombers during the 1980s, and tasked with flying air strikes on Mujahideen positions in Afghanistan, in 1986–1988. One of its senior officers, and the commander of the 326th in 1987–1991, was Colonel Dzhokhar Dudayev, a future major general. He was later the President of the ill-fated Republic of Ichkeria (colloquially Chechnya) and resistance leader in the First Chechen War. In the Aviation Regiment it is known that Dudayev's 'personal' jet bore the number 50, was decorated with a black bird carrying a red bomb, and a total of 16 red stars – as illustrated here. The latter represented 160 combat sorties, in turn illustrating the intensity of Tu-22M-3s involvement in the Afghan War. (Artwork by Tom Cooper)

The clothing of this Mujahideen identifies him as a Pashtun but the appearance was quite widespread all across Afghanistan in the 1970s and 1980s. It is dominated by his long shirt, loose-fitting trousers, comfortable leather sandals, and the characteristic lungi turban. Over these, he is shown wearing a fabric cloak and an old military jacket. In the early 1980s, while there was still a shortage of modern weaponry, many of the Mujahideen were still armed with outdated bolt-action rifles, like this Lee Enfield Mk 1 from the era of the First World War, magnificently adorned and probably reconfigured to fire bullets of a more modern calibre than the old British .303. Notable are the handmade ammunition bandoliers. (Artwork by Anderson Subtil)

Wearing the heavy uniform developed for Airborne Assault troops and introduced into service in the early 1980s, this paratrooper is well-equipped for the harsh Afghan winter. Widely distributed among Soviet forces, this rapidly became known as the Afghanka. This soldier combined it with a Ushanka hat made with blue/grey artificial fur. His equipment is from the RD-54 system, including a backpack, pouches for grenades and ammunition, and a leather belt, which in turn is used to carry the 6Ch4 bayonet with wire cutter, suitable for attachment on his AKS-74 assault rifle (chambered for 5.45 x 39mm bullets). (Artwork by Anderson Subtil)

This Razvednik (reconnaissance soldier) of the 108th MRD is shown wearing a jumpsuit in the distinctive RLMK pattern, widely used by elite Soviet troops in Afghanistan. Usually, this was worn over a regular uniform but in the summer heat of Afghanistan, it was frequently the sole clothing. His khaki cap is from the obr88 tropical uniform, while canvas sneaker boots with a rubber sole are from the USSR, and frequently worn both by special operators and helicopter pilots. His backpack contains the R-159 portable radio, while his armament includes an AKS-74 assault rifle with noise suppressor, and a GP-25 Kostyor 40mm grenade launcher. (Artwork by Anderson Subtil)

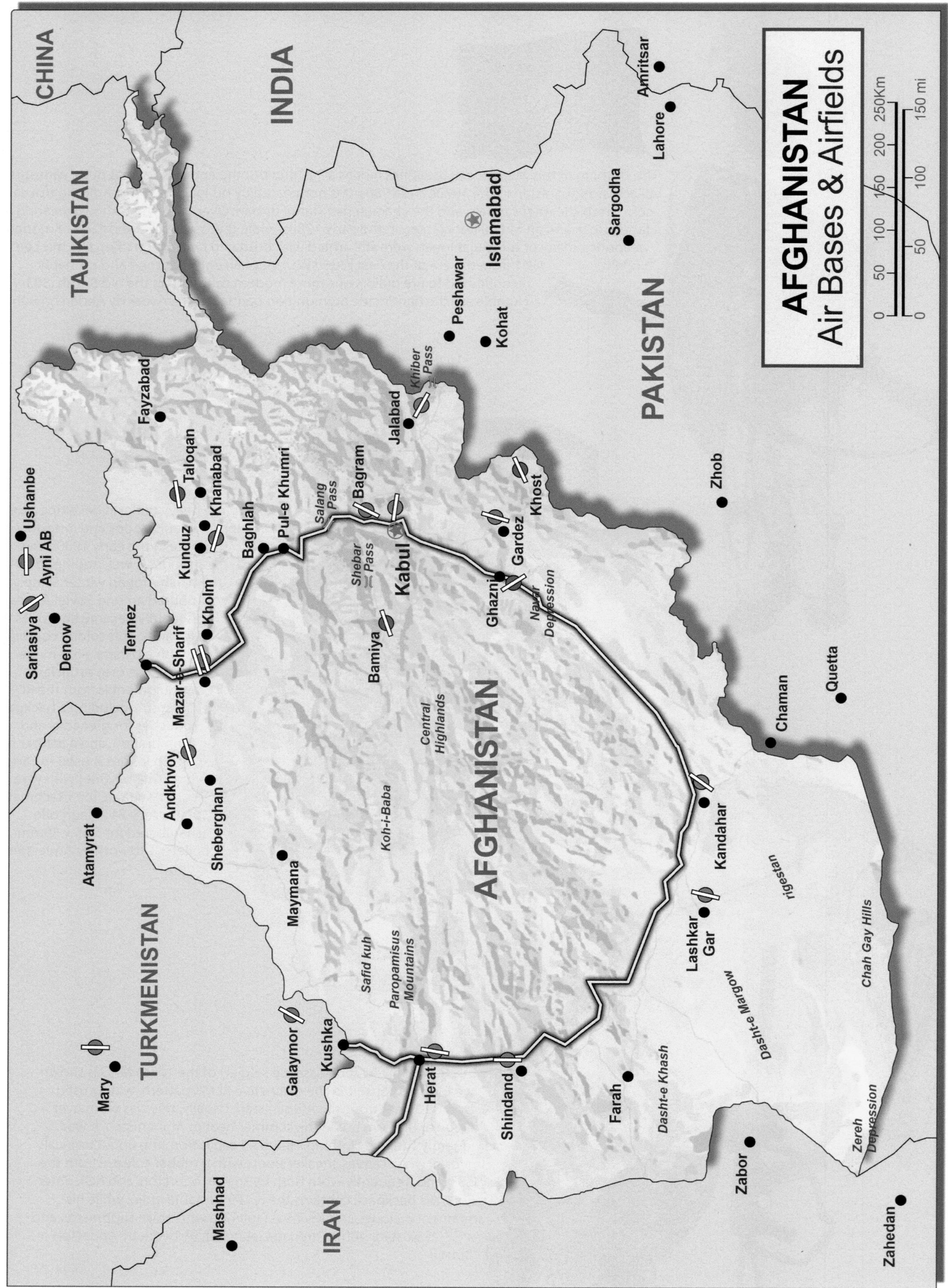

Map of Afghanistan with major air bases and airfields, and the 'ring road', circling the country, clockwise, from north, down to east, south, and then west. The northern section of the road, up to the Salang Pass – and the tunnel there – was constructed by the USSR in the 1960s. The rest of the road had been constructed by the USA at earlier times. (Map by Anderson Subtil)

Troops of the 149th Guards MRR, 201st MRD, with a ditched T-62 in the village of Mahajer, Baghlan Province, in January 1984. (ArtOfWar – Vladimir Shchennikov)

A clandestinely taken photograph of one of early Su-25s, in action in the Urgun area in early 1984. The jet can be seen making a hard right turn, while releasing decoy flares. (Central Intelligence Agency)

In February 1984 Soviet servicemen killed an unknown number of Afghan civilians, including women and children, in a village in Kunduz Province, in retaliation for the destruction of a Soviet tank near this settlement.

On 1 February 1984 a fight reportedly broke out in Kabul. One serviceman of the 103rd Separate Signal Regiment was killed. As an official source assures, a pole fell onto a Soviet BMP IFV in Kandahar on 4 February 1984. One soldier of the 3rd AA Company of the AABn, 70th Separate Guards MRBr was wounded and died in hospital later that day.[1] Four Privates from the 154th Separate Spetsnaz Detachment died on 6 February, when another BMP IFV fell off the cliff in the Salang Pass.

A heavy fight erupted on 15 February 1984 in Badakhshan Province. Seven soldiers of the 2nd MRBn of the 860th Separate MRR were killed and another went missing. The latter serviceman, Private Sergei Korshenko, reportedly participated in the later Badaber uprising. Twenty Soviet servicemen, including two officers, died on 17 February 1984 in five clashes, one accident and a friendly fire incident. Eight of them, belonging to the 66th Separate MRBr, were killed in one more heavy fight in Kabul Province.

Parwan Operation

In late January – late February 1984 the Soviet Command carried out an operation in Parwan Province. This involved:

- 191st Separate MRR
- 345th Separate GAR
- 180th MRR, 108th MRD
- 285th Tank Regiment, 108th MRD
- 781st Separate Reconnaissance Battalion, 108th MRD
- 271st Separate Engineering Battalion, 108th MRD
- 1003rd Separate Support Battalion, 108th MRD
- 357th GAR, 103rd GAD
- 1179th Guards Artillery Regiment, 103rd GAD
- 130th Separate Guards Engineering Battalion, 103rd GAD

Between 16 and 18 Soviet soldiers and officers were killed and at least one more soldier was wounded.

On 30 January 1984 11 servicemen of the 70th Separate Guards MRBr were killed in a single fight near the city of Kandahar.

Murderous February

Five events took place on 28 February 1984. One or two soldiers of the 781st Separate Reconnaissance Battalion of the 108th MRD and 13 Mujahideen were killed near the village of Kharoti in Parwan Province, 60km (37 miles) north of Kabul. Between five and seven servicemen of the 781st Separate Reconnaissance Battalion of the 108th MRD died near the town of Rodbar in Kabul Province, 70km (43 miles) east of Kabul, killing two Mujahideen. Three soldiers of the 317th GAR of the 103rd GAD were killed in a rebel mortar strike near the city of Nijrab in Kapisa Province, 60km (37 miles) northeast of Kabul. A fight also erupted near the town of Surobi in Kabul Province, leaving three soldiers of the 3rd MRBn of the 191st Separate MRR dead. And one more Soviet soldier, who belonged to the 2nd MR Coy of the 1st MRBn, 70th Separate Guards MRBr, was killed in a skirmish near the city of Kandahar.

A mixed convoy of BMP-1Ds and -2Ds of the 4th MR Coy, 2nd MRBn, 149th Guards MRR, 201st MRD, underway between Fayzabad and Kishim, in March 1984. (Kunduz.ru)

An attack on a densely packed Soviet convoy along a narrow road to Fayzabad, 1984. (ArtOfWar – Vladimir Shchennikov)

Massacres in Kapisa

In March 1984 Soviet servicemen killed several hundreds of Afghan civilians in two villages in Kapisa Province. On 10 March 1984 eight or nine soldiers and four or five officers of the 191st Separate MRR, including the commander of the 1st Battalion Major Sergei Sheremetov, were killed and at least one more soldier was wounded in a clash near the town of Surobi. On 11 March a self-propelled gun of the 1074th Artillery Regiment of the 108th MRD fell in the Kabul River, killing three Soviet servicemen. The next day an area near Surobi was the site of the death of seven soldiers of the 3rd MRBn of the 180th MRR, 108th MRD and three soldiers of the 459th Separate Spetsnaz Company. On 12 March 1984, rebels fired on a Soviet BRDM vehicle near the city of Herat, killing two military advisers, including one lieutenant colonel, and one private.

On 15 March 1984 the Chief of Intelligence of the 122nd MRR of the 201st MRD, Lieutenant Colonel Nikolai Zayets, was either taken prisoner or defected to the rebels near the city of Kunduz. He was reportedly killed by Mujahideen three days later, but his body was not found.

Soldiers of the 149th Guards MRR, 201st MRD, and a dead Afghan citizen in the village of Chim Tapah, Kunduz Province, April 1984. (ArtOfWar – Vladimir Shchennikov)

Gunners of the Reconnaissance Company, 181st MRR, 108th MRD, seen while resting in a position north of the Salang Pass, in 1984. (181msp.ru)

Soviet servicemen continued to kill Afghan civilians. On 18 March 1984 they murdered 75 people in several villages in Chaparhar District of Nangarhar Province. Fifteen Soviet servicemen, including five officers, and reportedly more than 20 Afghan guerrillas died on 23 March 1984. Six of them, belonging to the 1st Spetsnaz Company of the 154th Separate Spetsnaz Detachment, died in a road accident near the village of Madi Kats in Nangarhar Province, 155km (34 miles) east of Kabul. In late March 1984 (according to another source it may have been in 1986) Soviet soldiers killed around 350 Afghan civilians, including women and children, in four villages in Qara Bagh District of Ghazni Province. April of 1984 was the hardest month for the Soviet Army in Afghanistan, if we believe unofficial statistics, but even according to official sources the losses in that period were very high.

On 2 April 1984 rebels shot down a Mil Mi-8 helicopter with Soviet soldiers aboard near the city of Lashkar Gah. Three officers and nine soldiers of the 3rd ABn of the 350th GAR, 103rd GAD, including the commander of the battalion – Captain Nikolai Smirnov, and three pilots of the 3rd Helicopter Squadron, 280th Separate Helicopter Regiment were killed. One officer of the 335th Separate Combat Helicopter Regiment was killed, when a Mi-24 helicopter came under small arms fire near the city of Jalalabad. One soldier of the 3rd Reconnaissance Airborne Company of the 781st Separate Reconnaissance Battalion, 108th MRD was killed in a fight near the Surobi Dam, located not far from the town. A soldier of the 4th MR Coy of the 2nd MRBn of the 860th Separate MRR died of disease near the city of Fayzabad. On 4 April 1984 three soldiers of the 1st MRBn of the 149th Guards MRR, 201st MRD died of frostbite in the mountains near Fayzabad.

Six Soviet servicemen, including an officer, were killed in several clashes on 5 April 1984. A day later, 10 or 11 servicemen, mostly from the AABn of the 70th Separate Guards MRBr, died in clashes near the city of Kandahar. One soldier of the 62nd Separate Tank Battalion of the 103rd GAD hit a landmine near the city of Kabul. One Soviet soldier, belonging to the 3rd MRBn of the 682nd MRR, 108th MRD, committed suicide in the village of Qalah-ye Gulay in Parwan Province, 45km (28 miles) north of the capital. This last death was not unusual during the Soviet-Afghan War; many soldiers, especially young ones, took their own lives, tired of being bullied by their fellow soldiers, tired of the extremely

A convoy of the 181st MRR, 108th MRD passes by the Surobi Dam in 1984. (181msp.ru)

hard weather conditions of the country or unwilling to carry out the illegal orders of their superiors. These servicemen were often reported as killed in action.

Panjshir VII

From 8 April to 2 July 1984 (officially from 14 April to 5 May) the Soviet Command carried out Panjshir VII. The following units operated in the Panjshir Valley and in Baghlan Province and were to eliminate Ahmad Shah Massoud and his forces:

- 278th Road Control Brigade
- 191st Separate MRR
- 345th Separate GAR
- 45th Separate Engineering Regiment
- 177th MRR, 108th MRD
- 180th MRR, 108th MRD
- 181st MRR, 108th MRD
- 682nd MRR, 108th MRD
- 1074th Artillery Regiment, 108th MRD
- 781st Separate Reconnaissance Battalion, 108th MRD
- 271st Separate Engineering Battalion, 108th MRD
- 808th Separate Signal Battalion, 108th MRD
- 122nd MRR, 201st MRD
- 149th Guards MRR, 201st MRD
- 395th MRR, 201st MRD
- 541st Separate Engineering Battalion, 201st MRD
- 350th GAR, 103rd GAD
- 80th Separate Guards Reconnaissance Company, 103rd GAD
- 154th Separate Spetsnaz Detachment
- AABn, 66th Separate MRBr
- Reconnaissance Company, 66th Separate MRBr
- AABn, 70th Separate Guards MRBr
- 8th Infantry Division, Afghan Army
- 20th Infantry Division, Afghan Army
- 37th Commando Brigade, Afghan Army
- 444th Commando Regiment, Afghan Army

The bombardment of the valley with strategic bombers lasted for two days. Then the ground troops began to advance. Soviet troops reportedly destroyed the Mujahideen infrastructure in the Panjshir Valley. At least 118 Soviet soldiers and officers, including the deputy commander of the 345th Separate GAR – Lieutenant Colonel Sergei Rodionov and Chief of Staff of the 45th Separate Engineering Regiment, Lieutenant Colonel Pyotr Derid, and at least 10 rebels were killed, at least one Soviet soldier went missing. One Sukhoi Su-17M3R reconnaissance fighter-bomber and one Mi-24 helicopter were shot down.

Several fierce fights took place during the 7th Panjshir Offensive. On 23 April 1984 between eight and 17 men, mostly from the 1st MRBn of the 149th Guards MRR, 201st MRD and from the 541st Separate Engineering Battalion of the 201st MRD, and 28 rebels, were killed, and at least 50 more Soviet soldiers were wounded, near the town of Chowgani in Baghlan Province.

Deadly Hazara Gorge

Fifteen servicemen of the AABn of the 66th Separate MRBr, including one officer, died on 25 April in Baghlan Province. On 28 April 1984 between seven and 13 servicemen of the 191st Separate MRR were killed near the village of Dostum Khel in Parwan Province, 80km (50 miles) north of Kabul.

A serviceman of the 149th Guards MRR, 201st MRD and killed Afghans, reportedly Mujahideen, Baghlan Province, 1984. (ArtOfWar – Vladimir Shchennikov)

Smouldering wreckage of a Soviet Mi-24 helicopter. Clearly visible to the left is the boom with the fin, while the two engines and the front section are to the right. (Pit Weinert Collection)

On 30 April 1984 the action in which the highest number of Soviet casualties in the Soviet-Afghan War occurred broke out near the village of Malimah in Parwan Province, 100km (62 miles) north-east of Kabul. On 29 April the 1st MRBn of the 682nd MRR, 108th MRD, under the command of Captain Alexander Korolyov, received an order to investigate the Hazara Gorge in the Panjshir Valley and destroy an enemy ammunition depot. In the evening the 2nd and 3rd Motor Rifle Companies with several other units of the battalion began their raid, the 1st Company stayed to guard the headquarters of the regiment. The 2nd Company was advancing through the floor of the gorge, while the 3rd Company was taking control of the key heights. But soon the battalion was ordered to advance without taking the heights. The companies, marching until the morning of 30 April, passed by the settlement of Malimah and then ran into an ambush. The Mujahideen opened a heavy fire, and a lot of men, including Captain Korolyov, were killed almost immediately. Around 15 to 20 soldiers jumped into the Hazara River and swam away from the ambush site. The rest fought the rebels for several hours, and the V-VS rushed to the scene, to provide close air support. Eventually, between 45 and 86 officers and men of the Soviet Army, one KGB officer and an unknown number of Mujahideen were killed, between 58 and 105 other Soviet soldiers were wounded. Five more Soviet soldiers died in other parts of the country that day – near the city of Kabul, near the city of Kandahar and in the town of Shindand in Herat Province.

Soviet troops also suffered losses in other parts of Afghanistan: nine – including two officers – are known to have been killed in different clashes on 8 April 1984. Three days later, an intensive firefight erupted near the town of Surobi in Kabul Province. Between 11 and 15 officers and soldiers of the 7th MR Coy of the 3rd MRBn

Servicemen of the Reconnaissance Company of the 181st MRR, 108th MRD, with a BRDM-2 armoured car. The place is unknown, 1984. (181msp.ru)

of the 66th Separate MRBr died, killing and wounding an unknown number of Mujahideen. An additional six Soviet servicemen died on 17 April. Two soldiers of the 122nd MRR, 201st MRD were killed on 18 April, when a Soviet convoy was ambushed near the city of Andkhoy in Faryab Province, 455km (34 miles) north-west of Kabul. One serviceman of the Soviet Border Troops died in an explosion in Herat Province on 19 April. Three Soviet soldiers were killed on 20 April in Kabul and Kandahar Provinces. Two more Soviet soldiers died on 21 April. Eight more died on 22 April.

Red on Red

Another incident typical of the Afghan War occurred on 28 April 1984 near the border town of Hairatan in Northern Afghanistan. A Soviet unit mistakenly opened fire at, and then a few jets bombed, another group of Soviet soldiers, as a result, several men were killed and wounded. Between 11 and 13 servicemen of the 201st MRD, including three officers, were killed on 3 May 1984 in a fight near the town of Dushi in Baghlan Province. Another Soviet soldier, of the 8th MR Coy of the 3rd MRBn, 70th Separate Guards MRBr, died that day in a hospital in the city of Lvov in Ukraine (then the Ukrainian SSR).

From 4 May to 29 June 1984 the Soviet Command carried out an operation in Kandahar Province, involving the 70th Separate Guards MRBr, the 350th GAR of the 103rd GAD and the 173rd Separate Spetsnaz Detachment. Between 26 and 28 soldiers and officers were killed and at least two soldiers and one officer were wounded. On 7 May 1984 Soviet servicemen opened fire at a crowd of people at the Taimani bus depot in Kabul. At least six civilians were killed and 12 others, including a woman, four children, several elderly persons, one officer of the Afghan Army and several Afghan soldiers, were wounded. On 17 May 1984 an explosion occurred at Shindand Air Base; between five and 17 Soviet soldiers, mostly from ground personnel of the Soviet Air Force, died.

Mi-6s down

Seven Soviet soldiers died on 29 May 1984 – two of them committed suicide. Thirteen Soviet servicemen, including a lieutenant colonel who reportedly died as a result of a heart attack in combat, died on 31 May 1984. On 8 June 1984 a Soviet lecturer was killed by a soldier of the Afghan Army at the Kabul Polytechnic Institute. Between two and eight soldiers of the 66th Separate MRBr were killed in combat and between five and eight other servicemen of the brigade died from heat exhaustion on 26 June 1984 near the city of Jalalabad during a march towards their destination. On 6 July 1984, rebels shot down a Mil Mi-6 helicopter of the 280th Separate Helicopter Regiment near the town of Surobi in Kabul Province, killing 16 Soviet servicemen, including seven officers.

On 14 July 1984 another Soviet Mil Mi-6 helicopter, belonging to the 181st Separate Helicopter Regiment, was shot down by Mujahideen near the town of Bagram in Parwan Province – between eight and 12 people were killed. Two days later, on 16 July 1984, at least 14 men of the 59th Support Brigade and of the 180th MRR, 108th MRD were killed, and 11 more soldiers were wounded, in a fight near the city of Kabul. On 21 July 1984 the commander of the 333rd Separate Repair Battalion of the 108th MRD, Lieutenant Colonel Viktor Chervov, was killed by a Soviet sentry near Bagram, Parwan Province. On 2 August 1984 Soviet servicemen killed a boy of 10 or 12 years old in the village of Lalmah in Nangarhar Province, 120km (75 miles) north of Kabul, cutting his throat with a sickle after he pointed his toy rifle at a Soviet convoy. On 14 August 1984 Soviet aircraft bombed the village of Ambar Khana in Nangarhar Province, 150km (93 miles) east of Kabul, where a wedding ceremony was held. According to one group of witnesses, around 20 or 30 Afghan civilians died.[2] According to another account, 563 people were killed.[3]

In mid-August 1984 a Soviet jet conducted a strike on a village in Kandahar Province. Nine Afghan civilians, including one woman and two children, were killed.

On 16 August 1984 a private from the 10th AA Company of the 4th AABn, 56th Separate Guards AABr went missing in Logar Province. The same day 10 servicemen of the 56th Separate Guards AABr, including two officers, were engaged in heavy fighting and killed, near the village of Qalah-ye Taj Khan in the same province, 35km (22 miles) south of Kabul, when they were sent to find him.

On 18 August 1984 the Soviet Air Force carried out a bombing raid on a refugee camp in the Pashai Valley, near the border with Pakistan. Nine women and five children were killed and more than 60 civilians were wounded.

Seven soldiers of the 9th AA Company of the 3rd AABn, 56th Separate Guards AABr were killed on 22 August 1984, when a BTR-D airborne APC hit a landmine in the Waghjan Valley in Logar Province.

A Mi-6 transport helicopter landing at Bagram Air Base in the mid-1980s. (Pit Weinert Collection)

Gunners of the 149th Guards MRR, 201st MRD, with their 2S9B Vasilek 82mm automatic gun-mortar, photographed in 1984. (ArtOfWar – Vladimir Shchennikov)

In late August and early September 1984, the Soviet Command carried out an operation in Wardak Province. On 23 August eight paratroopers of the 350th GAR and the 357th GAR of the 103rd GAD were killed and at least one private was wounded in a fight near the town of Kotah-ye Ashro in Wardak Province. Three more Soviet servicemen died that day, when rebels shot down a Mi-24 helicopter of the 3rd Helicopter Squadron, 335th Separate Combat Helicopter Regiment that arrived in support. Nine servicemen of the 2nd ABn of the 350th GAR, 103rd GAD, including the commander of the battalion Lieutenant Colonel Valeri Spitsyn and one other officer, and three pilots of the 3rd Helicopter Squadron, 50th Separate Mixed Aviation Regiment were killed on 27 August in a skirmish and a Mil Mi-8 helicopter shot down near the same place.

During this offensive, in early September 1984, Soviet servicemen carried out a *zachistka* of the village of Awal Khel, 40km (25 miles) south-west of Kabul, after which they killed eight Afghan civilians, including several women and children. In total, around 500 Afghan civilians, mostly women and children, were killed by Soviet troops during this operation.

On 27 August 1984 Soviet aircraft conducted strikes on three villages in Bati Kot District of Nangarhar Province. A fight between a Soviet unit and Mujahideen broke out in one of them and after that Soviet soldiers started killing villagers. Between 120 and 140 Afghan civilians, including five children, were murdered.

In early September 1984 Soviet jets bombed a refugee caravan near the city of Jalalabad. Eight people, including one woman, were killed.

Fourteen Soviet servicemen, including one officer, died on 2 September 1984. Four of them, belonging to the Reconnaissance Company of the 149th Guards MRR of the 201st MRD, died when a BMP IFV collided with a tank near the village of Omar Khel in Kunduz Province, 250km (155 miles) north of Kabul.

Panjshir VIII

From 4 September to 8 November 1984 the Soviet Command carried out Panjshir VIII. In reality, the fighting in the Panjshir Valley had not stopped since early April. The operation involved:

- The 345th Separate GAR
- 45th Separate Engineering Regiment
- 177th MRR, 108th MRD
- 180th MRR, 108th MRD
- 181st MRR, 108th MRD
- 682nd MRR, 108th MRD
- 1074th Artillery Regiment, 108th MRD
- 781st Separate Reconnaissance Battalion, 108th MRD
- 1003rd Separate Support Battalion, 108th MRD
- 350th GAR, 103rd GAD
- 130th Separate Guards Engineering Battalion, 103rd GAD

Between 125 and 161 soldiers and officers were killed in action and in friendly fire incidents, died of diseases or committed suicide, one officer was taken prisoner and later killed, and at least 10 other officers and soldiers were wounded, two soldiers went missing and one or two more deserted from their units. A Mil Mi-24 helicopter of the 4th Helicopter Squadron, 181st Separate Helicopter Regiment was shot down.

A convoy of the 181st MRR, 108th MRD, in the Panjshir Valley, 1984. (181msp.ru)

From 4 September to 10 October 1984 the Soviet Command carried out an operation in Logar Province, involving the 56th Separate Guards AABr and the 191st Separate MRR in which 21 officers and soldiers were killed and one more soldier went missing. Two Mil Mi-8 helicopters of the 3rd Helicopter Squadron, 50th Separate Mixed Aviation Regiment were shot down. During this operation, on 11 September 1984, Soviet servicemen burnt 40 Afghan civilians alive, including children, in one of the villages in Baraki Barak District.

On 7 September 1984 Soviet servicemen stopped a caravan, which consisted of several cars, near the city of Herat. Soldiers inspected the cars and then shot everybody who was inside them, five Afghan civilians, and after that they took away the cargo. According to the official Soviet version, they were components for the production of explosives, according to the unofficial one, they were civilian goods.[4] The officer who led this operation, a senior lieutenant of the Soviet Army, was reportedly sentenced to death.[5]

On 9 September 1984 the Soviet Air Force bombed the city of Maidan Shahr, nine Afghan civilians were killed and 23 more were wounded. Four days later, a fire erupted at an ammunition depot at Bagram Air Base. Ground personnel of the Soviet Air Force started to extinguish it, but the depot exploded and eight Soviet servicemen, including one officer, died. Between 10 and 13 Soviet servicemen were killed on 19 September 1984 in the shooting down of a Mil Mi-8 helicopter of the 2nd Helicopter Squadron, 335th Separate Combat Helicopter Regiment near the Surobi Reservoir. On 23 September 1984 an Antonov An-12 transport airplane of the 930th Military Transport Aviation Regiment came under the fire of reportedly Iranian anti-aircraft artillery near Zaranj Air Base in Nimruz Province, and one Soviet officer was killed. On 25 September 1984 Soviet servicemen killed an unknown number of people near the town of Qara Bagh in Kabul Province. On 27 September 1984 a Soviet unit encountered mines near the town of Gundigan in Kandahar Province, 500km (311 miles) south-west of Kabul, and six or seven Soviet soldiers died. The rest of the servicemen entered the town and killed around 50 Afghan civilians, among who were two children.

In October 1984 Soviet airplanes and helicopters conducted a strike on a refugee convoy in a village in Ghor Province – an unknown number of civilians were killed and wounded. On 10 October 1984 the commander of the 860th Separate MRR, Lieutenant Colonel Valeri Sidorov, died near the village of Wekha in Badakhshan Province, 350km (217 miles) north of Kabul, when he reportedly mishandled a grenade. A Mil Mi-8 helicopter of the 254th Separate Helicopter Squadron was shot down by Mujahideen on 16 October 1984 near the town of Aibak; between seven and 17 officers and soldiers were killed.

On 27 October 1984 rebels shot down an Ilyushin Il-76 transport airplane of the 128th Guards Military Transport Aviation Regiment, 18th Guards Military Transport Aviation Division, near the city of Kabul, killing between five and 11 servicemen. In November 1984 Soviet servicemen killed around 40 Afghan civilians in the town of Ziruk in Paktika Province, 150km (93 miles) south of Kabul, after a bombardment that lasted for two weeks. Four Soviet servicemen, including a lieutenant colonel, died on 7 November 1984.

Kandahar Offensive

From 8 November to 7 December 1984 the Soviet Command carried out an offensive in Kandahar Province, involving:

- 70th Separate Guards MRBr
- 45th Separate Engineering Regiment
- 317th GAR, 103rd GAD
- 3rd ABn of the 350th GAR, 103rd GAD
- 173rd Separate Spetsnaz Detachment

Between 23 and 25 soldiers and officers were killed in action, two more soldiers and three pilots of the 4th Helicopter Squadron, 280th Separate Helicopter Regiment were wounded and later died. One Mi-24 helicopter was shot down.

During this operation, on 18 November 1984, Soviet helicopters conducted a strike in the city of Kandahar and mistakenly killed one soldier of the 3rd MRBn of the 70th Separate Guards MRBr. Nine Soviet servicemen, including one officer, were killed on 11 November 1984. Six of them, belonging to the Reconnaissance Company of the 149th Guards MRR, 201st MRD, died, when a BMP IFV hit a landmine in Baghlan Province.

On 19 November 1984 the Soviet Command carried out an operation on Tor Ghar Mountain in Nangarhar Province, 175km (109 miles) east of Kabul, involving the 66th Separate MRBr. One Mil Mi-8 helicopter of the 2nd Helicopter Squadron, 335th Separate Combat Helicopter Regiment and one Mil Mi-8 helicopter of the 3rd Helicopter Squadron, 50th Separate Mixed Aviation Regiment were shot down, after that, four servicemen, mostly of the AABn of the 66th Separate MRBr, were killed in a clash on the ground. Six Soviet servicemen, including a lieutenant colonel – a medical officer, who was reportedly poisoned along with his wife, died on 25

Servicemen of the 1st Spetsnaz Company of the 334th Separate Spetsnaz Detachment, 15th Separate Spetsnaz Brigade taking a rest after an operation, near the city of Jalalabad, the year is unknown. (ArtOfWar – Vladimir Lebedenko)

November 1984. From December 1984 to February 1985 the Soviet Air Force conducted strikes on the Zari Valley in Balkh Province, 270km (168 miles) north-west of Kabul. Between 13 and 15 Soviet servicemen, including one officer, died and at least one soldier was wounded on 4 December 1984. Between seven and nine of them, belonging to the 154th Separate Spetsnaz Detachment, were killed in a single fight near the city of Mehtar Lam.

Massacres in Kunduz

In December 1984 Soviet troops massacred hundreds of Afghan civilians in Kunduz Province. On 7 December 1984 a clash took place in Chahar Dara District of Kunduz Province. One resistance fighter was killed and seven more were wounded. In reprisal, Soviet soldiers, on 12 December, killed 154 men and women in the village of Tut Mazar, 250km (155 miles) north of Kabul. Two days later an unknown number of people were killed in Chahar Dara District. And on the 22 December 250 civilians, including several pregnant women and at least nine children, were slaughtered in the settlement of Haji Amanullah, 240km (149 miles) north of Kabul.[6] This village was set on fire and burnt for five days.

From 9 to 20 December 1984 the Soviet Command carried out an offensive near the village of Ali Khel in Paktia Province, involving the 56th Separate Guards AABr and the 191st Separate MRR; 17 officers and soldiers, including a lieutenant colonel, were killed in action. From 18 to 21 December 1984 the 66th Separate MRBr carried out an operation in Kunar Province and lost 12 officers and men. Eight of them were killed in a single fight. From 18 to 27 December 1984 Soviet troops stormed a rebel base in the Lur Kuh Mountains in Farah Province. The 101st MRR, 371st Guards MRR, 650th Separate Reconnaissance Battalion and 68th Separate Guards Engineering Battalion, all of the 5th Guards MRD, were involved in the assault.

Between nine and 11 soldiers were killed, at least one more soldier was wounded. On 20 December 1984 the deputy commander of the 276th Pipeline Brigade, Lieutenant Colonel Dmitri Lisovsky, was killed in an ambush near the village of Sang Sulakh in Baghlan Province, 140km (87 miles) north of Kabul. On 28 December 1984 four soldiers of the 2nd MRBn of the 180th MRR, 108th MRD were killed, when they hit a Soviet mine near the town of Bagram in Parwan Province.

8
1985

With hindsight, it can be said that 1985 was decisive for the outcome of the Soviet military intervention in Afghanistan. On one side, the Kremlin was already in negotiations with the Mujahideen representatives, but not yet ready to make any kind of serious compromises. On the other, the new Secretary General of the Communist Party of the Soviet Union, and the Head of State, Mikhail Sergeyevich Gorbachev, realised that the war was unwinnable. While granting the Soviet Armed Forces one additional year of all-out efforts to defeat the rebellion, in October 1985, he also met Afghan President Karmal and began urging him to acknowledge the lack of widespread public support and find a power-sharing agreement with the opposition. When Karmal refused, Gorbachev took the decision to find a way to withdraw from the war.

Winter Offensives

Exploiting the bad weather and snow to its advantage, the 40th Army opened 1985 with several offensive operations. In mid-January, and together with the Afghan Armed Forces, it carried out an offensive in the Zari Valley in Balkh Province. On 11 January 1985, Soviet airplanes and helicopters bombed two villages in Sayed Abad District of Wardak Province. Thirty-nine Afghan civilians, including several women, were killed, and 30 more people were seriously wounded. The villages were partially destroyed. Thirteen Soviet servicemen, including a lieutenant colonel and one other officer, died on 21 January 1985. Thirteen more Soviet servicemen died on 22 January 1985. Eight of them, including six officers, died when an Antonov An-26 transport airplane of the 1st Aviation Squadron, 50th Separate Mixed Aviation Regiment crashed near the town of Jabal Saraj in Parwan Province. The next day two soldiers of the 177th MRR, 108th MRD were killed in a fight near Jabal Saraj,

A destroyed Soviet D-30 howitzer, near the town of Asmar, Kunar Province, 1985. (Kunduz.ru)

when the Soviets tried to evacuate the bodies of those who died in the crash. Fifteen Soviet servicemen, including five officers, died on 29 January 1985. Seventeen Soviet servicemen, including three officers, died on 2 February 1985, nine of them, mostly from the 180th MRR, 108th MRD, were killed in a heavy firefight near the town of Charikar. The same day Soviet servicemen carried out a *zachistka* of a village in Nangarhar Province, after which they killed 20 Afghan civilians, including eight women.

From 5 to 10 February 1985 the Soviet Command carried out an operation in Samangan Province. The 122nd MRR, 149th Guards MRR, and 395th MRR, all of the 201st MRD were involved in the offensive. Fourteen Soviet soldiers and officers and an unknown number of Mujahideen were killed in action, and at least one more Soviet soldier was wounded. On 11 February 1985 eight servicemen of the 154th Separate Spetsnaz Detachment died near the village of Goshta in Nangarhar Province, 145km (90 miles) east of Kabul, when a BTR-70 armoured personnel carrier, crossing the Kabul River, was swept away by the current and sank. Two or three more Soviet soldiers went missing.

From 12 to 28 February 1985 the Soviet Command carried out an offensive in Kandahar Province, involving the 70th Separate Guards MRBr and the 59th Support Brigade, and had nine officers and men killed. Fourteen Soviet servicemen, including three officers, and two Afghan guerrillas died, and between one and four more Soviet servicemen were wounded on 15 February 1985. In spring 1985 the Soviets killed at least 30 Afghan civilians, including at least two women, two children and three elderly people, in the village of Fatehabad in Nangarhar Province, 100km (62 miles) east of Kabul. Most of the houses in the settlement were destroyed. From March to early April 1985 the Soviet Command carried out the 2nd Khulm Offensive, in Samangan Province. The 149th Guards MRR, the 395th MRR, and the 998th Artillery Regiment, all of the 201st MRD, and some units of the Soviet Border Troops with the units of the 18th Infantry Division and units of the 20th Infantry Division of the Afghan Army were to eliminate Mujahideen groups and to destroy their base near the town of Khulm. Soviet artillery and aircraft conducted strikes near the town, while Soviet and Afghan ground units were searching the settlement. Four Soviet soldiers and officers and reportedly around 300 rebels were killed, around 150 more rebels were taken prisoner.

On 4 March 1985 the commander of the 24th Guards Tank Regiment of the 5th Guards MRD, Lieutenant Colonel Anatoli Redechkin, was seriously wounded when his BTR APC hit a landmine near the town of Shindand in Herat Province. The lieutenant colonel died in the 46th Separate Medical Battalion of the 5th Guards MRD in Shindand, four days later. On 6 March 1985 a captain from the 173rd Separate Spetsnaz Detachment committed suicide at his unit base near the city of Kandahar.

Massacres in Laghman

From 11 to 18 March 1985 and in April 1985 Soviet troops committed another massacre in Afghanistan. They killed either around 500, or even more than 1,000, Afghan civilians, including

Rows of Mi-8 and Mi-24 helicopters at Pul-e Khumri airfield, photographed in 1985. (ArtOfWar – Vladimir Shchennikov)

women and children, in several districts of Laghman Province. The survivors described that the soldiers shot and blew up with grenades entire families in their houses, burnt people alive, raped women, killed the livestock and destroyed crops. According to one report, a three-week-old boy was hung on a tree and then stabbed by a rifle bayonet in front of his parents, who were then also killed.[1] On one day a rebel group arrived at one of the villages, and a skirmish broke out. Three Soviet servicemen were killed. The Soviet unit called for air support, and the jets dropped napalm bombs on the settlement, killing more people.

Servicemen of the Reconnaissance Company of the 181st MRR of the 108th MRD, the place and year are unknown. (181msp.ru)

On 14 March 1985 a Mil Mi-6 transport helicopter of the 2nd Helicopter Squadron, 181st Separate Helicopter Regiment collided with a Sukhoi Su-22M fighter-bomber of the Afghan Air Force at Pul-e Khumri Air Base. Six Soviet servicemen, including the commander of the squadron, Lieutenant Colonel Nikolai Lapshin, died in the crash.

Twelve Soviet servicemen, including one officer, died on 19 March 1985. On 20 March 1985 the Mujahideen shot down a Mil Mi-8 helicopter of the 335th Separate Combat Helicopter Regiment near the village of Rabat in Ghazni Province. Between 12 and 16 Soviet servicemen were killed. The same day a series of explosions began in and around the capital. The first bombing killed at least three people and wounded 25 others. Three days later, on 23 March, a bomb exploded near Kabul; four Soviet servicemen died and three more people were wounded. And on 29 March 1985 an explosion in Kabul killed one or two people.

On 23 March 1985 10 Soviet servicemen, including two officers, died and two more Soviet servicemen, including one officer, were wounded in one fight, one road accident and four explosions. Seventeen soldiers of the 2nd Troop Carrying Company of the 221st Separate Troop Carrying Battalion of the Soviet Air Force were killed and several more were wounded in a single fight on 24 March 1985, when a Soviet convoy was ambushed near the village of Qalah-ye Wulang in Parwan Province, 85km (53 miles) north of Kabul. Five more Soviet servicemen died that day in other regions of the country. On 29 March 1985 a lieutenant colonel, a military adviser, was killed in a shop in the city of Kabul. Two warrant officers from the 201st MRD, a father and son, were killed by a soldier of the Afghan Army in the city of Kunduz on 30 March 1985. In late March 1985 Soviet servicemen killed between 700 and 1,200 Afghan civilians in four villages in Khanabad District of Kunduz Province.

In April or May 1985 Soviet servicemen killed around 400 Afghan civilians in the village of Qarlugh in Kunduz Province, 290km (180 miles) north of Kabul. A fierce fight erupted on 5 April 1985 near the village of Wunamak in Parwan Province, 80km (50 miles) north of Kabul; eight servicemen of the 3rd MRBn of the 177th MRR, 108th

A soldier of the 1st Spetsnaz Company, 334th Separate Spetsnaz Detachment, 15th Separate Spetsnaz Brigade, in the process of defusing a mine. (ArtOfWar – Vladimir Lebedenko)

MRD, including one officer, were killed. In April/May 1985 the Soviet Air Force carried out a series of bombing raids on the settlements located in the Zari Valley in Balkh Province. On 11 April Soviet aircraft conducted a strike on one of the villages, wounding four Afghan civilians. On 20 April Soviet jets bombed the village of Amrakh, 270km (168 miles) northwest of Kabul. A six-year-old boy was killed, one woman, a two-year-old girl, and two men were wounded. On 23 April Soviet planes again bombed the valley and wounded two Afghan civilians. The next bombardment occurred on 24 April. On 29 May Soviet jets dropped incendiary bombs on a house near the Mujahideen base that was located in the valley. Nine Afghan civilians, including an 11-year-old boy, were killed and five more were badly burnt. On 30 May Soviet airplanes and helicopters bombed this Mujahideen base and destroyed it, one rebel was killed. Between 12 and 14 Soviet soldiers died on 17 April 1985. Between seven and nine of them, belonging to the 66th Separate MRBr, were killed in a single fight in Laghman Province.

Troops of the 149th Guards MRR, 201st MRD, crossing a stream in the Panjshir Valley, July 1985. (ArtOfWar – Vladimir Shchennikov)

A convoy of the 2nd MRBn, 149th Guards MRR, 201st MRD passes through an Afghan village, 1985. (Kunduz.ru)

Spetsnaz in Sangam

Another battle with a significant number of Soviet losses took place on 21 April 1985. The 334th Separate Spetsnaz Detachment of the 15th Separate Spetsnaz Brigade under the command of Major Viktor Terentiev was to investigate the village of Sangam in Kunar Province, 190km (118 miles) east of Kabul. The detachment launched a raid in the evening of 20 April, without armoured vehicles. Sometime later the 1st Spetsnaz Company of the 334th Separate Spetsnaz Detachment of the 15th Separate Spetsnaz Brigade under the command of Captain Nikolai Tsebruk and the 2nd Spetsnaz Company, 334th Separate Spetsnaz Detachment, 15th Separate Spetsnaz Brigade received an order to investigate another settlement, the village of Daridam, located 2km (1 mile) from Sangam, and to capture an American military instructor. On the night of 20/21 April the 1st Company searched Sangam and advanced to Daridam. The 1st and 2nd Groups[2] of the company started to investigate the village, while the 3rd and 4th Groups stayed to cover them. Several hours later, soldiers and officers finished the investigation and decided to return, but they were suddenly attacked by rebels. The 3rd and 4th Groups tried to come to their aid but were unable to break through the enemy fire; the 3rd Group was shelled with mortars. Captain Tsebruk also tried to come to the aid of his comrades, but he was soon killed. Soviet artillery conducted a strike near the settlement, but it was ineffective. As a result of the six-hour clash, between 26 and 31 Soviet servicemen and a number of insurgents were killed, only six soldiers of the 1st and 2nd Groups survived.

Badaber Prison Break

During the night of 26/27 April 1985 the Badaber prison break occurred. A group of Soviet and Afghan prisoners of war held in an ISI-run compound at Badaber fortress, near the town of Peshawar in Pakistan, managed to overpower their guards and attempted to escape. The ISI operatives attempted to negotiate with them, but in the course of the resulting talks, the prisoners saw several armed Mujahideen trying to sneak in their direction. The result was a fierce firefight that went on deep into the night. On the next morning, the Mujahideen bombarded the fortress with mortars: one of the bombs hit the local armoury, causing a major conflagration that obliterated the entire compound, and showered large parts of Peshawar with unexploded ammunition. While the Pakistanis greatly downplayed this affair, according to the Soviet reports, between 11 and 20 of their servicemen, 40 Afghan Army soldiers, at least 20 Mujahideen, and between 40 and 90 Pakistani servicemen – as well as six US advisers – were killed.

On 27 April 1985 a crowd of people on the central square of the city of Andkhoy in Faryab Province was shelled with mortars. Several dozen Afghan civilians, including children, were killed and wounded.

Kunar Offensive

From 16 May to 12 June 1985 (officially from 19 May) the Soviet Command carried out the Kunar Offensive. The troops listed below were to eliminate the rebel formations around the city of Asadabad and open the road from the city of Jalalabad to the village of Barikot:

- 66th Separate MRBr

Kunar Operation

Although one of the largest and most successful enterprises of the Soviet intervention in Afghanistan, the Kunar Operation remains one of the least known. In early March 1985, the Asadabad-based 2nd MRBn of the 66th Separate MRBr was reinforced by the 334th Separate Spetsnaz Detachment of the recently-established 15th Separate Spetsnaz Brigade. The two units then received the task of destroying a concentration of up to 6,000 Mujahideen led by Gulbuddin Hekmatyar, that were concentrating in the Kunar Valley, where they had also built-up huge stockpiles of ammunition and supplies, and thus secure the route connecting Asadabad with Jalalabad, and therefore relieve the Afghan garrison in Birkot that had been under siege since September 1984. The operation was planned by the staff of Lieutenant General Rodionov, of the 40th Army, and supervised by Army General Valentin Varennikov, Head of the Operation Group of the Ministry of Defence of Afghanistan. In essence it was a pincer attack, in which a mechanised group would enter the valley, while Airborne Assault forces would secure the dominating peaks and passes out of it, thus ambushing any rebels that might try to escape.

While centred on 600 troops of the 2nd Battalion of the 66th Separate MRBr, mounted on BMP-2D IFVs, and supported by a company of T-62M main battle tanks, a company of D-30 howitzers, and a platoon of BM-21 multiple rocket launchers, the Kunar Offensive included no fewer than 12,000 Soviet, and 5,000 Afghan, troops (the latter mostly from the 8th, 9th, and 11th Divisions of III Corps).

Although some preliminary operations had been undertaken since 13 April, officially this offensive was initiated on 19 May 1985, with massive air strikes by Tu-16 and Su-24 bombers, and then several vicious artillery barrages. Initially, the operation proceeded very fast, and the involved units managed to make an advance of nearly 30km along the Kunar and Pech Rivers. However, the Mujahideen then counterattacked and cut off the road connecting Asadabad with Jalalabad, destroying one Soviet and one Afghan engineering unit in the process. On 24 May, the 2nd Battalion of the 149th MRBn was sent to secure the high ground above the village of Konyak, several km north-west of Samir Kot, on the Pech River. While advancing at night, the unit ran into an ambush in which it lost 22 men of its 4th Company. That, however, remained the only major mishap in this offensive. The Kunar Operation continued through May and concluded only on 12 June, by when the Soviets had relieved the Birkot garrison and secured all of the road connecting Asadabad with Jalalabad. According to official reports from Moscow, by then Hekmatyar's force had suffered a loss of up to 4,200 killed and wounded. Precise numbers of Soviet and Afghan casualties were actually never released – partially because several officers of the 149th MRBn were subsequently court-martialled for cowardice. In turn, the 334th Separate Spetsnaz Detachment and its commander, Grigory Bykov, earned themselves a fearsome reputation with the Mujahideen, and became known as the 'Asadabad Hunters', because of their numerous intercepts of supply caravans.

One of four BMP-2s of the 2nd Battalion, 66th Separate MRBr, lost during a clash with the Mujahideen on 13 March 1985. (Efim Sandler Collection)

BMP-2Ds of the 103rd Airborne Division photographed during the Kunar Operation in May 1985. (Efim Sandler Collection)

- 56th Separate Guards AABr
- 45th Separate Engineering Regiment
- 149th Guards MRR, 201st MRD
- 317th GAR, 103rd GAD
- 350th GAR, 103rd GAD
- 357th GAR, 103rd GAD
- 1179th Guards Artillery Regiment, 103rd GAD
- 80th Separate Guards Reconnaissance Company, 103rd GAD
- 1074th Artillery Regiment, 108th MRD
- 334th Separate Spetsnaz Detachment, 15th Separate Spetsnaz Brigade
- 8th Infantry Division, 1st Army Corps, Afghan Army
- 9th Infantry Division, 1st Army Corps, Afghan Army
- 11th Infantry Division, 1st Army Corps, Afghan Army
- 10th Infantry Brigade, Afghan Army
- 37th Commando Brigade, Afghan Army
- 10th Engineering Regiment, Afghan Army

Vehicles of the 181st MRR, 108th MRD, underway in the Panjshir Gorge in 1985. (181msp.ru)

Soviet troops advanced through the Pech and Kunar Valleys and lost 63 officers and men, including the commander of the of the 4th Helicopter Squadron, 181st Separate Helicopter Regiment, Lieutenant Colonel Nikolai Kovalyov, killed or died from heat exhaustion, reportedly killing at least 4,200 Mujahideen. At least one other Soviet soldier was wounded and at least one more went missing. One Mi-24 helicopter was shot down.

A major fight between Soviet troops and Afghan guerrillas took place on 25 May 1985, during this offensive. The 4th MR Coy, 2nd MRBn, 149th Guards MRR of the 201st MRD under the command of Captain Alexander Peryatinets conducting a search and destroy operation was ambushed near the village of Konyak in Kunar Province, 80km (50 miles) east of Kabul. Twenty-two or 23 soldiers and officers, including Captain Peryatinets, were killed, and between 18 and 28 more were wounded. Ten Soviet servicemen, including one officer, died on 30 May 1985. In June 1985 Soviet servicemen killed around 300 Afghan civilians in Chahar Dara District of Kunduz Province. Six soldiers of the 2nd Mortar Battery, 2nd MRBn, 70th Separate Guards MRBr were killed, and one officer was wounded, on 5 June 1985, when a MT-LB amphibious vehicle hit a landmine near the village of Ghreh Kalachah in Kandahar Province, 460km (286 miles) south-west of Kabul.

A Su-25 seen while making a hard turn at low altitude over rebel positions and releasing flares. The aerodynamic configuration of this aircraft, with its large, straight wing, earned it the nickname 'Devil's Cross' with the Mujahideen.

Panjshir Offensive IX

From 7 June to 29 July 1985 the Soviet Command carried out Panjshir IX. This operation involved:

- 56th Separate Guards AABr
- 278th Road Control Brigade
- 191st Separate MRR
- 345th Separate GAR
- 177th MRR, 108th MRD
- 180th MRR, 108th MRD
- 181st MRR, 108th MRD
- 682nd MRR, 108th MRD
- 1074th Artillery Regiment, 108th MRD
- 781st Separate Reconnaissance Battalion, 108th MRD
- 271st Separate Engineering Battalion, 108th MRD
- the 1003rd Separate Support Battalion, 108th MRD
- 122nd MRR, 201st MRD
- 149th Guards MRR, 201st MRD
- 350th GAR, 103rd GAD
- 154th Separate Spetsnaz Detachment, 15th Separate Spetsnaz Brigade

Underneath view of a Su-22 fighter-bomber of the Democratic Republic of Afghanistan Air Force during an attack on the Mujahideen in the Panjshir Valley in 1986. (Tom Cooper Collection)

Soviet troops conducted heavy air and artillery strikes in the Panjshir Valley for about a month and reportedly took the village of Kijol, 105km (65 miles) north-east of Kabul. Between 116 and 134 Soviet officers and soldiers, and 21 Mujahideen were killed in action, one other Soviet soldier died in a friendly fire incident, and another Soviet soldier died in a road accident, at least 17 more Soviet officers and soldiers, including the commander of the 108th MRD, Major General Vasili Isayev, were wounded, three Soviet soldiers went missing and one Soviet officer deserted from his unit. One Sukhoi Su-25 airplane of the 378th Separate Assault Aviation Regiment and one Mil Mi-8 helicopter of the 3rd Helicopter Squadron, 181st Separate Helicopter Regiment were shot down. A BMP IFV, four BTR APCs and 96 trucks were destroyed, several tanks and AFVs were damaged.

During this offensive, on 16 June 1985, several rebel groups took 500 Afghan servicemen including 126 officers, prisoner at the village of Pashghur, 110km (68 miles) north-east of Kabul, but shortly afterwards they came under fire by Soviet helicopters, and most of the prisoners were killed. Some researchers have said that Panjshir IX began in reprisal for the destruction of this garrison, but in fact the fighting in the valley started before this event.

On 12 June 1985 an explosion occurred at Shindand Air Base. Thirteen Mikoyan-Gurevich MiG-21 fighters and six Sukhoi Su-17 fighter-bombers of the Afghan Air Force were destroyed.

A lieutenant colonel of the Soviet Army, a military adviser, was killed on 14 June 1985, when the rebels shot down a Mikoyan-Gurevich MiG-21MF fighter in Kandahar Province.

In July 1985 Soviet aircraft conducted a strike on one of the villages in Ghazni Province. A 2-year-old boy was heavily wounded; his family's house was completely destroyed.

Between six and 13 servicemen of the 12th Guards MRR and 101st MRR, both of the 5th Guards MRD, including one officer, were killed, and three more servicemen were wounded in a clash and a tank explosion in the city of Herat on 10 July 1985.

The next day 14 Soviet servicemen, including seven officers, were killed, when rebels shot down an Antonov An-12 airplane of the 111th Separate Mixed Aviation Regiment near the city of Kandahar.

From 13 July to 29 August 1985 the Soviet Command carried out the Khost Offensive. The 56th Separate Guards AABr, the 191st Separate MRR and the 345th Separate GAR were involved in this operation. Between 11 and 15 Soviet soldiers and officers and reportedly around 2,400 Mujahideen were killed, at least one Soviet soldier was wounded.

On 22 July 1985 a captain of the Soviet Army was killed by Soviet soldiers in Kabul, when he tried to arrest them for breaking curfew.

From 12 August to 4 September 1985 the Soviet Command carried out an operation in Kandahar Province, involving the 70th Separate Guards MRBr and the 1060th Guards Artillery Regiment of the 5th Guards MRD. Twenty-one officers and soldiers were killed and at least three more were wounded.

In late August 1985 Soviet jets heavily bombed a village in Jaji District of Paktia Province. An unknown number of people were killed.

4th Marmul Offensive and the First Battle of Zhawar

In September 1985 the Soviet Command carried out the 4th Marmul Offensive in Balkh Province. Units of the 201st MRD and some units of the Soviet Border Troops were involved in the operation.

At about the same time Soviet servicemen killed 17 Afghan civilians, including several women and children, in a village in Khogyani District of Nangarhar Province.

The First Battle of Zhawar was fought in September and October 1985. Units of the 12th Infantry Division and units of the 25th Infantry Division of the Afghan Army were to destroy a Mujahideen logistic base, located at Zhawar area in Paktia Province. Afghan troops took two villages around the base, but then retreated. The rebels lost 106 men killed and 321 wounded.

Fifteen Soviet servicemen died on 2 September 1985. Ten of them were killed in a single action near the village of Ali Khel in Paktia Province.

On 4 September 1985 the rebels mistakenly shot down a Bakhtar Afghan Airlines Antonov An-26 airplane near

A scene from the command post of the 201st MRD with BTR-60s and other command vehicles and captured Afghan citizens. (ArtOfWar – Vladimir Shchennikov)

Kandahar Airport. Fifty-two people, mostly civilians, were killed.

Thirteen Soviet servicemen died and one went missing on 18 September 1985. Ten of them, belonging to the 191st Separate MRR, were killed in a single explosion near the village of Sur Pul in Wardak Province.

Ten Soviet servicemen, including three officers, died on 19 September.

Charles E. Thornton, a correspondent for *The Arizona Republic* newspaper, was killed on 25 September 1985, when either a Soviet or an Afghan Army unit shot up the truck with him, his colleagues and resistance fighters on board near the city of Kandahar. One of the rebels was also killed, and three more American citizens, including Peter Schlueter, a photographer for the same newspaper, were wounded.

Military traffic along the road through the Macedonian Gorge, in Balkh Province. (ArtOfWar – Vladimir Shchennikov)

Two MiG-21bis of the 115th Guards Fighter Aviation Regiment seen lined up on the apron of Bagram Air Base in the mid-1980s. Notable in the background to the left is the fin of a MiG-21PFM of the Afghan Air Force, which wore no camouflage colours at the time. (Pit Weinert Collection)

From 26 September to 5 October 1985 Soviet troops stormed a Mujahideen fortress in Nangarhar Province. The 334th Separate Spetsnaz Detachment of the 15th Separate Spetsnaz Brigade was involved in the assault. A Soviet serviceman and reportedly 40 guerrillas were killed.

In October 1985 Soviet and Afghan soldiers carried out *zachistkas* of several villages in Ghazni Province, killing 20 people.

On 2 October 1985 two privates from the 66th Separate MRBr escaped from the brigade's guardhouse, located near the village of Samar Khel in Nangarhar Province, and officially went missing.

Ten Soviet servicemen, including three officers, died on 10 October 1985. Three of them, including the Chief of Staff of the 181st MRR of the 108th MRD, Major Valeri Cherevatenko, were killed by their fellow soldiers.

On 16 October 1985 the 682nd MRR of the 108th MRD was ambushed near the village of Rukhah in the Panjshir Valley, in Parwan Province. The regiment lost three or four men killed and 10 others wounded. Five BMP IFVs and six trucks were destroyed. The Soviet soldiers then halted for the night in the open, on the slope of a nearby mountain. By morning between five and 17 more Soviet soldiers had frozen to death and more than 30 others suffered frostbite of varying degrees of severity.

Twenty-two Soviet servicemen, including nine officers, died on 25 October 1985. Thirteen of them, including the deputy commander of the 201st MRD, Lieutenant Colonel Gennadi Bezuglov, and commander of the 3rd Helicopter Squadron, 181st Separate Helicopter Regiment, Lieutenant Colonel Nikolai Nuzhdin, were killed when rebels shot down a Mil Mi-8 helicopter of the 3rd Helicopter Squadron, 181st Separate Helicopter Regiment in Kunduz Province.

From 26 October to 3 November 1985 the Soviet Command carried out an operation in Baghlan Province. The 177th MRR of the 108th MRD, and the 149th Guards MRR and 395th MRR of the 201st MRD were involved. Six Soviet servicemen and an unknown number of rebels were killed.

Another Red on Red

Ten servicemen of the Soviet Army and three soldiers of the Soviet Border Troops, who were killed in a friendly fire incident in Takhar Province, died on 4 November 1985. A fourth Soviet general died in Afghanistan on 12 November 1985. The Adviser to the Commander of the Air Force of the Democratic Republic of Afghanistan,

Major General Nikolai Vlasov, was personally piloting a Mikoyan-Gurevich MiG-21 fighter, when the aircraft was shot down near the village of Deh Rawud in Uruzgan Province. The general had time to eject, but then was killed with small arms while in the air. Seven Soviet servicemen, including one officer, died that day in other parts of the country.

Nine Soviet servicemen, including a lieutenant colonel, died on 13 November 1985. Between 12 and 19 servicemen of the Soviet Border Troops were killed and at least three others were wounded on 22 November 1985 in a fierce fight with Mujahideen near the village of Afrij in Badakhshan Province, 320km (199 miles) north-east of Kabul. From 22 November to 12 December 1985 the Soviet Command carried out Operation Volna (Russian for 'Wave') in Kandahar and Uruzgan Provinces. The 70th Separate Guards MRBr, the 56th Separate Guards AABr, the 101st MRR and the 371st Guards MRR of the 5th Guards MRD were involved in the offensive. Twenty-six or 27 Soviet officers and soldiers, including the commander of the 280th Separate Helicopter Regiment, Colonel Yuri Filyushin, and 60 insurgents were killed. Two Mil Mi-8 helicopters of the 3rd Helicopter Squadron, 280th Separate Helicopter Regiment were shot down. During this offensive, on 6 December 1985, 13 servicemen of the 370th Separate Spetsnaz Detachment of the 22nd Separate Spetsnaz Brigade, including two officers, and three pilots of the 3rd Helicopter Squadron, 280th Separate Helicopter Regiment, were killed when a Mil Mi-8 helicopter was shot down near the village of Deh Rawud in Uruzgan Province. Nine Soviet servicemen, including one officer, died on 23 November 1985.

On 24 November 1985 a private from the 2nd Anti-Tank Battery of the 1377th Separate Anti-Tank Artillery *Divizion* of the 5th Guards MRD killed three of his fellow soldiers and then committed suicide near the village of Shahid-e Chahar Band-e Karwan Gah in Farah Province, 650km (404 miles) south-west of Kabul. Two soldiers of the 2nd MRBn of the 682nd MRR, 108th MRD were killed by a comrade near the village of Rukhah in Parwan Province. Eleven more Soviet soldiers, one KGB officer and one civilian contractor were killed that day in a single action near the Salang Pass.

On 8 December 1985 an explosion occurred at a weather station near the city of Kabul. Eight Afghan civilians were killed and 54 more were wounded. On 9 December 1985 a series of explosions occurred near the Kabul Polytechnic Institute and 21 people were wounded. On 14 December 1985 between 16 and 21 Soviet servicemen, mostly from the 3rd ABn of the 345th Separate GAR, were killed in a fierce firefight with rebels near the village of Pizgaran in Parwan Province, 90km (56 miles) north-east of Kabul. Five Soviet servicemen, including a lieutenant colonel, died on 16 December 1985. Six Soviet servicemen, including another lieutenant colonel – who was killed when a Mikoyan-Gurevich MiG-23MLD fighter was shot down near the town of Jabal Saraj in Parwan Province, died on 27 December 1985. The same day Soviet servicemen carried out a *zachistka* of a village in Kot District of Nangarhar Province, during which a large number of people were killed. After that, Soviet soldiers tied up 16 elderly villagers and took them to the helicopters, the helicopters took off, and then the soldiers began throwing the prisoners to the ground, while the servicemen who were still on the ground below fired their rifles at them. Eleven elderly people were killed and five survived, one of them managed to escape and reported this war crime. In late December 1985 Soviet aircraft conducted a strike near an airport in Parwan Province, killing more than 40 Afghan civilians.

9
1986

A MiG-21bis of the 115th Guards Fighter Aviation Regiment taxiing on the tarmac of Bagram Air Base. Although relatively short-range and limited in terms of its payload, this aircraft excelled in terms of maintainability and simplicity of operations, and thus continued in service with the V-VS throughout the duration of the Soviet military intervention in Afghanistan. MiG-21s of the 115th were replaced by MiG-29s in 1986–1987. (Pit Weinert Collection)

Ever since 1983, the leadership in the Kremlin had begun searching for a way to end its military intervention in Afghanistan: two years later, in October 1985, the Soviet Politburo – the government of the USSR – accepted Gorbachev's decision to withdraw from this conflict. The first step in any resultant strategy was to transfer the burden of fighting the Mujahideen to the Afghan Armed Forces, while restricting the involvement of the Soviet Armed Forces. Correspondingly, during 1986, and with extensive support from the USSR, the Afghan Army was built up to an official strength of over 300,000 officers and other ranks, while the Soviet 40th Army attempted to weaken the Mujahideen through a series of smaller offensives, which saw ever greater emphasis on deployment of carefully trained Spetsnaz units. Meanwhile, concluding that the government of President Karmal was ineffective and weakened by divisions from within, the Kremlin decided to replace him.

Scenes of a Soviet attack on an Afghan village, in 1986. (ArtOfWar – Vladimir Lebedenko)

Offensive in Nangarhar

Nine Soviet servicemen, including three pilots of the 3rd Helicopter Squadron, 50th Separate Mixed Aviation Regiment, were killed, and one officer was wounded on 13 January 1986. On 18 January 1986 Soviet troops stormed a Mujahideen fortress, located near the village of Goshta in Nangarhar Province – one soldier of the 3rd MRBn of the 66th Separate MRBr, one pilot of the 1st Helicopter Squadron, 335th Separate Combat Helicopter Regiment and reportedly around 60 Mujahideen were killed, one officer of the 7th MR Coy, 3rd MRBn, 66th Separate MRBr was wounded. Eleven Soviet servicemen, including three officers, died the next day; eight of them, five commandos of the 370th Separate Spetsnaz Detachment, 22nd Separate Spetsnaz Brigade and three pilots of the 3rd Helicopter Squadron, 280th Separate Helicopter Regiment, died in a Mil Mi-8 helicopter crash near Lashkar Gah Air Base. On 25 January 1986 a heavy firefight took place near the village of Dadah in Paktia Province, 90km (56 miles) south-east of Kabul, around the infamous Nari Mountain. Between 17 and 19 soldiers of the 1st Airborne Company of the 1st ABn, 56th Separate Guards AABr were killed.

From 9 February to 25 March 1986 the Soviet Command carried out an offensive in Nangarhar Province. The 66th Separate MRBr, the 154th and 334th Separate Spetsnaz Detachments of the 15th Separate Spetsnaz Brigade were involved in the operation. Fourteen soldiers and officers, including the commander of the AABn of the 66th Separate MRBr, Major Sergei Gorobets, were killed, and at least three more servicemen were wounded. On the first day of this operation, on 9 February 1986, Soviet helicopters conducted a strike on the village of Loyah Termay in Nangarhar Province, 90km (56 miles) east of Kabul, and mistakenly killed one soldier of the 154th Separate Spetsnaz Detachment of the 15th Separate Spetsnaz Brigade.

During this offensive, from 9 to 25 March, Soviet servicemen killed 180 Afghan civilians, including at least two women, six children and two elderly people, and wounded at least two more people in several villages in Darah-ye Nur District of Nangarhar Province. Fifty-six of the dead civilians were burnt alive. More than 200 houses in these settlements were destroyed. Three Soviet servicemen, including a GRU lieutenant colonel, died on 19 February 1986. Four Soviet servicemen, including the deputy commander of the 50th Separate Mixed Aviation Regiment, Lieutenant Colonel Ivan Piyanzin, died on 21 February 1986. Lieutenant Colonel Piyanzin was killed when a Mi-24 helicopter was shot down near Kabul. On 22 February 1986 Soviet aircraft conducted a strike near the village of Dowlat Shahi in Parwan Province, 50km (31 miles) north of Kabul, and mistakenly killed three Soviet soldiers. On 28 February 1986 Soviet troops stormed a Mujahideen base, located near the village of Wasati Chighnay in Kandahar Province. The 70th Separate Guards MRBr and the 173rd Separate Spetsnaz Detachment of the 22nd Separate Spetsnaz Brigade were involved in the assault. Three Soviet servicemen, including one officer, were killed.

Second Battle of Zhawar

The Second Battle of Zhawar took place from 28 February to 23 April 1986. The 56th Separate Guards AABr, the 191st Separate MRR, the 345th Separate GAR and the 45th Separate Engineering Regiment, with the 38th Commando Brigade of the Afghan Army, took part in the operation. Soviet and Afghan troops carried out several offensives, and the base was taken. By 10 April 1986, Soviet and Afghan ground troops had reached the Tani River, forcing the Mujahideen to organise a frontal defence and fight under circumstances for which they lacked both the training and the firepower. Moreover, they were subjected to continuous air strikes by Su-25s: additionally, Su-24s equipped with laser-guided bombs were deployed to hit their major fortifications. The operation proved costly for both sides: 25 Soviet officers and other ranks – including a colonel and three lieutenant colonels (all military advisers) – were killed, at least five other Soviet soldiers were wounded and one Soviet soldier went missing. Five hundred and thirty Afghan servicemen were taken prisoner, 78 of whom were later killed. The rebels lost 281 fighters killed and had 363 wounded. Two Sukhoi Su-25 attack aircraft, one Sukhoi Su-17M3R reconnaissance fighter-bomber of the Soviet Air Force and 24 helicopters of the Afghan Air Force were shot down.

On 6 April 1986, during this battle, a Sukhoi Su-25 aircraft of the commander of the 378th Separate Assault Aviation Regiment, Lieutenant Colonel Alexander Rutskoy, another future major general and Vice President of the Russian Federation, was shot down by a surface-to-air missile near the city of Khost. The lieutenant colonel had time to eject but suffered a fractured spine when he hit the ground, and then he reportedly was caught in a shootout

A crew posing with their 2S1 Gvozdika 122mm calibre howitzer. Note the camouflage paint applied to the vehicle. (Efim Sandler Collection)

and received two more wounds, before being evacuated by a Soviet helicopter.

Spetsnaz Operations in the Tani, Zhawar, and Kurukh Areas

In March 1986 Soviet jets bombed one of the villages near the city of Mazar-e Sharif. Sixty-seven Afghan civilians were killed and at least one more civilian, a 13-year-old boy, was wounded. Three Soviet servicemen, including a lieutenant colonel, a military adviser, and a civilian contractor died on 1 March 1986. Seven Soviet servicemen, including another lieutenant colonel, who was killed by his subordinate reportedly as a result of the negligent handling of a weapon, died on 4 March 1986. On 16 March 1986 Soviet helicopters conducted a strike in Kandahar Province and killed an unknown number of people. On 19 March 1986 Soviet servicemen killed several people with bayonets in the village of Siyah Wushan in Herat Province, 630km (391 miles) west of Kabul. On the same day, several waves of Su-22s of the Democratic Republic of Afghanistan Air Force, escorted by MiG-23MLDs of the V-VS, flew air strikes on targets inside Pakistan. Among others targets, they bombed several Pakistani border posts. This was a prelude for the next Soviet offensive, in which Mujahideen supply bases in the Tani and Zhawar area were the primary target. Two Soviet servicemen, including a lieutenant colonel, died on 21 March 1986. From 29 to 31 March 1986 Soviet troops stormed the Karera fortress in Kunar Province. The 154th and 334th Separate Spetsnaz Detachments of the 15th Separate Spetsnaz Brigade were involved in the assault. Between 42 and 50 Soviet servicemen, 70 Afghan soldiers and 26 insurgents were killed in several fights, three insurgents were taken prisoner.

The action was not limited to eastern Pakistan alone: on 4 April 1986 Soviet troops stormed a Mujahideen base located near the town of Karukh in Herat Province, 600km (373 miles) west of Kabul. The 12th Guards MRR and 650th Separate Reconnaissance Battalion of the 5th Guards MRD were involved in the assault. Seven or eight Soviet soldiers, including two officers, and at least four rebels were killed, between two and four other Soviet soldiers were wounded. Eleven Soviet servicemen died on 08 April 1986. Eight servicemen of the Soviet Army and two servicemen of the Soviet Border Troops, including one officer, died on 10 April.

On 12 April 1986 Soviet aircraft bombed numerous villages in the Andkhoy District of Faryab Province killing between 800 and 1,000 Afghan civilians. Ten Soviet servicemen died on 14 April 1986; four of them, soldiers of the 894th Separate Repair Battalion of the 59th Support Brigade, died when some oxygen tanks exploded during welding operations of the unit near the city of Pul-e Khumri. The next day seven servicemen of the Soviet Border Troops, including one officer and one KGB officer, were killed when a BTR APC hit a landmine near the village of Dasht-e Chinar in Takhar Province, 290km (180 miles) north of Kabul. Three Soviet servicemen, including a lieutenant colonel, died on 20 April 1986. Between 12 and 14 Soviet servicemen, including one officer, died on 25 April. Between six and 12 of them were killed in a single explosion near the village of Dandugi in Herat Province, 635km (395 miles) west of Kabul. Eight Soviet servicemen, including one officer, died on 28 April 1986.

On 4 May 1986 Soviet leaders replaced the General Secretary of the Central Committee of the People's Democratic Party of Afghanistan and Chairman of the Praesidium of the Revolutionary Council of the People's Democratic Party of Afghanistan, Babrak Karmal, with the Director of the KhAD, Mohammad Najibullah, who became the General Secretary of the Central Committee of the People's Democratic Party of Afghanistan (later also the Chairman of the Praesidium of the Revolutionary Council of the People's Democratic Party of Afghanistan and the President of the Republic of Afghanistan).

On 8 May 1986 Soviet servicemen killed six people near the town of Lyaz Khel in Laghman Province, 80km (50 miles) east of Kabul.

From 10 to 22 May 1986 the Soviet Command carried out an offensive near the village of Ali Khel in Paktia Province. The operation began with heavy air strikes by fighter-bombers of the V-VS and the Democratic Republic of Afghanistan Air Force, which targeted Mujahideen supply bases. Then the troops of the 66th Separate MRBr, the 56th Separate Guards AABr, the 345th Separate GAR, the 45th Separate Engineering Regiment, and the 181st MRR, 1074th Artillery Regiment and 1003rd Separate Support Battalion of the 108th MRD advanced on the ground. In support of this offensive, on 17 May 1986, Afghan and Soviet fighter-bombers also hit targets inside Pakistan. Eventually, between 11 and 13 officers and men, including a colonel, were killed and at least one more soldier was wounded in this operation. Another 10 Soviet servicemen, including three officers, died on 23 May 1986, while 11 Soviet servicemen, including two pilots of the 302nd Separate Helicopter Squadron,

A group of Afghan Mujahideen, the place and year are unknown. Note the 107mm Type 63 MRL of Chinese origin. (ArtOfWar – Vladimir Shchennikov)

died on 26 May. In reaction to the Soviet-Afghan offensive, the ISI ordered the Mujahideen to conduct numerous hit-and-run attacks. For example, on 29 May 1986 Mujahideen deployed their Type 85 single round rocket launchers to target the command post of one of the infantry regiments of the Afghan Army near the town of Urgun in Paktika Province. This attack killed five Soviet servicemen, including two lieutenant colonels – both were military advisers.

Elsewhere, the rebels planted numerous mines: 10 Soviet servicemen, including three officers, died on 2 June 1986. Five of them from the 177th Separate Spetsnaz Detachment of the 15th Separate Spetsnaz Brigade were killed when a BMP IFV hit a landmine near the village of Sheykhabad in Wardak Province, 60km (37 miles) south-west of Kabul. On 5 June 1986 around 100 Afghan civilians were killed in Faryab Province during fights between the Afghan troops and the Mujahideen.

Operation Manyovr

From 9 June to 14 July 1986 the Soviet Command carried out Operation Manyovr (Russian for 'Manoeuvre'). The objectives of the operation were to destroy rebel bases in the Ishkamish District of Takhar Province and to provide supplies to the 860th Separate MRR and the population of the city of Fayzabad. The offensive began with heavy and sustained air strikes by Tu-16 bombers, which were escorted by MiG-23MLDs. The ground operation involved:

- 66th Separate MRBr
- 56th Separate Guards AABr
- 191st Separate MRR
- 345th Separate GAR
- 45th Separate Engineering Regiment
- 180th MRR, 108th MRD
- 181st MRR, 108th MRD
- 122nd MRR, 201st MRD
- 149th Guards MRR, 201st MRD
- 395th MRR, 201st MRD
- 783rd Separate Reconnaissance Battalion, 201st MRD
- 541st Separate Engineering Battalion, 201st MRD
- 18th Infantry Division, Afghan Army
- 20th Infantry Division, Afghan Army
- 25th Infantry Division, Afghan Army

Between 20 and 27 Soviet soldiers and officers were killed, two or three other Soviet soldiers died from heat exhaustion, and between 19 and 40 more Soviet servicemen were wounded. Two Mil Mi-8 helicopters were shot down.

Grad multiple rocket launchers volley, date and location unknown. (Kunduz.ru)

Troops of the 149th Guards MRR, 201st MRD, with a prisoner and a collection of trophies captured from the Afghans – the latter including bolt-action rifles, two machine guns, and a number of RPG-rounds. (Kunduz.ru)

During this offensive, on 16 June 1986, the 783rd Separate Reconnaissance Battalion of the 201st MRD under the command of Major Pyotr Korytny was mistakenly landed at the enemy base and fought for almost 48 hours. Between 18 and 21 officers and men were killed. According to one report, the city of Taluqan was levelled during this operation.[1]

Ambushes and Minefields

Eight Soviet soldiers were killed on 20 June 1986, while 13 Soviet servicemen, belonging to the 181st MRR of the 108th MRD and to the Reconnaissance Company of the 371st Guards MRR, 5th Guards MRD, were killed in two explosions on 23 June 1986. From 1 to 31 July 1986 the Soviet Command carried out an operation in Kandahar Province, involving the 70th Separate Guards MRBr. Sixteen or 17 Soviet soldiers and officers, including a colonel and two lieutenant colonels, military advisers, were killed, and at least one soldier was wounded, one BTR APC was destroyed. During this offensive Soviet servicemen killed 25 Afghan civilians. A female civilian contractor, a nurse, was killed on 24 July 1986 in Kabul, when a Soviet sentry fired on a car with her aboard during a curfew.

In August 1986 fighting between the Afghan troops and the Mujahideen broke out in the Farkhar District of Takhar Province. Five servicemen of the 3rd MRBn of the 177th MRR, 108th MRD, including one officer, died on 4 August 1986, when a BTR APC fell off a cliff in Parwan Province. Ten Soviet servicemen were killed in six clashes on 7 August 1986. On 11 August 1986 a bomb exploded at Jalalabad Airport; around 20 people were killed and an unknown number of Afghan citizens were injured. In mid-August 1986 Soviet servicemen, in retaliation for the clash with insurgents, killed 30 Afghan civilians, including one woman and several children, in a village in Kunduz Province. According to one report, some children were kicked to death.[2] A few houses in this settlement were destroyed, and all livestock was also killed.

Troops of the 149th Guards MRR, 201st MRD, disembarking from a Mi-8MTV helicopter. Notably, the latter not only had machine gun in the nose, but also exhaust diffusers to the sides of its engines to make the helicopter less susceptible to such weapons as Stingers. (Kunduz.ru)

From 18 to 28 August 1986 the Soviet Command carried out Operation Zapadnya ('Trap' in Russian). The following, with some other units of the Afghan Army, were to destroy the Kokari-Sharshari fortress, located in the western part of the country, near the city of Herat:

- 345th Separate GAR
- 12th Guards MRR, 5th Guards MRD
- 101st MRR, 5th Guards MRD
- 371st Guards MRR, 5th Guards MRD
- 149th Guards MRR, 201st MRD
- 28th Artillery Regiment, 40th Army
- 17th Infantry Division, Afghan Army

While the appearance of FIM-92 Stingers made the life of Soviet helicopter crews much harder, they continued operating all around the battlefields. This example – equipped with exhaust diffusers and boom-mounted flare dispensers – was photographed while evacuating wounded troops. (ArtOfWar – Vladimir Shchennikov)

On 27 August 1986 an ammunition depot blew up near the town of Qarghah in Kabul Province, 10km (6 miles) west of Kabul. At least 50 people, including Afghan civilians, were killed, and several others were wounded. In early September 1986 the Soviet Air Force carried out a bombing raid on the town of Imam Sahib in Kunduz Province, 300km (186 miles) north of Kabul – around 500 Afghan civilians were killed. In September 1986 Soviet aircraft conducted a strike on a village in Badakhshan Province. Four Afghan civilians, including two women and one small child, were killed, a woman, seven children and an elderly man were wounded. At about the same time Soviet servicemen killed an unknown number of people and wounded two more children in two other villages in Badakhshan Province. Also at about the same time Soviet jets bombed several villages in Wardak Province. Seven Afghan civilians, including a child, were killed, and one woman was wounded. Many houses in those settlements were destroyed.

On 4 September 1986 a convoy of the 118th Separate Troop Carrying Battalion of the 58th Separate Troop Carrying Brigade that was reportedly carrying crushed stone for the construction of a school, was ambushed near the town of Paghman (not to be confused with Laghman Province) in Kabul Province, 20km (12 miles) west of Kabul. The trucks were fired upon and forced to stop. The soldiers and officers were reportedly unarmed. Either 17 or 18 of them were taken prisoner and killed later that day.

Seven Soviet servicemen, including one officer, died on 9 September 1986.

Seven more Soviet soldiers died the next day.

A checkpoint of the 3rd MR Company of the 1st MRB, 181st MRR, 108th MRD, the place and year are unknown. Note the three BTR-60PB APCs and the T-62 MBT. (181msp.ru)

- 5th Tank Brigade, Afghan Army

For nine consecutive days Soviet fighters, bombers and artillery continuously conducted strikes, the ground group stormed the fortress several times, and rebels were reportedly defeated. Soviet and Mujahideen casualties in this operation are not known exactly, sources speak of just one Soviet serviceman killed in action and at least five more wounded.[3] It is also known, that the Air Force of the 40th Army lost two Sukhoi Su-25 attack aircraft.

First Deployment of the FIM-92 Stinger

As both Soviet and modern Russian sources confirm, on 25 September 1986 Afghan rebels deployed US-made FIM-92 Stinger surface-to-air missiles for the first time to shoot down either two or three Soviet helicopters near the city of Jalalabad, killing three pilots of the 335th Separate Combat Helicopter Regiment.[4]

On 26 September 1986 one officer and one warrant officer from the 2nd MR Coy of the 1st MRBn of the 371st Guards MRR of the 5th Guards MRD were killed by a Soviet sentry in Farah Province.

In October and December 1986 Soviet jets bombed a village in the Khost wa Firing District of Baghlan Province. Around 15 Afghan civilians, including four women, around nine children, and two insurgents were killed. Twelve servicemen of the Soviet Army, two soldiers of the Soviet Border Troops and 10 Mujahideen died, and one officer of the Soviet Army was wounded on 11 October 1986. On 13 October 1986 Soviet and Afghan servicemen carried out a *zachistka* of the village of Chahar Deh in Paktika Province, 160km (99 miles) south of Kabul, and killed two Afghan civilians.

Show Withdrawal

In the second half of October 1986 the Soviet Command carried out an operation which was referred to as *pokazukha* ('for show') in the Soviet Union. It manned two non-existing regiments with soldiers whose enlistments were due to expire, named them '220th Guards MRR of the 5th Guards MRD' and '620th MRR of the 201st MRD' and defiantly, in front of the cameras, withdrew them from Afghanistan along with the 24th Guards Tank Regiment of the 5th Guards MRD, the 1122nd Anti-Aircraft Missile Regiment of the 5th Guards MRD, the 1415th Anti-Aircraft Missile Regiment of the 108th MRD and the 990th Anti-Aircraft Artillery Regiment of the 201st MRD.

On 16 October 1986 the Chief of Staff of the 180th MRR, 108th MRD, Lieutenant Colonel Ruslan Aushev, another future lieutenant general and the president of the Russian Republic of Ingushetia, was wounded in a firefight in the Salang Pass. Seven Soviet servicemen, including four officers, died that day in other regions of the country. Five Soviet servicemen, including Colonel Vladimir Denisov, the Chief of the Operations Directorate of the Staff of the 40th Army and another officer, died on 21 October 1986. In November 1986 Soviet servicemen shot-up a bus near the town of Khayr Kot in Paktika Province, killing 14 people, including two women and a child.

In November or December 1986 Soviet jets conducted a strike on the village of Nowabad in Kunduz Province, 240km (149 miles) north of Kabul. Twelve Afghan civilians, including five women and four children, were killed, three more civilians, including a woman and a child, were wounded.

Ten Soviet servicemen, including one officer, died on 1 November 1986. Six of them, belonging to the 1st Mortar Battery of the 1st MRBn of the 70th Separate Guards MRBr, were killed in a single explosion in Kandahar Province.

Eight servicemen of the Soviet Army, including a colonel and one other officer, two servicemen of the Soviet Border Troops and a woman civilian contractor died on 12 November 1986. Another woman civilian contractor was raped and then killed by a soldier from the 70th Separate Guards MRBr in the city of Kandahar on 13 November 1986.

Nine Soviet servicemen, including one officer, died on 20 November 1986, while a lieutenant colonel, a military adviser, was killed in combat on 21 November. From 21 November to 28 December 1986 the Soviet Command carried out an operation in Nangarhar Province, involving the 66th Separate MRBr, the 345th Separate GAR and the 28th Artillery Regiment. Between 17 and 19 officers and men were killed, three other soldiers were wounded and two more soldiers went missing. One Mil Mi-24 helicopter of the 1st Helicopter Squadron, 335th Separate Combat Helicopter Regiment was shot down. During this offensive, on 25 November 1986, Soviet aircraft conducted a strike on a hospital in the village of Shinwar in Nangarhar Province, 70km (43 miles) southeast of Kabul.

Renewed Soviet Offensive in Kandahar

From 24 November to 15 December 1986 the Soviet Command carried out an offensive in Kandahar Province. The 70th Separate Guards MRBr, the 191st Separate MRR and the 173rd Separate Spetsnaz Detachment of the 22nd Separate Spetsnaz Brigade were involved. Eighteen or 19 officers and men were killed in action or died in road accidents. On 25 and 26 November 1986 the 186th Separate Spetsnaz Detachment of the 22nd Separate Spetsnaz Brigade carried out an operation in Zabul Province, South Afghanistan. Soviet commandos fought with rebels for about 40 hours and reportedly killed 24 of them, losing one officer and one soldier killed and several more wounded.

On 29 November 1986, a Mujahideen Stinger team sneaked into Kabul International Airport, and fired a missile to shoot down an An-12B transport aircraft of the 1st Aviation Squadron, 50th Separate Mixed Aviation Regiment. Between 30 and 32 of those on board, including two lieutenant colonels, were killed.

In late November 1986 Soviet aircraft bombed a hospital in Tani District of Paktia Province three times.

The deaths of several participants in the Soviet-Afghan War occurred in the border town of Kushka in the Turkmen SSR on 20 and 21 December 1986. Two young women, one a warrant officer of the Soviet Army and one a civilian contractor, were going to the Soviet Union from Afghanistan on vacation by train and accompanying a demobilised conscript soldier (it appears that demobilised conscript had to be accompanied by an officer when returning home). In Kushka all three of them went to a restaurant, where an unknown lieutenant colonel began extorting money from a soldier on the grounds that there was a problem with his papers – that was a 'tradition', unfortunately. The soldier had to give money to the lieutenant colonel, who turned out to be the Chief of the Operations Directorate of the 88th MRD, based in Kushka, and the women complained about him to the Military Commandant's Office (according to another source – to his superiors, which could be the same thing). The lieutenant colonel somehow managed to find out where the women were, and in the evening of 20 December came to their hotel room, where he shot and killed them with his pistol and seriously wounded a senior lieutenant, who was attracted by the gunfire and decided to help; he later died in a hospital. Then the lieutenant colonel left the town and, according to some reports, tried to cross the border, but a Soviet patrol the next day found his body in the desert – the lieutenant colonel had shot himself. When the soldiers started to pick up the body, there was an explosion, because the lieutenant colonel had placed a grenade with the pin removed underneath himself, and three servicemen were wounded.[5]

Ten Soviet servicemen, including two officers, died on 27 December 1986. Six of them (including one officer), belonging to the 334th Separate Spetsnaz Detachment of the 15th Separate Spetsnaz Brigade, were killed, when they hit a Soviet mine in Kunar Province.

10
1987

Throughout 1987, Mikhail Gorbachev, searching for a way to reform the failing economy of the USSR, intensified his efforts to lessen the tensions of the Cold War with the West, and also ended the strategy of confrontation, changing to that of an avoidance of conflict whenever possible. Indeed, in mid-1987, the Kremlin announced that it would start withdrawing its forces from Afghanistan, although even the new government in Kabul was opposed to the idea. For their part, under the guidance of the ISI, the seven major

An up-armoured T-62M knocked out during the fighting in the Delaram area in February 1987. (Efim Sandler Collection)

Mujahideen factions had opened negotiations into establishing their own, interim, government.

Slow Start

In January, and either in February or in March 1987, Soviet aircraft bombed several villages in Khost wa Firing District of Baghlan Province. Seven Afghan civilians, including two women and two children, were killed and six more were wounded. Five Soviet servicemen and one female civilian contractor, a nurse, died on 17 January 1987. Six Soviet servicemen, including a lieutenant colonel, died on 24 January 1987. Another lieutenant colonel died of disease on 1 February 1987. The same day an explosion occurred in the city of Kabul, and four Afghan civilians were killed and an unknown number of people were injured.

Meena Keshwar Kamal, an Afghan revolutionary political activist, women's rights activist, feminist and founder of the Revolutionary Association of the Women of Afghanistan – an organisation formed to promote equality and education for women in Afghanistan – was assassinated in the city of Quetta in Pakistan on 4 February 1987. According to one source, she was killed by KhAD agents, according to another, by the henchmen of Gulbuddin Hekmatyar, one of the Mujahideen leaders. From 4 February to 11 March 1987 the Soviet Command carried out Operation Shkval (Russian for 'Squall') in Kandahar Province, involving the 70th Separate Guards MRBr and the 59th Support Brigade. Eight or nine soldiers were killed, and one Sukhoi Su-25 attack aircraft of the 378th Separate Assault Aviation Regiment was shot down. Eight Soviet servicemen died on 12 February 1987; seven of them, including a lieutenant colonel, were killed in a single action in Farah Province. From 16 to 21 February 1987 the Soviet Command carried out Operation Udar-2 ('Strike-2' in Russian) in Kunduz Province. From 25 to 27 February 1987 Soviet Border Troops carried out an operation on Darqad Island, located on the Panj River, in Darqad District of Takhar Province. Two soldiers were killed in action and one more was wounded.

Trading Hot Punches

Concerned about a possible Mujahideen offensive in the spring, in late February and through March of 1987 the Soviet Air Force carried out a series of raids on targets in the Zhawar area, and on several of the refugee camps that were located inside Pakistan, close to the Pakistan-Afghan border. On 26 February Soviet aircraft bombed the towns of Ghulam Khan and Saigai. On 27 February, 40 Afghan men and women and seven Pakistani civilians were killed and 57 more were wounded in an air strike on the town of Matta Sanga. On 3 March Soviet aircraft dropped bombs near the town of Drosh, killing five Afghan refugees and wounding five more. Four Soviet servicemen, including three officers – one a lieutenant colonel, were killed on 27 February 1987. From 2 to 21 March 1987 the Soviet Command carried out Operation Groza (Russian for 'Thunderstorm') in Ghazni Province, involving the 56th Separate Guards AABr. Three soldiers were killed in action. Eleven Soviet servicemen, including a lieutenant colonel and nine other officers with another lieutenant colonel, and four insurgents died, and two or three more were wounded on 4 March 1987. Eleven additional Soviet servicemen, including two officers, died on 8 March 1987.

The same day, on orders from the ISI, the Mujahideen shelled the town of Panj in the Tajik SSR, killing one Soviet civilian and wounding several others. In retaliation, from 10 to 18 March 1987 units of the Soviet Border Troops with some units of the Afghan Army carried out an operation near the town of Alchin in Kunduz Province, 290km (180 miles) north of Kabul: one Soviet soldier, 17 servicemen of the Afghan Army and (reportedly) up to 151 rebels were killed, 18 other Soviet servicemen were wounded and 28 more rebels were taken prisoner. After finding evidence that the attack on Pani was organised by the ISI, Moscow issued a strenuous warning to Islamabad, forcing the Pakistanis to discontinue attacks into the USSR.

From 8 to 24 March 1987 the Soviet Command carried out Operation Krug ('Circle' in Russian) in Kabul and Logar Provinces. The 181st MRR and the 1074th Artillery Regiment of the 108th MRD, and the 668th Separate Spetsnaz Detachment of the 15th Separate Spetsnaz Brigade were involved in the operation. Eight or nine servicemen were killed and at least one more soldier was wounded. Five Soviet servicemen, including a lieutenant colonel, a medical officer, died on 10 March 1987, while three Soviet servicemen, including a GRU lieutenant colonel, died on 14 March. Seven Soviet servicemen, including four officers, died on 23 March, and 39 or 40 people, including two children, died on 30 March 1987 when an Antonov An-26 aircraft of the 373rd Transport Aviation Regiment of the Afghan Air Force was attacked near Khost Airport by a Pakistani F-16 fighter, and crashed in Tsamkani District of Paktia Province.

Toy Bombs

In April 1987, fighting and shelling between Afghan troops and insurgents took place in the city of Kandahar, one woman was wounded. Later the same month and in early May 1987 nine boys

A machine gun team of the Reconnaissance Company, 181st MRR, 108th MRD. (181msp.ru)

Engineers of the 181st MRR, 108th MRD, with a BMR-1 mine-clearing vehicle. Visible in the foreground is the KMT-7 mine-clearing set, which entered service in 1987. As clear from the damage to the rollers, it served its purpose. (181msp.ru)

were killed and seven others were wounded in Khost wa Firing District, Baghlan Province, in two incidents that occurred within the same day, when they were playing with Soviet mines. Soviet and Afghan troops indiscriminately used anti-personnel mines and booby-traps and used bombs disguised as toys throughout the entire Soviet-Afghan War.

On 9 April 1987 a two-hour fight erupted on Soviet territory, near the ruins of the village of Ivalk in the Tajik SSR. Two soldiers of the Soviet Border Troops and between 15 and 20 Mujahideen were killed, an unknown number of rebels were taken prisoner.

From 11 to 21 April 1987 the Soviet Command carried out an operation in Herat Province.

From 11 April to 8 June 1987 the Soviet Command carried out an offensive in Nangarhar Province. The 66th Separate MRBr, the 56th Separate Guards AABr, the 345th Separate GAR and the 154th Separate Spetsnaz Detachment of the 15th Separate Spetsnaz Brigade were involved. Between 22 and 25 Soviet soldiers and officers and an unknown number of Mujahideen were killed and at least four more Soviet servicemen were wounded. Two Mil Mi-24 helicopters of the 1st Helicopter Squadron, 335th Separate Combat Helicopter Regiment were shot down.

On 24 May 1987, during this operation, seven soldiers of the 1st AA Company of the AABn, 66th Separate MRBr were killed in a single engagement in Nangarhar Province.

From 12 to 24 April 1987 the Soviet Command carried out Operation Vesna ('Spring' in Russian) in Kabul Province, involving the 181st MRR of the 108th MRD. Five Soviet officers and soldiers and three insurgents were killed. One Mi-8 helicopter of the 262nd Separate Helicopter Squadron was shot down.

From 17 April to 13 June 1987 the Battle of Jaji took place, in which the following units were to eliminate Mujahideen in Jaji District of Paktia Province:

56th Separate Guards AABr
345th Separate GAR
180th MRR, 108th MRD
181st MRR, 108th MRD
682nd MRR, 108th MRD
1074th Artillery Regiment, 108th MRD
808th Separate Signal Battalion, 108th MRD

Between 27 and 37 Soviet officers and men, including a GRU lieutenant colonel, and reportedly more than 120 rebels, were killed, one other Soviet soldier died of disease and at least six more Soviet servicemen were wounded. Two Mil Mi-24 helicopters of the 3rd Helicopter Squadron, 50th Separate Mixed Aviation Regiment were shot down.

On 29 May 1987, during this operation, eight paratroopers of the 345th Separate GAR were killed in a heavy fight near the village of Ali Khel in Paktia Province. According to some reports, Osama bin Laden and Arab volunteers took part in this battle and bin Laden was wounded.[1]

Servicemen of the 1st Spetsnaz Company of the 334th Separate Spetsnaz Detachment, 15th Separate Spetsnaz Brigade inspecting an Afghan caravan near the village of Daruntah, Nangarhar Province, 1987. (ArtOfWar – Vladimir Lebedenko)

- 68th Separate Guards Engineering Battalion, 5th Guards MRD
- 173rd Separate Spetsnaz Detachment, 22nd Separate Spetsnaz Brigade

Between 54 and 59 officers and men, including the commander of the 3rd Helicopter Squadron, 280th Separate Helicopter Regiment, Lieutenant Colonel Viktor Klimkin, were killed in action and in a friendly fire incident or died in accidents or of disease, at least four more soldiers and one officer were wounded. One Mil Mi-24 helicopter and three Mi-8 helicopters were shot down. On 21 April 1987, during this operation, 15 officers and soldiers of the 173rd Separate Spetsnaz Detachment of the 22nd Separate Spetsnaz Brigade and four pilots of the 3rd Helicopter Squadron, 280th Separate Helicopter Regiment died when two Mi-8 helicopters collided in the air near Kandahar Air Base. Also during this operation, in May 1987, a fight broke out in a village near the city of Kandahar. In retaliation, the next day Soviet helicopters conducted a strike on the neighbouring village, wounding three children, a six-month-old girl and one- and 12-year-old boys. On 9 June 1987, also during this operation, 10 servicemen of the 191st Separate MRR, including one officer, were killed in a fierce firefight in Kandahar Province. Two Soviet servicemen, including a lieutenant colonel, died on 24 April 1987.

Troops of the 149th Guards MRR, 201st MRD, seen during a break in a march in 1987. (Kunduz.ru)

In May 1987 around 130 bodies of Afghan citizens, reportedly refugees who were shot dead, were found in Charkh District of Logar Province. Fifteen Soviet servicemen, including six officers, died on 7 May 1987, 14 of them died when a Mi-8 helicopter of the 3rd Helicopter Squadron, 280th Separate Helicopter Regiment crashed near Lashkar Gah Air Base. Thirteen Soviet servicemen, including one officer, died and another officer was wounded on 12 May 1987. Eleven of them, belonging to the 180th MRR of the 108th MRD, were killed in a fierce fight near the town of Charikar.

From 25 May to 24 August 1987 the Soviet Command carried out a sweeping operation in Kabul and Logar Provinces involving:

56th Separate Guards AABr
59th Support Brigade
278th Road Control Brigade
180th MRR, 108th MRD
181st MRR, 108th MRD
738th Separate Anti-Tank Artillery *Divizion*, 108th MRD
334th Separate Spetsnaz Detachment, 15th Separate Spetsnaz Brigade
668th Separate Spetsnaz Detachment, 15th Separate Spetsnaz Brigade

In May – June 1987 the Battle of Arghandab took place. The Afghan Army, supported by the Soviet 70th Separate Guards MRBr, tried to destroy Mujahideen strongholds in Arghandab District of Kandahar Province. Afghan troops campaigned for a month and suffered heavy casualties and 1,200 servicemen defected to the rebels. The rebels lost more than 60 fighters. On 13 June 1987, during this offensive, Soviet aircraft bombed several villages in Arghandab District and killed at least 50 Afghan civilians.

From 18 April to 2 July 1987, almost simultaneously with the Battle of Arghandab, the Soviet Command carried out Operation Yug or Yug-87 ('South' or 'South-87' in Russian) in some other districts of Kandahar Province. The offensive involved:

- 70th Separate Guards MRBr
- 59th Support Brigade
- 191st Separate MRR
- 371st Guards MRR, 5th Guards MRD

Servicemen of the 149th Guards MRR, 201st MRD, and captured Afghans. (Kunduz.ru)

Servicemen of the 149th Guards MRR with another captured Afghan. (ArtOfWar – Vladimir Shchennikov)

Between 20 and 30 Soviet soldiers and officers and an unknown number of insurgents were killed, at least five other Soviet soldiers and officers were wounded and one Soviet soldier was taken prisoner. One Mi-8 helicopter of the 4th Helicopter Squadron, 50th Separate Mixed Aviation Regiment and one Mi-8 helicopter of the 262nd Separate Helicopter Squadron were shot down. Three Soviet servicemen, including a lieutenant colonel, died on 12 June 1987. Two Soviet servicemen, including a colonel, a medical officer, died on 22 June 1987.

In July 1987 Soviet and Afghan troops carried out another sweeping operation in Helmand Province. During this offensive several villages in Helmand Province were heavily shelled. An unknown number of Afghan civilians were killed and around 40 more people were wounded. At about the same time either Soviet or Afghan artillery shelled a village near the city of Herat. An unknown number of Afghan civilians were killed and at least six were wounded, between 50 and 60 houses in this settlement were destroyed. On 8 July 1987 an Antonov An-26 aircraft of the 339th Separate Mixed Aviation Squadron mistakenly entered the territory of Iran and landed at Zabol Air Base. Soon after, soldiers of the Iranian Army attacked the plane and killed one Soviet pilot.

On 12 July 1987 at Kandahar Air Base an Antonov An-12 airplane with ammunition aboard caught fire. Officers and men began to extinguish it, but sometime later the plane blew up and 13 Soviet servicemen, including three officers, died, and up to 38 others were injured. Three Soviet servicemen, including the commander of the 1st Helicopter Squadron, 181st Separate Helicopter Regiment, Lieutenant Colonel Anatoli Kosenko, died on 13 July 1987.

In mid-July 1987 a clash between Soviet troops and Mujahideen took place in Ghazni Province. The rebels captured 27 Soviet servicemen and brought them through one of the neighbouring villages. In retaliation, the next day Soviet aircraft conducted a strike on this village. Seven Afghan civilians were killed and one young woman was severely wounded. Ten Soviet servicemen, including two officers, died on 19 July 1987. Between seven and nine of them, belonging to the 1st MRBn of the 149th Guards MRR, 201st MRD, were killed and more than 50 others were wounded in a fierce battle near the town of Kalafgan in Takhar Province, 260km (162 miles) north of Kabul.

Continuous Losses

In August 1987 Afghan soldiers killed 17 Afghan civilians in Mir Bacha Kot District of Kabul Province in retaliation for a rebel attack on an Afghan Army unit. In turn, sometime midway through that month, Afghan artillery, answering a rebel attack, shelled a neighbourhood in the city of Kandahar, one elderly woman was wounded.

In September 1987 the Soviet Air Force bombed several villages in Badakhshan Province. Seventeen Afghan civilians, including five women and seven children, plus one Mujahid were killed, an unknown number of people were wounded.

At about the same time Soviet aircraft conducted strikes on three villages located in Wardak and Ghazni Provinces. Seven Afghan civilians – three women and four children – were killed, and 45 more, also including women and children, were wounded, one woman later died.

In September or October 1987 Afghan servicemen in Herat Province shelled a refugee group, heading to Pakistan; 19 Afghan civilians, including five women and seven children, were killed. Two weeks later Soviet helicopters conducted a strike on this group in Helmand Province, killing a further five people.

On 6 September 1987 a village in Nahrin District of Baghlan Province was shelled. Eight Afghan civilians were killed, including two women and four children.

A unique case even by Soviet standards happened on 8 September 1987 in the town of Chowgani[2] (according to another source, in the town of Khinjan[3]) in Baghlan Province. A political officer of the 278th Road Control Brigade, Senior Lieutenant Dmitri Kolyabin, killed the commander of the brigade, Colonel Nikolai Ostapenko, with a shot from a service pistol, reportedly in front of soldiers and officers of the brigade, and then either shot himself or was brought before a military court. According to one version, this happened as a result of a domestic dispute.[4] According to another, Colonel Ostapenko mistreated his subordinates.[5]

Between six and seven people, including a lieutenant colonel of the Soviet Army, were killed on 13 September 1987 when rebels shot down a Su-25 attack aircraft of the 378th Separate Assault Aviation Regiment and an An-26 transport airplane of the Afghan Air Force. Eight Soviet servicemen, including two officers, died, one other soldier was wounded and one more went missing on 15 September 1987. Seven of them died, when a Mi-8 helicopter of the 4th Helicopter Squadron, 50th Separate Mixed Aviation Regiment crashed in Wardak Province. In mid-September 1987, Soviet aircraft conducted a strike on a nomad family in Kandahar Province, killing one woman and wounding eight children. In late September 1987 Soviet aircraft bombed one of the villages in Nangarhar Province, and a nine-year-old boy was killed.

On 2 October 1987 a fight between Afghan troops and Mujahideen erupted in the city of Kandahar. During this skirmish, artillery shells hit a bus carrying a wedding party and three Afghan civilians were killed and six more were wounded. A day later, two Afghan crews flew their Mi-4 helicopters to Pakistan and landed near Chihal. Although both helicopters were subsequently returned to Afghanistan, their crews were granted political asylum. From 6 to 16 October 1987 units of the Soviet Border Troops carried out an operation near the village of Sakhsa Kol in Kunduz Province, 285km (177 miles) north of Kabul. One Soviet serviceman and an unknown number of rebels were killed. On 9 October 1987 an explosion occurred in the city of Kabul and 27 people were killed.

The same day Soviet helicopters conducted a strike near one of the villages in Kunar Province, killing eight people. Three Soviet servicemen, including the commander of the 1179th Guards Artillery Regiment of the 103rd GAD, Lieutenant Colonel Yuri Kalinin, died on that day in other parts of the country. On 10 October 1987 Soviet soldiers burnt a bus carrying 29 Afghan civilians, near the town of Khushi in Logar Province, 60km (37 miles) south of Kabul, in retaliation for a Mujahideen attack on a Soviet unit that had been carried out at the same location the day before.

A soldier of the 2nd MRBn of the 181st MRR, 108th MRD, serving his 82mm mortar at the central outpost in 1987. (181msp.ru)

From 16 to 28 October 1987 units of the Soviet Border Troops carried out an operation in Kunduz Province. At least seven insurgents were killed and one more was taken prisoner. Twenty Soviet servicemen died on 21 October 1987: 18 of them, including 12 officers (three of whom were lieutenant colonels), when an An-12B transport of the 1st Aviation Squadron, 50th Separate Mixed Aviation Regiment collided with a Mi-24 helicopter at Kabul Air Base.

From 21 October to 2 November 1987 Soviet servicemen killed 206 Afghan civilians, including women, children and elderly people, in Logar Province, and more than 1,000 houses were destroyed. Nine servicemen of the Soviet Army, one lieutenant colonel of the Soviet Border Troops, one KGB officer and a woman civilian contractor died on 22 October 1987. Ten of them, including five officers of the Soviet Army, a KGB officer and a woman civilian contractor, were killed when rebels shot down an An-26 transport aircraft of the 2nd Aviation Squadron, 50th Separate Mixed Aviation Regiment near Jalalabad Air Base.

Spetsnaz Ambushes in Kubay and Duri

In October 1987 two major actions involving Soviet Army Spetsnaz took place. On 23 October the 3rd Spetsnaz Company of the 173rd Separate Spetsnaz Detachment of the 22nd Separate Spetsnaz Brigade, under the command of the deputy commander of the 173rd Detachment Major Vladimir Udovichenko, was to eliminate a rebel group near the city of Kandahar. The officers decided to organise an ambush in the abandoned village of Kubay, 460km (286 miles) south-west of Kabul. On the night of 23/24 October the 3rd Company investigated the settlement and dug-in there. When the resistance fighters, who were, according to some sources, also looking for the Soviet commandos,[6] entered Kubay a serious engagement, lasting for five hours, broke out. Soviet soldiers reportedly killed at least 34 Mujahideen and wounded 60 more, and left nine men dead on the field, including Major Udovichenko, and suffered a further between 11 and 17 wounded.

A week later another clash occurred near the border village of Duri in Zabul Province, 310km (193 miles) south-west of Kabul. In late October 1987 the 4th Group of the 2nd Reconnaissance Company, 186th Separate Spetsnaz Detachment, 22nd Separate Spetsnaz Brigade, under the command of Senior Lieutenant Oleg Onishchuk, was ordered to arrange an ambush on a caravan road near Duri. In the evening of 29 October, the group reached the settlement and organised the first ambush – it was ineffective. Twenty-four hours later commandos organised a second ambush. Sometime later a caravan of three trucks appeared on the road. The soldiers hit one of them, while the two others drove away. On the night of 31 October Senior Lieutenant Onishchuk decided to examine the disabled vehicle. There are two versions of what happened next. According to the first one, Onishchuk ordered four soldiers to cover them from a neighbouring hill, and then he and six other soldiers approached the truck, but they were ambushed and put up a fierce fight for 15 minutes, as a result of which they and then the soldiers on the hill were killed; Senior Lieutenant Onishchuk and Junior Sergeant Yuri Islamov blew themselves up with grenades, killing reportedly at least 100 Mujahideen and wounding an unknown number in

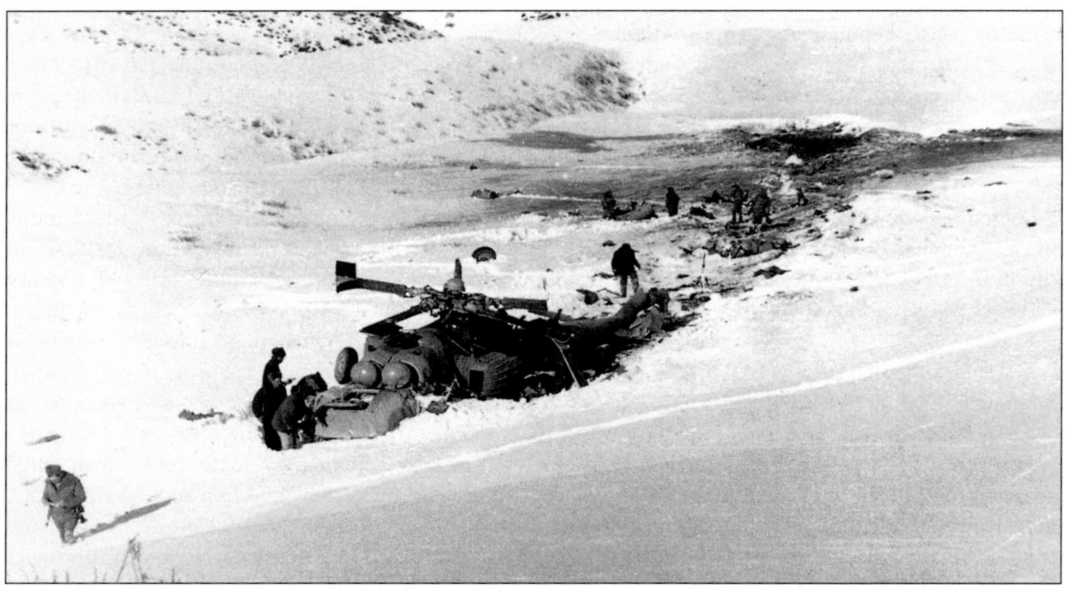

Soviet troops inspecting the wreckage of a downed Mi-8MTV assault helicopter, in early 1988. (Pit Weinert Collection)

addition.[7] According to the second version, Soviet servicemen were also ambushed near the truck, but were killed with knives, and then the covering group on the hill with Senior Lieutenant Onishchuk was killed after a brief shootout, and Onishchuk and Islamov did not blow themselves up with grenades.[8]

Operation Magistral

Ten Soviet servicemen, including three officers, died on 30 October 1987. On 9 November 1987 a Sukhoi Su-25 mistakenly attacked a Soviet outpost near the village of Sufiyan-e Pa'in in Parwan Province, 50km (31 miles) north of Kabul, and either seven or eight soldiers were killed.

From 23 November 1987 to 10 January 1988 40th Army carried out Operation Magistral ('Highway' in Russian) to relieve the city of Khost, besieged by Mujahideen and the Jadran Tribe, involving:

- 66th Separate MRBr
- 56th Separate Guards AABr
- 191st Separate MRR
- 345th Separate GAR
- 45th Separate Engineering Regiment
- 103rd Separate Signal Regiment
- 180th MRR, 108th MRD

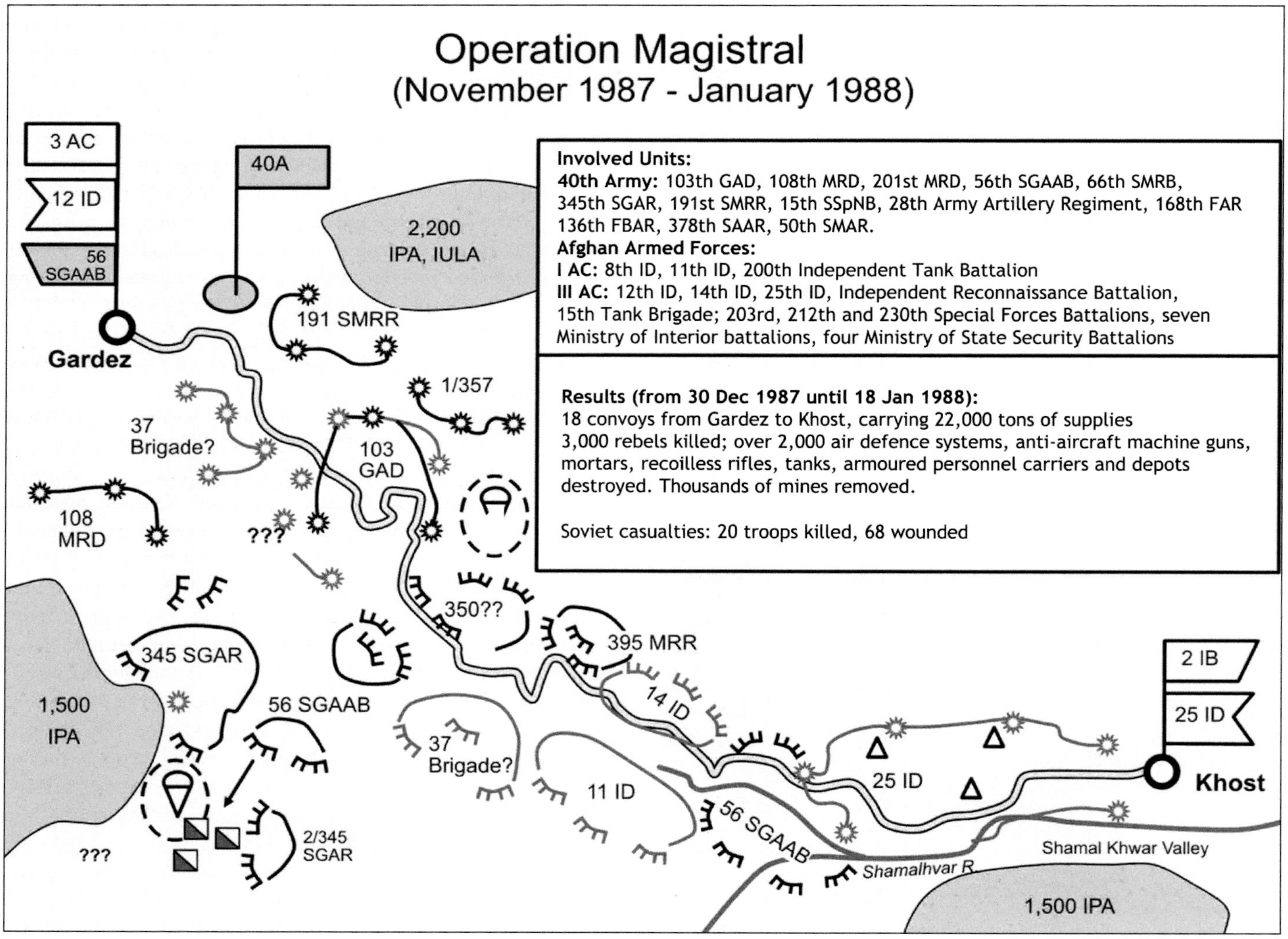

Operation Magistral
(November 1987 - January 1988)
3 AC
12 ID
56 SGAAB
40A
2,200
IPA, IULA
Involved Units:
40th Army: 103th GAD, 108th MRD, 201st MRD, 56th SGAAB, 66th SMRB, 345th SGAR, 191st SMRR, 15th SSpNB, 28th Army Artillery Regiment, 168th FAR 136th FBAR, 378th SAAR, 50th SMAR.
Afghan Armed Forces:
I AC: 8th ID, 11th ID, 200th Independent Tank Battalion
III AC: 12th ID, 14th ID, 25th ID, Independent Reconnaissance Battalion, 15th Tank Brigade; 203rd, 212th and 230th Special Forces Battalions, seven Ministry of Interior battalions, four Ministry of State Security Battalions
Results (from 30 Dec 1987 until 18 Jan 1988):
18 convoys from Gardez to Khost, carrying 22,000 tons of supplies
3,000 rebels killed; over 2,000 air defence systems, anti-aircraft machine guns, mortars, recoilless rifles, tanks, armoured personnel carriers and depots destroyed. Thousands of mines removed.
Soviet casualties: 20 troops killed, 68 wounded
191 SMRR
Gardez
1/357
37 Brigade?
103 GAD
108 MRD
???
350??
395 MRR
345 SGAR
14 ID
2 IB
25 ID
1,500 IPA
56 SGAAB
37 Brigade?
11 ID
25 ID
Khost
2/345 SGAR
???
56 SGAAB
Shamalhvar R
Shamal Khwar Valley
1,500 IPA

The Soviet Army's Operation Magistral, which ran from November 1987 until January 1988. (Map by Mark Thompson)

Commander of the tank battalion of the 181st MRR, 108th MRD, the town of Bagram, Parwan Province, 1988. (181msp.ru)

- 181st MRR, 108th MRD
- 1074th Artillery Regiment, 108th MRD
- 781st Separate Reconnaissance Battalion, 108th MRD
- 149th Guards MRR, 201st MRD
- 395th MRR, 201st MRD
- 783rd Separate Reconnaissance Battalion, 201st MRD
- 317th GAR, 103rd GAD
- 350th GAR, 103rd GAD
- 357th GAR, 103rd GAD
- 1179th Guards Artillery Regiment, 103rd GAD
- 742nd Separate Guards Signal Battalion, 103rd GAD

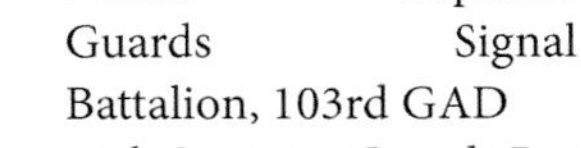

- 80th Separate Guards Reconnaissance Company, 103rd GAD

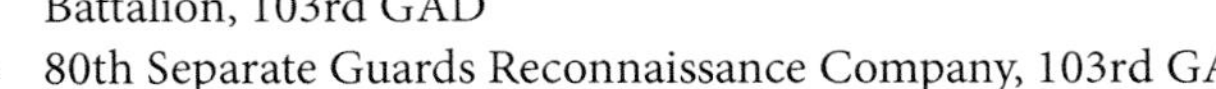

- 334th Separate Spetsnaz Detachment, 15th Separate Spetsnaz Brigade
- 668th Separate Spetsnaz Detachment, 15th Separate Spetsnaz Brigade
- some units and formations of the 1st and 3rd Army Corps, Afghan Army
- 15th Tank Brigade, Afghan Army
- 37th Commando Brigade, Afghan Army
- 666th Commando Regiment, Afghan Army
- 203rd Special Forces Battalion, Afghan Army

A street scene in Asadabad, in 1986. (ArtOfWar – Vladimir Lebedenko)

There were rumours that the new commander of the army, Boris Gromov, being promoted to lieutenant general, was to receive a Gold Star of the Hero of the Soviet Union for this operation. Before the offensive, there were negotiations with some of the Afghan rebel commanders that were blockading the town: although conducted for several weeks, these failed. There is a story that the Soviet Command paid the rebel commanders, and that they agreed to lift the siege of Khost for two weeks, but that the environment of the town was so heavily mined that when Afghan and Soviet troops attempted to reach it, many of them were killed.

Eventually, massive formations of Soviet and Afghan ground forces advanced from Kabul in the direction of Khost over the course of a month, and the first convoy entered the town on 30 December 1987. Gromov's offensive proved very costly for both sides: between 24 and 33 Soviet soldiers, 300 Afghan servicemen and between 150 and 300 insurgents were killed during this operation and 56 Soviet soldiers and 700 Afghan soldiers were wounded. One Mi-8 helicopter of the 4th Helicopter Squadron, 50th Separate Mixed Aviation Regiment was shot down.

One of the notable clashes of this operation – the Battle for Hill 3234, between the towns of Gardez and Khost – was fought on 7 and 8 January 1988, when the 9th Airborne Company of the 3rd ABn of the 345th Separate GAR, under the command of the deputy commander of the 9th Company Senior Lieutenant Sergei Tkachyov, made a heliborne landing near the peak. Their task was to create a strongpoint from which they could observe and control the road below their position and thus secure it for the safe passage of convoys. Shortly after landing, around noon on 7 January, they were attacked by rebels, who were trying, unsuccessfully, to drive the Soviet airborne troops from their positions. The fighting went on, with the Soviets counting a total of 12 assaults on their position by the following morning. By then, five of the airborne soldiers and, reportedly, up to 250 Mujahideen had been killed: the Mujahideen acknowledged losing only 10. Another Soviet soldier died in a

Undeclared Air War

Ever since the number of V-VS units assigned to the 40th Army began increasing in 1981, and they expanded their operations ever closer to the border with Pakistan, and then undertook air strikes on refugee camps and the training camps for the Mujahideen maintained by the ISI inside that country, tensions in the sky along the borders between Afghanistan and Pakistan increased exponentially. The Pakistan Air Force initially reacted by deploying forward its Shenyang F-6 interceptors from Peshawar air base. For example, it is known that the F-6 equipped No.15 Squadron of the Pakistan Air Force served a tour at Peshawar in 1982–1983; it was replaced by No.23 Squadron; in turn was replaced by No.17 Squadron, and in October 1984, No.26 Squadron arrived, also equipped with F-6s. However, the majority of Soviet incursions were relatively shallow: targeting positions as little as two or three kilometres inside Pakistan. Moreover, the Pakistan Air Force's radar network along the border with Afghanistan was poor, and the service usually scrambled its interceptors too late to catch Soviet jets violating Pakistani airspace. Finally, before securing full US support, the Pakistani government was not keen to provoke the USSR, and thus its pilots were strictly prohibited from opening fire. Unsurprisingly, when a Sukhoi Su-22 fighter-bomber of the Afghan Air Force crashed outside the village of Dal Bandin on 20 November 1983; a MiG-17 crash-landed at Mushab on 25 March 1984; and when an Afghan crew landed its Mi-25 inside Pakistan on 16 July 1984, Pakistan Air Force interceptors were nowhere near.

The situation changed only in November 1985, when the Soviets intensified their operations against the Mujahideen bases along the border with Pakistan. Heavily supported by tactical aircraft, the offensives in question put the rebels under severe pressure and cost them numerous positions. Until that point in time, the Pakistan Air Force interceptors were operating under peacetime rules of engagement, by which they always had to remain inside Pakistani airspace and first had to identify any foreign aircraft before asking for permission to engage. Due to the significant increase in the number of Afghan and Soviet violations of Pakistani airspace, the government in Islamabad took the decision to adapt. Starting in early 1986, flights of Dassault Mirage IIIEP and Mirage 5P interceptors from No.5 and No.18 Squadrons regularly rotated to Peshawar, in addition to the F-6s, and their pilots were granted permission to open fire provided this was confirmed by ground control.

On 11 February 1986, a pair of F-6s encountered a total of eight MiG-23MLDs of the V-VS, but the Soviets withdrew into Afghan airspace before either side could open fire. The first time the Pakistan Air Force pilots opened fire at Soviet and Afghan aircraft inside Pakistani airspace was on 12 April 1986, during the Soviet-Afghan offensive in the Zhawar area. On that occasion, a pair of F-6s intercepted a formation of Soviet Su-25s. However, both of the AIM-9P Sidewinders they fired were released well outside their engagement envelopes and missed their targets. Four days later, Pakistani Mirages were more successful: on 16 April 1986, they claimed an Afghan MiG-21 as shot down. This claim was followed by another one, from 10 May 1986. Interestingly, although both incidents were widely reported in the Pakistani press, neither was ever officially confirmed by Islamabad.

Meanwhile, in December 1981, Washington decided to sponsor the delivery of 40 General Dynamics F-16 fighter-bombers to

hospital several days later, while 29 – and an unknown number of insurgents – were wounded.

Minor Offensives in Faryab and Kandahar

From 26 November to 14 December 1987 units of the Soviet Border Troops stormed a Mujahideen base in Faryab Province: one Soviet serviceman and reportedly at least 23 insurgents were killed, several other Soviet servicemen and four Afghan servicemen were wounded and three rebels were taken prisoner, one Mil Mi-8 helicopter was shot down. Nine Soviet servicemen, including three officers, were killed on 27 November 1987. Seven of them died when guerrillas shot down a Mil Mi-8 helicopter of the 2nd Helicopter Squadron, 335th Separate Combat Helicopter Regiment near the city of Asadabad. A fierce fight erupted in Deh-e Sabz District of Kabul Province on 18 December 1987, and 13 or 14 Soviet servicemen were reportedly killed.

From 25 December 1987 to 5 January 1988 the Soviet Command carried out an operation in Daman District of Kandahar Province, involving the 70th Separate Guards MRBr and the 371st Guards MRR of the 5th Guards MRD. Five soldiers and officers were killed in several clashes and at least two more soldiers were wounded.

Islamabad: the first of an eventual 28 F-16A single-seater and 12 F-16B two-seaters reached Pakistan in October 1982. The first two F-16 squadrons of the Pakistan Air Force, No.9 and No.11 Squadrons, were operational by 1985, and the following year Islamabad made the decision to adapt the rules of engagement for its pilots. Henceforth, they were granted permission to not only open fire at any Afghan or Soviet aircraft violating Pakistani airspace, but also to fly over Afghanistan. On 17 May 1986, when Soviet and Afghan aircraft bombed camps up to 10km deep inside north-west Pakistan, a pair of F-16As intercepted a formation of Su-22M-3s of the Democratic Republic of Afghanistan Air Force, and claimed one as shot down by a combination of AIM-9L Sidewinder air-to-air missiles and fire from their 20mm guns. On 19 June 1986, a pair of F-16As from No.9 Squadron, Pakistan Air Force, intercepted a formation of Soviet MiG-23MLDs: although reaching a favourable position behind their opponents, the Pakistani pilots failed to fire because of several technical malfunctions.

On 30 March 1987, Pakistani ground control vectored two F-16As into an attack on a transport aircraft assumed to be equipped for electronic intelligence gathering, airborne west of Parachinar. One of the aircraft approached the target and claimed it was shot down by a single AIM-9L Sidewinder air-to-air missile. While the Pakistanis celebrated a victory, the aircraft in question turned out to have been an An-26 of the 373rd Transport Aviation Regiment of the Afghan Air Force, approaching Khost airport: all 39 (or 40) occupants were killed. Two weeks later, on 16 April 1987, two F-16As of the third Pakistan Air Force unit operating this type, No.14 Squadron, were vectored to intercept a formation of Su-22s of the Afghan Air Force bombing a camp inside Pakistan. The leader of the Pakistan Air Force formation fired two AIM-9L Sidewinders, claiming two enemy fighters as shot down. Actually, he downed only one; Lieutenant Colonel Abdul Jameel ejected safely and landed by parachute well inside Afghanistan.

Throughout early 1987, Islamabad officially reported nearly 100 airspace violations by Afghan and Soviet aircraft. In reply, the commander of the Democratic Republic of Afghanistan Air Force, Lieutenant General Abdul Kadir, claimed 30 violations by Pakistani aircraft. Although ignored in the West, Kadir's report was confirmed on 29 April 1987, when a pair of F-16As from No.9 Squadron intercepted a formation of MiG-23MLDs from the 120th Fighter Aviation Regiment, led by Lieutenant Colonel Pochitalkin in a mission to mine one of the paths used by caravans transhipping supplies from ISI bases in Pakistan to the Djaware area. Approaching undetected, the F-16s caught the Soviets by surprise, as they were flying a shallow dive to deploy their KMGU cluster bomb containers: the lead Pakistani aircraft released a single AIM-9L. However, as the Soviet formation then made a climbing turn to return to higher altitude, the Pakistani Number 2 flew in between it and the approaching missile and was hit by the Sidewinder. Flight Lieutenant Shahid Sikander was left with no choice but to eject from the F-16A serial number 85-720. He descended on a parachute deep into Afghanistan, but landed safely within an area controlled by the Mujahideen and was subsequently returned to Pakistan – together with many parts of his aircraft, including an AIM-9L still attached to its rail. Combined with the warnings from Moscow in reaction to the ISI-instigated Mujahideen attack on Panj in the USSR, this faux-paus prompted Islamabad to curtail further incursions of its F-16s into Afghan airspace. Indeed, no confirmed aerial incidents are known to have occurred for over a year.

11
1988–1989

Unknown to most of the participants, 1988 was to see the first phase of the Soviet withdrawal from Afghanistan. On 14 April 1988 the Geneva Accords on Afghanistan were signed by representatives of the governments of Afghanistan and Pakistan. The Minister of Foreign Affairs of the USSR, Eduard Shevardnadze, and the United States Secretary of State, George Shultz, were the co-guarantors of the Accords. Soviet troops had to be withdrawn from Afghanistan within nine months, beginning on 15 May 1988, and then in two stages: the first stage, from 15 May to 15 August 1988, and the second stage, from 15 August 1988 to 15 February 1989.

A Soviet Il-76 transport deploying flares while on approach to Kabul International in late 1987. (Mark Lepko Collection)

The 40th Army had already made the first move in April, when it withdrew the garrison of Barikot to Jalalabad. Through late May 1988, other Soviet units withdrew from south and

A column of BTR-70s from the 3rd MRBn, 181st MRR, 108th MRD, underway in 1988. (181msp.ru)

A gunner of the 2nd MRBn, 181st MRR, 108th MRD, on his 2S3 152mm calibre howitzer at the 1-A outpost in 1988. (181msp.ru)

south-west Afghanistan. In turn, Moscow initiated a massive airlift to significantly bolster the arsenals of the government in Kabul, delivering hundreds of thousands of additional arms, ammunition, equipment, and supplies. Meanwhile, and although withdrawing from a number of other bases, Soviet troops continued to operate all over the country.

On the Defensive

In January 1988 Soviet and Afghan servicemen blew up 12 captured Mujahideen in a mosque in one of the villages in Paktia Province; nine were killed and three survived. Seven Soviet servicemen, including four officers, died on 17 January 1988. Twelve Soviet servicemen, including seven officers, and one female civilian contractor, died on 21 January 1988. Three Soviet soldiers were killed and the deputy commander of the 101st MRR of the 5th Guards MRD, Lieutenant Colonel Valeri Babich, was wounded on 29 January. Nine Soviet servicemen, including two officers, died on 31 January 1988. Fourteen Soviet servicemen, including six officers, died on 6 February 1988. On 11 February 1988 Sayd Bahauddin Majrooh, Director of the Afghan Information Centre, an Afghan independent media outlet, was assassinated in his home in the city of Peshawar in Pakistan. On 12 February 1988 Soviet helicopters carried out a strike near the village of Shiwu Kala in Laghman Province, 70km (43 miles) east of Kabul; 23 people were killed. On 11 March 1988 Soviet troops conducted air and artillery strikes near the village of Chichkah in Kunduz Province, 280km (174 miles) north of Kabul, killing an unknown number of people. Eight Soviet servicemen, including the commander of the 4th MRBn, 70th Separate Guards MRBr, Lieutenant Colonel Konstantin Lyashenko, died on 4 April 1988. Six Soviet servicemen, including two officers, died, and one more soldier went missing on 9 April 1988. On 12 April 1988 Soviet artillery shelled the vicinity of the town of Rustaq in Takhar Province, 295km (183 miles) north of Kabul, killing an unknown number of people.

Eight servicemen of the Soviet Army, including the deputy commander of the 682nd MRR, 108th MRD – Lieutenant Colonel Mikhail Krivorotko, and two soldiers of the Soviet Border Troops died on 26 April 1988. On 27 April 1988 a bomb exploded in Kabul and six people were killed. On 13 May 1988 a Soviet convoy was ambushed near the town of Marmul in Balkh Province, 280km (174 miles) north-west of Kabul. Six servicemen of the Soviet Border Troops and two Mujahideen were killed in the ensuing clash, and another Soviet serviceman was wounded. Nine Soviet servicemen died on 25 May 1988. Seven of them, including five officers, died in the Soviet Union, when a Mil Mi-8 helicopter of the 2nd Helicopter Squadron, 335th Separate Combat Helicopter Regiment crashed in Saratov Oblast en route from Afghanistan. Three Soviet servicemen, including two lieutenant colonels, military advisers, were killed when rebels shot up a BTR APC in Kandahar Province on 30 May 1988. Two more Soviet servicemen, including a lieutenant colonel, also a military adviser, were taken prisoner and later killed. The fifth and the last of the Soviet Generals to do so died in Afghanistan on 2 June 1988. The adviser to the commander of the

By the summer of 1988, the threat of Mujaheddin Stinger teams attacking transport aircraft and civilian airliners was high enough for every aircraft taking off or landing to receive escort in the form of Mi-24 helicopters equipped with flare dispensers. This Il-76 of Aeroflot – although probably in service with the Transport Aviation of the V-VS – was photographed taking off, escorted by a Mi-24. (Efim Sandler Collection)

A trio of 9P140 Uragan (also known as BM-27) 220mm multiple rocket launchers in position, waiting for the order to open fire. (Efim Sandler Collection)

A convoy of the 181st MRR (108th MRD), led by a ZSU-23-4, travelling along the road connecting Kabul with Jalalabad in 1987. (181msp.ru)

Artillery of the Armed Forces of the Republic of Afghanistan, Major General Leonid Tsukanov, died in Kabul, officially of disease.

The Hot Summer of 1988

Thirteen Soviet servicemen, including five officers, died on 24 June 1988. Six of them, including the commander of the 1st Helicopter Squadron, 50th Separate Mixed Aviation Regiment, Lieutenant Colonel Alexander Kosyanenko, were killed when insurgents shot down an Antonov An-26 aircraft at Bagram Air Base. Seven Soviet servicemen, including one officer, died on 26 June 1988, while five Soviet soldiers were killed a day later, and another five – including two officers – were killed on 28 June. Seven Soviet soldiers, including three officers – two of whom were lieutenant colonels, and one female civilian contractor died on 29 June 1988. Three Soviet servicemen, including another lieutenant colonel, were killed, and one more soldier went missing on 6 July 1988. Eleven Soviet servicemen, including three officers, died on 18 July. Six Soviet servicemen, including one officer, died on 24 July. Starting in late July 1988, aircraft of the V-VS were unleashed into a renewed series of strikes on refugee and ISI-controlled training camps inside Pakistan.

On 2 August 1988 a female civilian contractor was killed by a Soviet soldier in the town of Bagram in Parwan Province as the result of a dispute. On 4 August 1988 Alexander Rutskoy, by then promoted to colonel and to deputy commander of the Air Force of the 40th Army, was shot down for the second time, when his jet either mistakenly or intending to bomb refugee camps, entered the air space of Pakistan and was attacked by a Pakistani fighter. The Colonel ejected, but he was taken prisoner. According to some sources, he was exchanged for a large quantity of weapons, including a BMP IFV.[1] Rutskoy returned to the USSR two weeks later, on 20 August.

Rutskoy's Dogfight

Despite the Mujahideen siege of Khost, and the resulting Soviet counteroffensives, the situation in the air along the border between Afghanistan and Pakistan remained relatively quiet for most of 1987 and well into 1988. Arguably, Operation Magistral was supported by Tu-22M-3 medium bombers of the Soviet Strategic Aviation: forward deployed to Mary-2 air base, they targeted rebel positions with all available bomb types up to 3,000 kilogramme FAB-3000M-54s. Because the Tu-22s operated very closely to the Pakistani border, they were supported by four Tu-22PD electronic warfare aircraft of the 341st Bomber Division, forward deployed to Mary-2, as well. Despite claims published in the Pakistani media ever since, the Pakistan Air Force is not known to have ever attempted to disrupt any of the Soviet operations that resulted in the lifting of the siege of Khost in late December 1987. This changed only when the V-VS was unleashed into a renewed series of strikes on refugee camps and ISI-controlled training camps inside Pakistan in late July 1988.

In the late afternoon of 4 August 1988, a section of Su-25s was underway to attack an Afghan refugee camp near Miranshah. Half an hour before sunset they were detected by Pakistani radars, and two F-16As from No.14 Squadron of the Pakistani Air Force were scrambled to intercept. Approaching to about 15 nautical miles from the enemy formation, the pilots were granted permission to open fire, and the leader attacked a single aircraft underway at high altitude. The Soviet pilot of the aircraft in question, Colonel Alexander Rutskoy, was then warned about the approach of two Pakistani interceptors, and made a hard, 6.5G turn into the threat. However, the sky was already dark and he lost the sight of his opponents, which turned even harder: seconds later, his Su-25 was hit by a single AIM-9L Sidewinder. The Su-25 broke into two: the wreckage was found the following morning, but the cockpit was empty. Both the Soviets and Pakistanis initiated a search operation, but Rutskoy was caught by the locals who handed him over to the Pakistani authorities. Under interrogation, the Russian pilot claimed he was shot down by a radar-guided missile fired from the front hemisphere and refused to believe his Su-25 was felled by an AIM-9L actually fired from behind him.

If the clash that resulted in the downing and arrest of Colonel Rutskoy – who was returned to Moscow, a few weeks later – marked the high point of aerial clashes between the V-VS and the Pakistani Air Force, it did not mean their end. On 12 September 1988, a pair of F-16As from No.14 Squadron was vectored to

A row of Su-25 close support aircraft photographed at Bagram Air Base in 1987, together with long rows of UB-32-57 pods for unguided 57mm calibre rockets. (Pit Weinert Collection)

Bloody Withdrawal

On 10 August 1988 a series of explosions and the ensuing huge fire destroyed a Soviet ammunition depot near the city of Pul-e Khumri. Between five and eight Soviet soldiers and one female civilian contractor died and a large number of others were wounded or went missing. A Mil Mi-8 helicopter of the 254th Separate Helicopter Squadron and more than 100 vehicles were destroyed, seven Mil Mi-24 and seven Mil Mi-8 helicopters of the 254th Separate Helicopter Squadron were damaged. According to the official version, the explosions and fire were the result of a rebel shelling of the depot, some witnesses think that the reason that happened was a safety violation during welding operations, but there were rumours that the Soviet Command wrote off stolen and sold shells that way.[2]

On 17 August 1988 the President of the Islamic Republic of Pakistan Muhammad, Zia-ul-Haq, died in a plane crash near the city of Bahawalpur in Pakistan. The aircraft, a Lockheed C-130 Hercules, hit the ground and exploded shortly after take-off. Between 29 and 36 more people, including the United States Ambassador to Pakistan, Arnold Lewis Raphel, the Chairman of the Joint Chiefs of Staff Committee of the Islamic Republic of Pakistan, General Akhtar Abdur Rahman Khan, Chief of the United States Military Mission in Pakistan, Brigadier General Herbert M. Wassom, and a group of senior officers of the Pakistan Army, who were on board the plane, also died. There were several investigations into the causes of this crash, but the exact cause was never officially established. According to some sources, the crash was an assassination organised by the Soviet Union.[3]

intercept a formation of 12 MiG-23MLDs from the 120th Fighter Aviation Regiment approaching the border at an altitude of 10,000 metres (32,808ft). Eight of the MiGs were loaded with bombs and tasked with striking targets in the Kunar Valley, while two pairs acted as escorts. The Soviet ground control detected the Pakistanis in time and advised one pair of escorting MiG-23MLD to block them, while turning the other jets away from the border. Nevertheless, the F-16s decided to engage and their leader locked-on its radar on the leading MiG from a range of 22km (12 nautical miles), from the forward hemisphere. However, the AIM-9L the Pakistani released was decoyed by flares deployed by the two Soviet fighters. The Pakistani attempted twice to achieve a lock-on with his other missile, but without success. Finally, his fourth effort was successful, and he fired again. The missile trailed the MiG-23MLD with bort number 55, piloted by Captain Sergey Privalov, and – decoyed by additional flares – detonated above the target, spraying it with shrapnel, but failing to cause enough damage to bring it down. The Soviet pair then turned west, covered by the other pair of escorting MiG-23MLDs, the pilots of which attempted to achieve a lock-on on the two disengaging Pakistani fighters and attack them with R-24 missiles, but without success. Privalov managed to land his MiG-23MLD in Bagram, however the jet suffered additional damage when the nose leg of its undercarriage collapsed. Curiously, the Pakistanis subsequently claimed two kills against Soviet MiG-23MLDs, and their lead F-16 pilot was credited with these. Indeed, the US officials that reviewed the video- and radar recordings of this engagement, 'confirmed' two aerial victories for the Pakistani Air Force. However, an extensive search by the Mujahideen and ISI operatives provided no trace of any kind of wreckage: the official explanation was that this was scattered over much too wide an area, which was mined. Unsurprisingly, Moscow found it rather easy to deny suffering any kind of losses.

The Soviets were keen to exact their revenge but never found a suitable opportunity. Nevertheless, another incident occurred on 3 November 1988, when a pair of F-16s from No.14 Squadron was vectored to intercept a formation of Afghan MiG-21s and Su-22s approaching the border. As the Pakistanis approached, the ground control advised the Afghan pilots to make a 180-degrees turn, and they did so, but too late: the F-16s were much too close. Therefore, the leader of the Democratic Republic of Afghanistan Air Force formation, Captain Abdul Hashim, made another turn, and attempted to confront the nearest enemy. To his misfortune, his opponents were armed with AIM-9Ls that had a front-aspect capability, and one of two missiles fired by the lead Pakistani jet disabled his Sukhoi. Hashim ejected and was captured by the Pakistani Army: his jet crashed no less than 18km (9.7 nautical miles) east of the border.

A MiG-23MLD of the 655th Fighter Aviation Regiment, photographed high above Afghanistan, armed with R-24R (ASCC/NATO reporting name 'AA-7 Apex'; nearest the camera, installed underwing) and R-60M ('AA-8 Aphid') air-to-air missiles. Noticeable is the installation of large chaff and flare dispensers on top of the centre fuselage, in front of the fin. (Pit Weinert Collection)

Ten Soviet soldiers died on 20 August 1988, eight of them belonging to the Engineering Company of the 345th Separate GAR were killed in a single explosion near the town of Baghlan. In September 1988 Soviet troops stormed a rebel base located near the city of Maidan Shahr. In September and October 1988, 22 Afghan servicemen were killed by guerrillas in the town of Asmar in Kunar Province after they had surrendered. Ten Soviet servicemen, including four officers, died on 4 September 1988. On 26 September 1988, a pair of MiG-23MLDs from the 120th Guards Fighter Aviation Regiment, V-VS was scrambled in reaction to reports about the activity of Iranian helicopters along the border. Eventually, Major Vladimir Astakhov and Captain Boris Gavrilov detected two Bell AH-1J Cobra attack helicopters, about 75km south-east of Shindand, and claimed both as shot down with R-24R missiles.

The final few Months

Seven Soviet servicemen, including one officer, died on 20 October 1988. From 21 to 28 October 1988 the Soviet Command carried out the last major offensive in Afghanistan, near the Kajaki Reservoir in Helmand Province, 450km (280 miles) southwest of Kabul. The units involved were the 371st Guards MRR, 1060th Guards Artillery Regiment and the 650th Separate Reconnaissance Battalion, all of the 5th Guards MRD. Six Soviet soldiers and at least three insurgents were killed.

From 23 October to 7 November 1988 the Mujahideen carried out Operation Ghashey ('Arrow' in Pashto) in Laghman Province.

Two TOS-1 Buratino multiple rocket launchers, moving along a road, escorted by two BMP–2Ds and three BTR-70s of the 345th Separate GAR, during Operation Tayfun, undertaken from 23 to 26 January 1989. (Efim Sandler Collection)

Another view of an early TOS-1 vehicle together with BMP-2Ds of the 345th Separate GAR, in Parwan Province in January 1989. (Efim Sandler Collection)

TOS-1 and BTR-70s photographed during Operation Tayfun. This offensive saw the first combat deployment of the TOS-1. (Efim Sandler Collection)

A Su-17M-4 of the 302nd Fighter-Bomber Aviation Regiment: this unit was deployed at Kokayty Air Base in late 1988 in the Turkmen SSR, to provide cover for Soviet ground units withdrawing from Afghanistan. (Pit Weinert Collection)

An An-26 transport of the 382nd Transport Aviation Regiment, Democratic Republic of Afghanistan Air Force, seen at Kabul International Airport in the early 1980s. Visible in the rear is a Mi-4 helicopter of the 377th Separate Helicopter Regiment. (Pit Weinert Collection)

Its objective was to seize and hold part of the Kabul – Jalalabad Road for two months and to prevent the arrival of reinforcements for the Afghan Army in Jalalabad, because the Soviet troops had already withdrawn from Nangarhar Province. The rebels at first advanced for a week, capturing a number of Afghan Army outposts, and then defended them for one more week; after which they ambushed a large military convoy. Eighteen guerrillas were killed, 53 other insurgents were wounded and 223 Afghan servicemen were taken prisoner.

From 3 to 11 November 1988, 79 Afghan servicemen were killed by rebels near the Torkham Border Crossing in Nangarhar Province, 180km (112 miles) south-east of Kabul, after they had surrendered.

On 13 November 1988 guerrillas shelled Kabul Airport with surface-to-surface rockets, killing 11 Soviet servicemen, mostly pilots of the 4th Helicopter Squadron, 50th Separate Mixed Aviation Regiment, and one civilian contractor. On 19 November 1988 Soviet helicopters carried out a strike near the village of Darakht-e Tut in Herat Province, 720km (447 miles) west of Kabul, and killed 12 people.

In December 1988, when amid the Soviet withdrawal, the Mujahideen threatened the hydro-electric power plant south-west of Kabul, the 40th Army requested air strikes by all available aircraft. Dozens of fighter-bombers from Bagram, Mazar-e-Sharif and even Shindand, and also Tu-22M-3 bombers from Mary-2 joined the fight. The sky was so packed with aircraft, that several times, collisions were avoided only narrowly. Guided by two An-30 reconnaissance aircraft of the 50th Separate Long Range Reconnaissance Squadron (an element of the 50th Mixed Aviation Regiment), and despite 4,000–5,000-metre-high mountains (13,120–16,400 feet) around the Afghan capital, they continued striking the rebels until they gave up.

Although withdrawing from Afghanistan, according to the official statistics, the Soviet forces had 47 officers and men killed in January 1989 and 21 more servicemen in February 1989. In early January 1989 several Afghan servicemen and 22 women were killed by insurgents in Nangarhar Province. On 13 and 14 January 1989 a group of Mujahideen, including Arab volunteers, massacred most of the inhabitants of the village of Kuhnah Deh in Nangarhar Province, 130km (81 miles) east of Kabul. From 20 January to 24 January 1989 rebels shelled Kandahar Airport and shot down an An-12 of the 930th Military Transport Aviation Regiment.

From 23 January to 26 January 1989 Soviet Command carried out Operation Tayfun (Typhoon in Russian). Artillery and aircraft bombed villages around the Salang Pass, according to the official version, to provide cover for the withdrawing units and formations. Depending on the source, between 600 and 1,500 Afghan civilians were killed. Four Soviet servicemen, including three officers with the commander of the 50th Separate Mixed Aviation Regiment, Colonel Alexander Golovanov, died on 1 February 1989. On 15 February 1989 the last Soviet Army unit, the 1st MRBn of the 180th MRR, 108th MRD, was withdrawn from Afghanistan. Lieutenant General Boris Gromov crossed the border bridge over the Panj River on foot after the last armoured personnel carrier. At least for the Union of Soviet Socialist Republics, the War in Afghanistan was officially over.

12 CONCLUSIONS

Depending on the source, between 13,835 and 30,000 officers and men of the Soviet Army, the Soviet Border Troops and KGB, between 18,000 and 58,951 Afghan soldiers, up to 90,000 Mujahideen and between 562,000 and 2,000,000 Afghan civilians – including at least 20,700 children – died during the Soviet-Afghan War. Between 17,892 and 53,753 Soviet officers and men, 77,000 Afghan soldiers, between 17,000 and 75,000 resistance fighters and at least 1,500,000 Afghan civilians suffered wounds of varying degrees of severity. Four hundred and fifteen thousand, nine hundred and thirty-two Soviet servicemen suffered from various diseases. Between 264 and 417 Soviet servicemen went missing or were captured, between 119 and 130 of them were released. Between 5,000,000 and 10,000,000 Afghan men, women and children became refugees.

The Soviet Army lost between 147 and 385 tanks, between 1,314 and 2,530 AFVs, 433 artillery guns and mortars, 11,369 trucks, between 103 and 122 aircraft and between 267 and 340 helicopters. The Afghan Army lost 362 tanks, 804 AFVs, 120 aircraft and 169 helicopters. Between one-third and one-half of all of the settlements in Afghanistan were destroyed. Afghan citizens lost their homes, property and fields. At the end, large numbers of uncleared mines still littered the countryside.

Around 620,000 Soviet service personnel took part in the war. Thousands of them returned to Soviet towns and villages disabled, and the authorities did not always provide them with the right kind of care. Thousands more returned physically healthy, but with serious mental problems, with a lot of experience in killing and torturing, including killing of women and children. They entered mental hospitals, drank and died, and many of them forever stayed in a life of crime.

Afghanistan is still at war, and for more than 40 years, generations of people, who saw nothing except war, have grown up in this country.

The Soviet-Afghan War is often compared to the Vietnam War, one can even see expressions such as 'Soviet Vietnam', 'our Vietnam' and similar. At first sight, there really are several grounds for this comparison – the war between a large, developed country and a small, underdeveloped country, the war between a country with a continental climate and a country with a hot climate, the guerrilla war between a regular army and irregular armed formations, many young men involved in fighting and many young men returning home in coffins. But if you look closely at these two wars, it turns out that they are completely different.

First and foremost, the United States of America really helped the South Vietnamese, no matter what anybody says. The people of South Vietnam defended themselves from their enemies. Many American soldiers and officers did not know what they were doing in Vietnam, maybe not all South Vietnamese wanted those foreign troops in their country, but the American government did well. There is a theory that the Vietnam War was launched in the interests of the Soviet Union and even on the direct orders of the Soviet leaders; because they knew that the United States had a security treaty with South Vietnam and would send their troops to defend the country if it suffered aggression, and the Soviet leaders wanted to draw the USA into a war so that the country would waste money that was allegedly intended to otherwise strike against the USSR (through military and economic means). But it is just a theory, as some researchers say – 'a conspiracy theory.' Anyway, the United States helped the countries in South-East Asia to fight communist expansion. The Soviet Union in Afghanistan helped only its own puppet government, and it helped it to fight against its own people.

Secondly, the United States of America were not alone. The forces of several countries fought in the Vietnam War. The Soviet Union was not just alone in Afghanistan, its actions were condemned by dozens of countries across the world, they were explicitly named as an aggressor and occupier, and many countries imposed sanctions against the USSR.

Thirdly, the Soviet Union supplied North Vietnam much more than the United States supplied the Afghan Mujahideen, and it did that in an entirely official way. Thousands of Soviet officers and soldiers were in North Vietnam for years. It was much harder for the United States to fight against North Vietnamese troops and guerrillas both militarily, and the most important thing, politically,

A destroyed BMP-2D IFV of the Reconnaissance Company of the 149th Guards MRR of the 201st MRD, the location and year are unknown. (Kunduz.ru)

A BTR-70 (closest to the camera) and two BTR-80s, probably of the 181st MRR on approach to a bridge on the Amu Darya River, photographed during the withdrawal from Afghanistan. (Efim Sandler Collection)

Helsinki Watch in its first report about the Soviet-Afghan War cited one of the former servicemen of the 40th Army:

> We were ordered by our officers that when we attack a village, not one person must be left alive to tell the tale. If we refused to carry out these orders, we got it in the neck ourselves.[1]

Helsinki Watch, the human rights organisation, provides another testimony:

> Sgt Igor Rykov, a defector from the Soviet Army, described the searches conducted by his unit in Kandahar Province: "The officer would decide to have the village searched, and if it was found it contained a single bullet, the officer would say: 'This is a bandit village: it must be destroyed.' The men and young boys would be shot, and the women and small children would be put in a separate room and killed with grenades."[2]

And one more quote from the same report:

> Pvt. Vladislav Naumov, who served in a battalion specialising in punitive expeditions near Jalalabad, Ningrahar Province, described his training in the use of the bayonet to attack villagers: "At Termez [Soviet Uzbekistan, just north of Mazar-e Sharif across Amu Darya (Oxus River)] we built models of Afghan villages. Before every combat exercise, Major Makarov would constantly repeat: 'Look in the direction of the village: there are the dushmans [*dushman* is the Persian word for enemy, used by the Soviet press to refer to the Afghan insurgents]. Forward! Kill them! They kill completely innocent people.' And then the truly punitive operations would start .... Under the cover of the infantry combat vehicles we would raze the village to the ground. Then, working under the scorching sun, we would rebuild the model, all over again .... We had bayonets and silencers attached to our rifles, and we learned to use them pretty skilfully. The major often repeated Suvorov's words: 'The bullet is a fool, the bayonet – a stalwart. Hit with the bayonet and try to turn it around in the body.'"[3]

because any direct clash with Soviet troops risked causing a new world war.

That American servicemen committed war crimes during the Vietnam War is well-known and has been described many times, but it is as nothing compared to what the Soviets did in Afghanistan. Firstly, there were many fewer of these crimes by America troops. Secondly, Soviet troops not only wiped-out entire Afghan settlements together with the inhabitants, if there was a single shot from the direction of some village towards a Soviet convoy, or even if there was the slightest suspicion of sympathy for rebels: they did it on the direct orders of the Soviet Command. There was a saying in the Soviet Army, 'initiative is punishable', and most of the Soviet soldiers, not to mention officers, did not want to take the initiative in anything, the more so in the things, which – even according to Soviet legislation – were subject to severe punishments.

In their second report about the Soviet-Afghan War Helsinki Watch provided the following words of the Afghan refugee:

> They announced it by loudspeaker when the troops came. I heard this from the Russian soldiers, 'We don't need the people, we want the land.'[4]

These were the Soviet State's policies, like selling weapons. Soviet leaders in Moscow and the Soviet Command in Kabul regarded those Afghan citizens, who did not wish to obey them (that means, almost the whole population of the country) as their enemies, and acted accordingly, in the same way as they acted during the Russian Civil War towards the population of their own country, and during many other wars.

And last, but not the least, that the Vietnam War caused a split in American society is another well-known fact. University students demonstrated and protested against the war, other young men refused to join the army. The American media called the officers and soldiers a variety of names and described massacres perpetrated by them. American public figures showed solidarity with the people of Vietnam, and some politicians even called the President of the United States a 'madman.' There is the real story. Maybe there was nothing good about it, but it actually happened. Was there a split in Soviet society because of the Soviet-Afghan War? No! Were there any demonstrations, rallies, marches or at least any public statements? Everyone knows that there was not anything of the kind. But what happened in the Soviet Union in connection with the Soviet-Afghan War? Nothing – nothing at all. There was silence in Soviet society, a silence like the silence of the tomb. One person even said about it that there was no society in the Soviet Union. And it turns out that the American civil society has split into two parts, and was at war with itself, but there was no civil society in the USSR. According to some reports, most of the Soviet people did not know that there was a war in Afghanistan until 1985, and even when they became aware of it, Soviet mothers, receiving bodies of their dead sons, did not demonstrate against the government and did not sign letters of protest.

America was divided, but the Soviet Union collapsed and dissolved.

Many researchers think that the war in Afghanistan was one of the main causes of the dissolution of the Soviet Union. This statement seems to be true, but with one caveat – not so much the war itself, but rather its cost. Soviet leaders were bankrupt with that war, as they were bankrupt with the arms race. The final irony is that the Soviet Union went bankrupt selling weapons.

Have the people who ruled the Soviet Union, learned any lessons from the Soviet-Afghan War? It seems they have not. They did not even acknowledge that there was a war in Afghanistan – soldiers and officers were told about 'international duty,' and the paper said that the army planted trees in the streets of Kabul. Maybe those who rule the Russian Federation now have learned anything? Judging by what they are doing, they understand even less; see the story with the Chechen War. And a lot of them have obviously stated that they wish to recreate that very Soviet Union, having absolutely no idea what kind of country it was, that its collapse and dissolution were only natural and that the Soviet-Afghan War, which was launched by their former bosses, played a major, if not the greatest, role in it.

Igor Bunich wrote,

> Really, Soviet troops, for a reason that even today nobody is able to explain, invaded the neighbouring Muslim country, rampaged there for 10 years, killing one-third of the population and razing roughly a half of the settlements to the ground, were finally knocked out of there by an unconquerable spirit of popular resistance, and, having left this place, decided that the war was now over.[5]

BIBLIOGRAPHY

Alexievich, Svetlana, *Cinkovye mal'chiki* [*Boys in Zinc*] (Moscow: Molodaya Gvardiya, 1989)

Avtorkhanov, Abdurakhman et al., *Vojna v Afganistane* [*The War in Afghanistan*] (Frankfurt/Main: Possev-Verlag, 1981)

Balenko, Sergei, *Afganistan. Chest' imeju!* [*Afghanistan: The Honour Is Mine!*] (Moscow: Algoritm, 2015)

Bobrov, Gleb, *Snajper v Afgane. Porvannye dushi* [*A Sniper in Afghan. Ripped Souls*] (Moscow: Yauza; Eksmo, 2014)

Borovik, Artyom, *Sprjatannaja vojna* [*The Hidden War*] (Moscow: PIK, 1992)

Boyarkin, Sergei, *Soldaty Afganskoj vojny* [*Soldiers of the Afghan War*] (Novosibirsk: Asteiya, 1999)

Braithwaite, Rodric. *Afgan: russkie na vojne* [*Afghan: The Russians at War, 1979–89*] (Moscow: Corpus, 2013)

Bukovsky, Vladimir, *Moskovskij process* [*Judgement in Moscow. Moscow*] (Paris: MIK; Russkaya Mysl, 1996)

Bunich, Igor, *Hronika Chechenskoj bojni i Shest' dnej v Budennovske* [*Chronicle of the Chechen Massacre and Six Days in Budyonnovsk*] (Saint-Petersburg: Oblik, 1995)

Bunich, Igor, *Mech Prezidenta (v sbornike «Poligon satany»)* [*Sword of the President* (in *The Satan's Testing Ground. A Collection)*] (Saint-Petersburg: Shans, 1994)

Bunich, Igor, *Zoloto partii (v sbornike «Poligon satany»)* [*The Party Gold* (in *The Satan's Testing Ground. A Collection)*] (Saint-Petersburg: Shans, 1994)

Chikishev, Alexei, *Specnaz v Afganistane* [*Spetsnaz in Afghanistan*] (Moscow: Veche, 2018)

Drogovoz, Igor, *Tankovyj mech Strany Sovetov* [*The Tank Sword of the Soviet Country*] (Minsk: Harvest, 2004)

Drogovoz, Igor, *Vozdushnyj shhit Strany Sovetov* [*The Air Shield of the Soviet Country*] (Minsk: Harvest, 2007)

Feifer, Gregory, *Bol'shaja igra. Vojna SSSR v Afganistane* [*The Great Gamble: The Soviet War in Afghanistan*] (Moscow: Eksmo, 2013)

Galitsky, Sergei, *Fotoal'bom o desantnikah v Afganistane i Chechne* [*A Photo Album about Paratroopers in Afghanistan and Chechnya*] (Saint-Petersburg: Grad Dukhovny, 2008)

Gareyev, Makhmut, *Moja poslednjaja vojna (Afganistan bez sovetskih vojsk)* [*My Last War (Afghanistan without Soviet Troops)*] (Moscow: INSAN, 1996)

Grau, Lester W, *The Bear Went Over the Mountain: Soviet Combat Tactics in Afghanistan* (Washington: National Defense University Press, 1996)

Gromov, Boris, *Ogranichennyj kontingent* [*The Limited Contingent*] (Moscow: Progress, 1994)

Jalali, Ali Ahmad and Grau, Lester W, *The Other Side of the Mountain: Mujahideen Tactics in the Soviet-Afghan War* (Quantico: USMC Studies and Analysis Division, 1998)

Kakar, Mohammad Hassan, *Afghanistan: The Soviet Invasion and the Afghan Response, 1979–1982* (Berkeley: University of California Press, 1995)

Karelin, Alexander, *Afganskaja vojna glazami voennogo hirurga* [*The Afghan War through the Eyes of a Military Surgeon*] (Moscow: Litmir, 2009)

Kolpakidi, Alexander and Sever, Alexander, *Specnaz GRU* [*Spetsnaz GRU*] (Moscow: Eksmo, 2008)

Korotkov, Andrey, *Rooks in Afghanistan, Volume 1: Sukhoi Su-25 in the Afghanistan War, 1981–1985* (Warwick: Helion & Co., 2023)

Kozhukhov, Mikhail, *Nad Kabulom chuzhie zvezdy* [*Foreign Stars over Kabul*] (Moscow: Eksmo; Olimp, 2010)

Kozlov, Sergei et al., *SPECNAZ GRU: Ocherki istorii. Istoricheskaja jenciklopedija v 5 knigah Kniga 3: Afganistan – zvezdnyj chas specnaza. 1979-1989 gg.* [*SPETSNAZ GRU: Essays on the History. Historical Encyclopedia in 5 Books, Book 3: Afghanistan – Spetsnaz's Finest Hour, 1979–1989*] (Moscow: SPSL; Russkaya Panorama, 2013)

Kozlov, Sergei, *Specnaz GRU. Pjat'desjat let istorii, dvadcat' let vojny* [*Spetsnaz GRU. Fifty Years of History, Twenty Years of War*] (Moscow: Russkaya Panorama, 2000)

Kuzmin, Nikolai, *Vojskovye razvedchiki. Zapiski nachal'nika razvedki divizii* [*Recons in Afgan. A Diary of a Chief of Intelligence of a Division*] (Moscow: Yauza; Eksmo, 2013)

Lebed, Alexander, *Za derzhavu obidno… Za derzhavu obidno…* [*I Feel Hurt for My Country…*] (Moscow: Moskovskaya Pravda, 1995)

Lyakhovsky, Alexander and Nekrasov, Vyacheslav, *Grazhdanin, politik, voin* [*Citizen, Politician, Warrior: In Memoriam Ahmad Shah Massoud*] (Tula: Grif and K, 2007)

Lyakhovsky, Alexander and Zabrodin, Vyacheslav, *Tajny Afganskoj vojny* [*Secrets of the Afghan War*] (Moscow: Planeta, 1991)

Lyakhovsky, Alexander, *Tragedija i doblest' Afgana* [*Tragedy and Valour of Afgan*] (Moscow: Iskona, 1995)

Marchenko, Valeri, *Afganskij razlom. Istoki mirovogo terrorizma* [*Afghan Break, Origins of World Terrorism*] (Saint-Petersburg: Piter, 2018)

Markovsky, Viktor, *Boevaja aviacija v Afganskoj vojne* [*Combat Aviation in the Afghan War*] (Moscow: Eksmo, 2016)

Mayorov, Alexander, *Pravda ob Afganskoj vojne* [*The Truth About the Afghan War*] (Moscow: Prava Cheloveka, 1996)

Merimsky, Viktor, *V pogone za «L'vom Pandzhshera»* [*In the Pursuit of the 'Panjshir Lion'*] (Moscow, 1993)

Merimsky, Viktor, *Zagadki afganskoj vojny* [*Riddle of the Afghan War*] (Moscow: Veche, 2006)

Okorokov, Alexander, *Sekretnye vojny Sovetskogo Sojuza* [*Secret Wars of the Soviet Union*] (Moscow: Yauza; Eksmo, 2008)

Orlov, Alexei, *Afganskij dnevnik pehotnogo lejtenanta. «Okopnaja pravda» vojny* [*The Afghan Diary of an Infantry Lieutenant. 'The Trench Truth' of the War*] (Moscow: Yauza; Eksmo, 2014)

Pilon, Juliana Geran, *The Report that the U.N. Wants to Suppress: Soviet Atrocities in Afghanistan* (Washington: The Heritage Foundation, 1986)

Ramazanov, Aleskender, *Tragedija v ushhel'e Shaesta* [*Tragedy in the Shayesta Gorge*] (Moscow: Eksmo, 2011)

Runov, Valentin, *Afganskaja vojna. Vse boevye operacii* [*The Afghan War. All Combat Operations*] (Moscow: Yauza; Eksmo, 2008)

Severin, Maxim and Ilyushechkin, Alexander, *Ja dralsja v Afgane. Front bez linii fronta* [*I Fought in Afghan: A Front without a Front Line*] (Moscow: Yauza; Eksmo, 2014)

Sheynin, Artyom, *Desantno-shturmovaja brigada. Nepridumannyj Afgan* [*The Airborne Assault Brigade: The Uninvented Afgan*] (Moscow: Eksmo, 2015)

Shipunov, Alexander, *Specnaz GRU v Kandagare. Voennaja hronika* [*Spetsnaz GRU in Kandahar: A Military Chronicle*] (Moscow: Yauza; Eksmo, 2014)

Skrynnikov, Mikhail, *Specnaz VDV. Diversionno-razvedyvatel'nye operacii v Afgane* [*Airborne Spetsnaz: Sabotage and Reconnaissance Operations in Afghan*] (Moscow: Yauza; Eksmo, 2005)

Sokolov, Boris, *SSSR i Rossija na bojne. Ljudskie poteri v vojnah HH veka* [*USSR and Russia Got Slaughtered: Human Losses in the Wars of the 20th Century*] (Moscow: Yauza-Press, 2013)

Stoderevsky, Igor, *Avtobiografija (Zapiski oficera specnaza GRU)* [*The Autobiography (A Diary of a Spetsnaz GRU officer)*] (Moscow: Fintrex, 2006)

Sukholessky, Alexander and Musiyenko, Alexander, *SPECNAZ GRU v Afganistane. 1979-1989 gg* [*Spetsnaz GRU in Afghanistan. 1979–1989*] (Moscow: Russkaya Panorama, 2012)

Suvorov, Viktor, *Rasskazy osvoboditelja* [*The Tales of the Liberator*] (Moscow: Dobraya Kniga, 2015)

Suvorov, Viktor, *Sovetskaja voennaja razvedka* [*Soviet Military Intelligence*] (Moscow: Dobraya Kniga, 2016)

Suvorov, Viktor, *Specnaz* [*Spetsnaz*] (Moscow: Dobraya Kniga, 2018)

Tikhonov, Yuri, *Afganskaja vojna Stalina* [*Stalin's Afghan War*] (Moscow: Yauza; Eksmo, 2008)

Tobolyak, Gennadi, *Afganskaja vojna GRU. Grif sekretnosti snjat* [*The Afghan War of the GRU. Declassified!*] (Moscow: Yauza; Eksmo, 2010)

Yousaf, Mohammad and Adkin, Mark, *Afghanistan: The Bear Trap, the Defeat of a Superpower* (London: Casemate, 2001)

Zhirokhov, Mikhail, *Opasnoe nebo Afganistana. Opyt boevogo primenenija sovetskoj aviacii v lokal'noj vojne* [*A Dangerous Sky of Afghanistan. Experience of a Combat Use of the Soviet Aviation in a Local War*] (Moscow: Tsentrpoligraf, 2012)

Zhirokhov, Mikhail, *Pogranichnaja aviacija v Afganskoj vojne* [*The Border Aviation in the Afghan War*] (Moscow: Yauza; Eksmo, 2015)

NOTES

Introduction

1 Wikipedia 'Afghanistan'.
2 Raimo Vayrynen, 'Afghanistan' in *Journal of Peace Research*, 1980, 17 (2), pp. 93–102.
3 Igor Bunich, 'The Party Gold' in *The Satan's Testing Ground. A Collection* (Saint-Petersburg: Shans, 1994), p. 230.

Chapter 1

1 J. Bruce Amtstutz, *Afghanistan: The First Five Years of Soviet Occupation* (Collingdale: DIANE Publishing, 1994), pp. 181–189 & 312; David Isby, *Russia's War in Afghanistan* (Oxford: Osprey Publishing, 1986), pp. 18–19.
2 *Divizion* is a military unit in the artillery of the Soviet Army, equivalent of battalion, deploying between 12 and 24 weapons, depending upon the type equipped.
3 A Spetsnaz Detachment is a military unit equivalent to a battalion.
4 See Andrey Korotkov, *Rooks in Afghanistan*, Volume 1 (Warwick: Helion & Co, 2023). Future volumes forthcoming at the time of writing.

Chapter 2

1 Igor Bunich, 'The Party Gold,' in *The Satan's Testing Ground. A Collection* (Saint-Petersburg: Shans, 1994), p. 249.

Chapter 3

1 Viktor Suvorov, *Soviet Military Intelligence* (Moscow: Dobraya Kniga, 2016).
2 Alexander Lyakhovsky, *Tragedy and Valor of Afgan* (Moscow: Iskona, 1995); ArtOfWar, Eduard Viktorovich Beresnev: 'Fatalities, Afghanistan, 1978–1979.'
3 Vladimir Bukovsky, *Judgement in Moscow* (Paris: MIK; Russkaya Mysl, 1996).
4 'News from the USSR,' 15 January 1980 (1).
5 ArtOfWar, Eduard Viktorovich Beresnev: Fatalities, Afghanistan, 1980.
6 Aleskender Ramazanov, *Tragedy in the Shayesta Gorge* (Moscow: Eksmo, 2011)
7 ArtOfWar – Beresnev, 1980.
8 Sergei Boyarkin, *Soldiers of the Afghan War* (Novosibirsk: Asteiya, 1999).
9 This would be the first of nine such offensive operations, numbered I to IX.
10 Mohammad Hassan Kakar. *Afghanistan: The Soviet Invasion and the Afghan Response, 1979–1982* (Berkeley: University of California Press, 1995).
11 Kakar.
12 Kakar.
13 Kakar.
14 ArtOfWar – Beresnev, 1980.
15 *Samizdat Magazine* – Zhukov's List, 1980.
16 Afghan-war-soldiers.ru – Veterans' Reminiscences.

Chapter 4

1 Alexander Mayorov, *The Truth About the Afghan War* (Moscow: Prava Cheloveka, 1996).
2 Kakar.
3 ArtOfWar – Eduard Viktorovich Beresnev: Fatalities, Afghanistan, 1981.
4 Kakar.

Chapter 5

1 *The Washington Post*, '3,000 Afghans Reported Slain by Soviet Chemicals,' 09 March 1982; *The New York Times*, 'U.S. Accuses Soviet of Poisoning 3,000,' 9 March 1982.
2 Igor Stoderevsky, *The Autobiography (A Diary of a Spetsnaz GRU officer)* (Moscow: Fintrex, 2006).
3 ArtOfWar – Eduard Viktorovich Beresnev, Fatalities, Afghanistan, 1982.
4 Technically a room by room sweep but often as well used for a house by house.
5 ArtOfWar – Beresnev, 1982; *Samizdat Magazine* – Zhukov's List, 1982.
6 *The New York Times*, 'Afghan Blast Toll is Put in Hundreds,' 10 November 1982.

Chapter 6

1 *Russian Seven – History*, 05 April 2019.
2 Rodric Braithwaite, *Afgan: The Russians at War, 1979–89* (Moscow: Corpus, 2013).
3 Braithwaite.

Chapter 7

1 ArtOfWar – Beresnev Eduard Viktorovich: Fatalities, Afghanistan, 1984.
2 Helsinki Watch. 'Tears, Blood and Cries': Human Rights in Afghanistan Since the Invasion, 1979–1984.
3 Helsinki Watch. 'Tears, Blood and Cries'.
4 Russian Seven – History,' 24 April 2017.
5 Russian Seven – History, 24 April 2017.
6 Haji Rahmatullah, according to Helsinki Watch. 'To Die in Afghanistan,' p. 19.

Chapter 8

1 Helsinki Watch. 'To Die in Afghanistan.'
2 Spetsnaz Group is a military unit, being an equivalent of a platoon.

Chapter 9

1 *Current Time TV*, 13 February 2019.
2 Juliana Geran Pilon, *The Report that the U.N. Wants to Suppress: Soviet Atrocities in Afghanistan* (Washington: The Heritage Foundation, 1986).
3 ArtOfWar – Eduard Viktorovich Beresnev: Fatalities, Afghanistan, 1986; *Samizdat Magazine* – Zhukov's List, 1986.
4 Viktor Markovsky, *Combat Aviation in the Afghan War* (Moscow: Eksmo, 2016); ArtOfWar – Beresnev, 1986.
5 ArtOfWar – Alla Smolina: "Afganki". Shot. Blown up. Burned. Defamed.

Chapter 10

1 Peter Bergen, *The Rise and Fall of Osama bin Laden: The Biography* (New York: Simon & Schuster, 2021), p. 38; Steve Coll, *Ghost Wars: The Secret History of the CIA, Afghanistan, and bin Laden, from the Soviet Invasion to September 10, 2001* (London: Penguin Books, 2004), p. 163.
2 Kviu.3dn.ru – Articles, Alumni, 1965, Ostapenko N.I.
3 ArtOfWar – Eduard Viktorovich Beresnev: Fatalities, Afghanistan, 1987.
4 ArtOfWar – Beresnev, 1987.
5 Kviu.3dn.ru – Articles, Alumni, 1965, Ostapenko N.I.
6 Afgan.ru – Book of Memory, Udovichenko V.M.
7 Sergei Kozlov et al., *SPETSNAZ GRU: Essays on the History. Historical Encyclopedia in 5 Books, Book 3: Afghanistan – Spetsnaz's Finest Hour, 1979–1989* (Moscow: SPSL; Russkaya Panorama, 2013), pp. 494–504.
8 Kozlov et al., pp. 494–504.

Chapter 11

1 Igor Bunich, 'Sword of the President,' in *The Satan's Testing Ground. A Collection* (Saint-Petersburg, Shans, 1994), p. 409.
2 ArtOfWar – Eduard Viktorovich Beresnev, Fatalities, Afghanistan, 1988; ArtOfWar – Alla Smolina. Give me your Address, "Afganka," part 44 (Nos 461–470).
3 Russian Seven – History, 4 July 2019.

Chapter 12

1 Helsinki Watch. 'Tears, Blood and Cries,' p. 41.
2 Helsinki Watch. 'Tears, Blood and Cries,' pp. 42–43.
3 Helsinki Watch. 'Tears, Blood and Cries': pp. 38–39.
4 Helsinki Watch, 'To Die in Afghanistan,' p. 7.
5 Igor Bunich, *Chronicle of the Chechen Massacre and Six Days in Budyonnovsk* (Saint-Petersburg: Oblik, 1995), p. 31.